Mission under
SCRUTINY

"Kirk . . . charts a convincing course for mission in a post-Christian environment. In an era when the Christian faith has no special advantage or prestige in the West, Kirk reminds us of how we can be faithful followers of Jesus and witness with confidence in a spirit of epistemological humility to the transforming power of the Gospel. He takes on the tough issues of how the Gospel connects to our culture in addressing the role of the Bible, evangelism, religious violence, homosexuality, and other social and religious controversies."

—Darrell Whiteman, Wesleyan Mission Society

Also by J. Andrew Kirk:

What Is Mission?

Mission under
SCRUTINY

Confronting Contemporary Challenges

J. Andrew Kirk

Fortress Press
Minneapolis

MISSION UNDER SCRUTINY
Confronting Contemporary Challenges

First Fortress Press edition 2006.

Cover image: © Frédéric Cirou / PhotoAlto
Cover design: Kevin van der Leek

Library of Congress Cataloging-in-Publication Data

Kirk, J. Andrew.
  Mission under scrutiny : confronting contemporary challenges /
  J. Andrew Kirk.
    p. cm.
Includes bibliographical references and index.
ISBN-13: 978–0–8006–3800–9 (alk. paper)
ISBN-10: 0–8006–3800–X (alk. paper)
  I. Missions—Theory. I. Title.
BV2063.K57   2006
266.001—dc22

                                                    2006011707

Printed in Great Britain

08   07   06   1   2   3   4   5   6   7   8   9   10

Contents

Acknowledgements

Having already beeen invited to write about my pilgrimage in mission,[1] it is not necessary to repeat here the countless contributions others have made to my thinking. I am indebted not only to those with whom I largely agree but also those who may well diverge sharply from my views. I endeavour to engage with the thinking of those whose basic assumptions I do not share. This is a hard but necessary discipline. It would be easy, but basically dishonest, either to encounter their ideas at second hand or to ignore them altogether. More importantly, I would miss the crucial insights and genuine challenges that are to be found in places where, because of preconceptions, one might not expect to find them. So, I am grateful to those, both known and unknown to me, who are likely to find my opinions difficult to accept. I hope that I have succeeded in representing their views fairly.

A friend is, among other things, a person who is willing to spend time and effort in meeting the needs of another. Friendships flourish when people are prepared to forego legitimate interests and tasks to help someone else. I am fortunate to count among mine three people who have nobly and cheerfully (as far as I know) given time and expertise to comment on

[1] J. Andrew Kirk, 'My Pilgrimage in Mission' in *International Bulletin of Missionary Research*, Vol. 28, No. 2, April 2004.

portions of this book. They are Colin Chapman, Darrell Jackson and Alan Kreider. Their remarks have been more incisive than, in their modesty, they will probably realise. I have considered them carefully and, as a result, made important changes to the original draft. Needless to say, the result is all my fault, not theirs!

It has been a delight to work with Virginia Hearn and Liz Piercy of Darton, Longman and Todd. Their professionalism as editors and their personal enthusiasm and support have been exemplary. Happy is the person who has two such competent colleagues to guide him!

Now that I am retired, my wife Gillian expected perhaps that I would spend just a little less time in the study and a little more with her tending the vegetables, or wherever. I have tried to be in both places, though not simultaneously! I thank her for her patience and forbearance, or perhaps resignation, to my writing compulsion.

Finally, I owe a deep debt of gratitude to students and staff of various institutions where I continue to teach and supervise on a part-time basis: the International Baptist Theological Seminary in Prague, the Protestant Institute for Mission Studies in Budapest, the Baptist Seminary in Bucharest, the Oxford Centre for Mission Studies. I would also like to mention with affection and appreciation many members of the International Association for Mission Studies, whom I also count as friends, especially the members of its various Executive Committees from 1990-2004, of which I was also a part. Chapter 6, in particular, owes a good deal to all that I have learnt over 20 years as a member of the International Board of the Life and Peace Institute (Uppsala). My association with its work has been one of the main reasons why I am convinced that the resolution of conflict and the pursuit of reconciliation are fundamental tasks of mission. I have and continue to learn much from them all. It is a privilege to be part of such communities of Christian faith, hope and love. They have all helped shape and sharpen my missiological convictions. Thank you all for your fellowship in the Gospel.

Andrew Kirk

Introduction

I hope the title of the book speaks for itself. Mission is an essential part of the response of Christians to the good news of Jesus Christ. However, it is not always immediately obvious what forms it should take. What may be right for one generation or situation may be unsuitable at another time or place. So, what is appropriate mission in each context has to be constantly evaluated. It is inevitable that, wherever human beings do not heed God's testimony to his nature and action in the world, the mission of Jesus' disciples will always be challenged. The questioning, however, does not come only from outside. Queries, reservations and debates about a proper approach to mission in different circumstances are also heard within.

I can well imagine that ten or so years from now someone else might write a book with exactly the same title as this one, yet having a completely different content. What is current today may have faded by then into distant memories of the past. The likelihood, however, is that some of the topics that I cover here will still be relevant, for good or ill, for some time to come. Whatever the case, each generation of Christians needs to select and focus on those aspects of mission which are most pressing in its moment of history. Whether my choice of current challenges is the most pertinent is obviously a matter of debate. I can imagine some reviewers suggesting that other issues should have been included. I also suspect that some will point to the limited ground that is covered, given the global reach of Christian mission. My only defence is that I am who I am, a particular individual with a limited experience of the world and a restricted vision.

Nevertheless, without pretending to be comprehensive, I believe that many of the subjects covered are relevant today to broad sections of the church across the world. I realise that for Christians in continents either having a largely Christian population (Africa and Latin America) or where the majority profess another religion (Asia) concentrating so much on the challenges of secularism may seem highly parochial.

I argue, however, that secularising forces are influential, and even dominant, even in places where religious beliefs and values are taken seriously in everyday life. Their impact cannot be measured simply by looking at the statistics of religiously engaged people. Is not the intense debate about the nature and place of Islamic faith and practice in the world today largely due to the assumption that it has to come to terms with 'modern' (i.e. secular) societies? It has to face its own current challenges in areas of life where secular cultures have set the agenda: for example, democracy, human rights, the situation of women, law and punishment, the use of violence, the scope of science and technology, the moral limits of art forms, freedom of speech and association. In many parts of Africa and Asia, the future of Islam is of intense interest to Christians living there. The latter will be watching with exceptional interest its various responses to secularising processes.

Unlike my last book on mission,[1] this present one is not designed to cover systematically the various component parts of missiological reflection and mission practice. However, in the course of discussing the various challenges, I refer to most of the substantial issues - such as the significance of specific contexts, the relationship between Gospel and culture, and between mission and evangelism, the encounter between different living faiths, a missionary understanding of the church and of

What is Mission? Theological Explorations (London: Darton, Longman & Todd, 1999)

Scripture - which would be encompassed in any standard educational programme on mission. In some cases, particularly where missiological reflection still has some catching up to do, like the issue of conflict, violence and peace-making, I tackle the subject head-on.

This book has a different rationale. It endeavours to reconsider what appear to me to be some of the most pressing problems facing the Church in mission. They are not necessarily new, although they constantly show fresh dimensions. As circumstances change so some matters become more complicated. There can be little doubt, for example, that the recent intensification of militant forms of religion has made relationships between faith communities more complex. This certainly affects the agenda for both dialogue with and evangelistic witness to people of different religious convictions. It also throws into sharp relief the role that different religions play in fomenting or overcoming violence. I am attempting to reconsider each of these massive challenges from the perspective of the Christian community's call to share in God's mission. Given the nature of the various situations, what specifically should the church be doing?

In a way, each of these chapters is self-contained. The reader is at liberty to dip into any of the subjects being discussed according to personal interest. I believe that s/he will find in each case a coherent presentation of a particular subject. The book does not pretend, therefore, to advance one overall major thesis, but tackles a number of sub-themes, each of which forms part of the church's complete missionary task. At the same time, the reader will note a fairly constant cross-referencing going on between the different topics. In this sense, s/he may have to read more than one chapter to appreciate the full nature of the discussion. Unlike some books, this is not simply a compilation of individual, unrelated articles; none of them has appeared in print before. Perhaps, because missiology is an integrated discipline and mission a unified act across a number of activities, each aspect has repercussions for every other.

To illustrate this point, one might consider the influence of secular thought on a number of ethical, political, social and cultural realities. One may suspect, for example, that current Islamic assertiveness has something to do with the repugnance felt by many Muslims to the way many secular people appear to abandon themselves to an inane and trivial pursuit of pleasure for its own sake. They may also fear the long-term repercussions of secular assumptions (as I have traced them in chapters 1 and 2) on their communities. At the same time, a secular outlook has been influential in curbing the church's illegitimate striving after political and social influence, which has often led to its endorsing ethnic conflict. Moreover, secular societies are not about to concede ground to Islamists who demand that laws and legal processes reflect the teaching of their traditions.

The underlying naturalistic assumption of the secular viewpoint has damaged reliance on the testimony of Scripture to the acts of God in time and space. This in turn has undermined confidence in its reliability as an accurate portrayal of God's communication to his creatures. As a result, reliance on the text to deliver clear ethical principles in cases such as justice for the poor and human sexuality has been eroded.

Unlike many other Christian commentators, I am not persuaded that the cultural condition of post-modernity is the major factor in shaping how people think and live in so-called post-industrial societies. I recognise that it offers an intriguing and ingenious interpretation of certain developments in social and cultural history in the West. However, contrary to the hype, I am not convinced that it represents a decisive rupture with the life forms of modernity. Rather, it seems to act as its complement. On the one hand, it shares the same basic secular assumption as modernity, namely that human life is not shaped or guided by a personal divine being. On the other hand, it seeks to ameliorate the deep sense of loss that such a belief engenders. Unlike modernity, it allows some space for a spiritual dimension to life. Having abandoned apparently the rigid division between approaches to life based either on reason alone or on faith, it has been lauded for having a more holistic outlook.

---

[2] I take up again certain aspects of post-modern thought in chapter 10.

In my opinion, the belief that post-modernity represents a significant move away from modernity is deceptive.[2] Post-modern consciousness is no less secular than its alleged fore-runner. Its attitude to the uncompromising claims of theistic faiths, that they are based on a reality touching but beyond our universe, is the same as that of modernity. Such a parallel reality does not exist; or, if it does, we can know nothing about it. The only real difference lies in the fact that post-modern thought allows for the cultural and 'spiritual' value of the use of symbolic language and rites, if some people find these help-ful in coping with the enigma of life. It is more sympathetic, perhaps, to the view that human beings function best if they hold to certain beliefs *as if* they were true. Or, to reverse the argument, beliefs may be counted as *true*, if they work for people's well-being.

This personal evaluation of current trends in intellectual and practical life is the reason why I have devoted considerable space to secular culture as a pivotal context in which Christian mission has to take place. I am arguing that, for all practical purposes, most people in the West live within a world in which the per-sonal, infinite, creating and redeeming God of the Christian faith is not a part. Although I am convinced that such a stance is intel-lectually and ethically untenable, I do not want to imply that everything that a secular outlook has brought is untrue or invalid. I wish to make a distinction between recognising an overwhelming reality and adopting a predominantly negative attitude to it.

I write from a position that believes that established Trinitarian theism, based on a written text that faithfully trans-mits God's word, applicable to all peoples and cultures, is the only sustainable charter for the mission of God's people. I hope that such a confession will not entice people to hang any theo-logical or ecclesiastical labels on me. Some of them I might be willing to own, but only if allowed to define them in my own way! In response to the question 'do you belong to such a body or tradition in the church?' I am inclined to say it all depends on who is said to share the same bed!

This book is written for any group within the church which

may find its various discussions helpful in its own wrestling with current challenges to mission. The purpose ultimately, of course, is not to discover intellectually satisfying formulae for judging the rightness or wrongness of missiological theories, but to practise day in and day out an honest and faithful discipleship in the way of Jesus Christ.

CHAPTER 1

Christian Mission and the
Sacredness of Secular Freedom

It is now a universal truism that mission is severely impaired without an adequate understanding of the context in which it takes place. We may proceed, therefore, to make a number of assumptions about the relationship between mission and the present context, as long as these are open to careful examination. We might refer to them as law-like generalisations that can be confirmed or denied by adequate evidence. Firstly, mission is effective always in proportion to a valid understanding of the mechanisms that drive contemporary cultures. These latter include basic beliefs, values, traditions, customs and institutions, that tend to interact in complex and often unpredictable ways. Secondly, the dominant global force driving human cultures for the last quarter of a millennium has been the pursuit of freedom. In the celebrated trilogy of human rights, 'life, liberty and the pursuit of happiness', the middle virtue is deemed the necessary condition for the exercise of the other two. Without genuine freedom, both life and happiness are severely compromised. Thirdly, and as a consequence of the previous assumptions, productive mission will depend upon grasping the historical and social significance of modern notions of freedom.

Given the impulse, over the last three centuries, to construct a view of human life without recourse to any reality beyond the natural world, there has been an increasing tendency to see freedom as release from the imposition of beliefs and values not personally decided on. In this sense, the concept of freedom, in all societies affected by the ideas of the Enlightenment, is secular in nature.[1] It presumes an innate independence from external controls decided by some institution – such as religious bodies or political establishments – without individual consent.

Due to the limits of space, we will only touch upon the two main notions of freedom that have arisen in the course of the modern history of the West.[2] Although increasingly important in the controversy over the relationship between the brain, mind and will, the technical philosophical argument about free will and determinism is beyond the confines of this particular debate.[3]

The liberal tradition (freedom from . . .)

By the beginning of the eighteenth century, a number of important factors in the cultural and social life of Europe had begun seriously to undermine the hierarchical and authoritarian structures of the existing social order. Firstly, there was a growing acknowledgement of the sovereignty of individual conscience, arising mainly from the struggle for the recognition of religious

---

[1] Secular is used to describe a society in which the following conditions prevail: (i) there is an effective separation of the state and public life from the domination of religious belief; (ii) human life is interpreted and conducted normally without reference to any supernatural agency; (iii) the majority of the population do not even exercise a minimal attachment to formal religious institutions and symbols. I explore further the nature and scope of secular belief in chapter 2.

[2] A much fuller account of modern concepts of freedom is given in J. Andrew Kirk, *The Meaning of Freedom: A Study of Secular, Muslim and Christian Views* (Carlisle: Paternoster Press, 1998); see also, A. Ryan (ed.), *The Idea of Freedom* (Oxford: OUP, 1979); J. Gray, *Liberalism* (Milton Keynes: Open University Press, 1986). Restricting the discussion to concepts that have arisen in the West may appear to assume that European civilisation is the reference-point for change throughout the world. However, although aspects of the liberal tradition are highly attractive to people in many other cultures, especially the young, I am careful to show that the presumed gains are often ambiguous and even harmful, and that there are other credible interpretations.

[3] For a useful discussion of some of the main issues, see Roger Trigg, *Reality at Risk: A defence of realism in philosophy and the sciences* (Hemel Hempstead: Harvester Wheatsheaf, 1989), pp. 142–152.

toleration. Chronologically speaking, freedom of religious belief and practice was the first civil freedom to be contended for. Then, secondly, the beginning of modern science, based on disciplined investigation of the natural world, presupposed an unfettered approach to intellectual research and discovery. By its very nature, the scientific enterprise could not be directed to fit preconceived beliefs. Its method demanded freedom from external supervision and constraint. Thirdly, incipient notions of political democracy, that challenged the divine right of some to rule and that used the language of accountability to the will of the people, were beginning to emerge.

During the eighteenth century, these factors translated into forces, which gathered strength. They were fuelled by the writings of political philosophers like John Locke, Jean-Jacques Rousseau and Thomas Paine. Though called 'The Age of Reason', it might just as well have been known as 'The Age of Revolt'. It marked a fundamental change of mood in society, externalised to some degree in the American and French Revolutions, in which people were demanding freedom from all kinds of external restrictions, limitations and impositions, and in particular from the detailed regulation by the state of most aspects of life. Although not always articulated in this way, the mood reflected a challenge to all forms of 'elitism', in which some group, alien to oneself, assumed a right or duty to determine the limits of personal choice and self-determination.

Ever since, the liberal tradition within Western societies has campaigned for this as the fundamental concept of freedom. It is classically defined by Isaiah Berlin as, 'freedom from any agent external to myself determining what is in my best interests and forcing me to comply'.[4] He calls this *negative* freedom. We are free to the degree that no individual or group interferes with our activities. The obstruction or prevention of doing what I would otherwise do is to be unfree, coerced or enslaved.[5] 'The only freedom which deserves the name is that of pursuing our own good in our own way.'[6]

[4] *Four Essays on Liberty* (Oxford: OUP, 1969), p. 122.
[5] Ibid. p. 122.
[6] Ibid. p. 127.

According to this way of thinking, as logically it must be, negative freedom is dependent on society accepting a strong separation between private belief and public authority. This in turn springs from the notion of the intrinsic worth, or sanctity, of individual selves. They are self-contained, autonomous units, always to be treated as an end in themselves, never used as the means to other ends, especially those of the state.[7]

In the course of time, the 'sacred' nature of private space and time has led, as indeed it must, to society awarding the highest values to permissiveness and tolerance. The claim to a natural, self-evident right to manage one's own life, free from external interference, is also a claim that society must permit and tolerate my own self-chosen life-style, as long as this is compatible with an equal freedom accorded to others. Two manifestations of self-determination - the public right freely to elect and dismiss the governing powers and the private right freely to choose and change the government of one's own life – have become mutually reinforcing. As we shall see, however, the recognition of the right to political self-determination, as in the case of former colonies,[8] was not met by an equal ability to gain freedoms in the sphere of personal life.

The socialist tradition (freedom for . . .)

Another major social tradition, that of 'human rights', also saw its beginning in the eighteenth century. The language of rights has become, perhaps, one of the most persistent and significant pieces of vocabulary to be used in modern political and civil life. The notion is enshrined in the Bill of Rights which accompanied the American Declaration of Independence: 'All men are born free, and have the right to life, liberty and the pursuit of happi-

---

[7] 'Act in such a way that you always treat humanity, whether in your own person or that of another, never simply as a means but always at the same time as an end' (Immanuel Kant), see Garrett Thomson, *On Kant* (London: Wadsworth, 2003), pp. 66–67.

[8] The move to political emancipation for all peoples became irresistible once the Atlantic Charter of 1941 accorded to people subjugated by the Nazi regime the right to be free from foreign domination.

ness.' In this proposition, human rights are set out in the form of what most people must be free to do, in the light of what they are by their very nature. Hence, it takes the form of what is called *positive* freedom. According to this vision, freedom is about possibilities, potential and potency.

Negative freedom, on the other hand, could be interpreted as being reductionist. It really comprises a double negative: *not* being *prohibited* from certain courses of action (for example, women not being forbidden to join a hitherto all-male club or society). But a non-prohibition is quite different from a positive opportunity. The women in question may be free to join the club, in the sense that the rules no longer bar them from membership, but not free in the sense that they do not have the ability to pay the exorbitantly high entrance fee.

Positive freedom can be understood as 'the power of acting . . . according to the determination of the will'.[9] In this sense, part of actual freedom is the creation of conditions that make a choice a real, open possibility. For this to happen, sometimes negative freedoms may have to be curtailed so that freedoms overall may be increased. The classic example of multiplying the positive aspects of freedom in a social setting is the income tax system. Negatively, a citizen might argue that nobody has the right to interfere in the use of his or her accumulated wealth legitimately acquired. Nevertheless, positively, the redistribution of wealth through tax is intended to allow otherwise disadvantaged people an opportunity to develop skills and knowledge that give them access to more possibilities for their lives. Other examples of the same principle working might be a ban on smoking in public places, to guarantee the positive freedom of breathing unpolluted air, and land reform, to enable more people to earn a livelihood in agriculture. In both cases people's right to be free of sanctions against smoking wherever they please or holding huge tracts of uncultivated land are overturned.

So, positive freedom is about widening access to resources, such as education, healthcare, sanitation, job opportunities and minimum financial support when work is not available, to

[9] *International Encyclopaedia of the Social Sciences: Vol.5* (London: Macmillan, 1972)

enable wider choices to be made. If freedom is closely related to power, increasing freedoms means equalising power. This, in turn, implies the redistribution of the means of power, i.e. wealth, privilege, patronage, knowledge, status in the community and decision-making mechanisms. It is recognised that redistribution is coercive and inevitably restrictive of some individual freedoms.[10] In political philosophy, it is justified on the utilitarian grounds that it is aimed at the expansion of the sum total of freedoms. One of the main debates between advocates of the 'left' and the 'right' in politics concerns the balance between negative and positive freedoms.

Existential freedom

Alongside the long and intense discussion of the meaning and scope of civil liberties and rights a major question exists about the existence of an inner freedom to choose, and choose meaningfully, without which external freedoms would be merely formal and conventional. From time to time the human spirit revolts against the constraints seemingly imposed by an enclosed materialist and rationalist account of reality. Human self-awareness strives to reach beyond the notion that an empirical reading of the natural world is the measure of our ability to know and comprehend the meaning of life. The experience of being human appears to transcend an explanation of the human condition that sees it entirely as the sum of its biological parts in nature. Important though a reasoned interpretation of human history and social development may be, human beings struggle to encounter a world that is not wholly encompassed by the powers of the mind.

The experience of living in a culture that has been dominated by a particular kind of rationalist view of reality is that modern human beings encounter the world as a series of unrelated experiences of the material that fail to explain the deep and permanent sense of personhood. If, in the philosopher Heidegger's

---

[10] This argument does not mean that individual freedom is a zero-sum game, in which there will always be some losers. An increase of positive freedoms can be of benefit to all.

famous phrase, human beings are simply 'thrown into being', as if by chance, and have to learn to live with the irresolvable predicament of a life without any predetermined meaning,[11] they are of all creatures the most miserable and unfulfilled. They alone, apparently, live daily with the massive contradiction between what modern thought allows them to believe and an intense yearning for something much more significant. This is unquestionably a fundamental aspect of the longing to be free: free from the poverty of a diminished view of life.[12]

Secular accounts of freedom do not seem to offer any escape from the ceaseless flux of existence in which meaning, purpose, moral values and human relations are constantly, and arbitrarily, changing on a daily basis. Such a life is actually experienced as loss of freedom. Freedom, to be genuine, has to be related to what is worth choosing and, without an end in view that will eventually be vindicated as true meaning, we cannot know what is of value. Otherwise, every choice and every action is equally meaningful and equally absurd.

There have been a number of attempts to come to terms with what appears, without a constant, external point of reference, to be a vacuous life in an absurd universe. Albert Camus, in his celebrated book *The Myth of Sisyphus*,[13] proclaims the message that the true revolt against the futility of existence is not consummated in suicide, but in continuing to live. So, the recommendation is that human beings attempt to regain the freedom threatened by absurdity through their own voluntary, unforced, fully conscious decision to create their own meaning and values and to shoulder the consequences of their own actions.

[11] Heidegger, *Being and Time* (Oxford: Blackwell, 1962), p. 174; also, Peter Sedgwick, *Descartes to Derrida: An Introduction to European Philosophy* (Oxford: Blackwell, 2001), pp. 113–115.

[12] There can be no escape from the poverty of a secular view of reality, until science is accorded a proper place in culture. As long as it is given the task of explaining the *whole* breadth of human reality in the universe, it will fail. It does not possess the tools for such an undertaking. Better that it be allowed to fulfil a more limited mission, otherwise people will become disillusioned with an enterprise, in which *too* much has been invested, see, J. C. Somerville, 'Post-Secularism marginalizes the University' in *Church History*, 71:4 (December 2002), p. 848.

[13] A. Camus, *The Myth of Sisyphus* (Harmondsworth: Penguin Books, 1975).

> Only the 'lucid' recognition of the absurdity of existence
> liberates us from belief in another life and permits us to live
> for the instant, for beauty, pleasure and the 'implacable
> grandeur' of existence. Lucidity . . . is the counterpart of the
> notion . . . of anguish as the self-conscious and unflinching
> apprehension of freedom.[14]

The only freedom that is open to us is that of personal integrity
and authenticity: to be free from the hypocrisy of submitting to
imposed meanings and values, of being the willing slave of a culture that decides on our behalf what is the good-life, what is
('politically') correct, what is normal.

The mechanics of freedom

One powerful image of contemporary perceptions of freedom is
the solitary individual sitting in front of the TV screen with
remote control in hand, able to switch at will from channel to
channel.[15] By pressing a button he or she has instant access to an
amazing kaleidoscope of programmes. However, there is a problem with this view of freedom as extended choice. Supposing
that freedom is interpreted as the unrestricted decision to sit
down one evening to watch whatever programme captures the
imagination, yet on that particular evening nothing seems
worthwhile viewing. Has not that particular freedom been
thwarted? Then there is the dilemma that the impossibility of
watching properly more than one programme at a time actually
leads to the loss of freedom implicit in being unable to view all
the most desirable channels simultaneously. Here we encounter
the common experience of the paradox of freedom: extended
choice results in extended limitations on freedom.

A yet more powerful image might be that of the same person,
sitting in front of the same TV set, devouring a carefully chosen
pre-prepared meal cooked in two minutes in the microwave or

---

[14] David West, *An Introduction to Continental Philosophy* (Cambridge: Polity Press, 1996), p.152.

[15] Or, increasingly, moving from one web page or one computer game to another, at the click of the mouse.

brought to one's front door by the local take-away! Perhaps these images are partly the result of mass-advertising, which projects the (well-camouflaged) illusion that affluent members of advanced industrial societies have a freedom of choice that is only limited by the disposable wealth available to them to consume their preferred goods and services.

In terms of political theory, notions of freedom in a liberal democratic society are based on the idea of social contract.[16] Members of society implicitly contract with one another, through due legal process, to respect one another's rights to control personal decision-making processes, in ways compatible with everyone else's rights to do the same. According to the reigning philosophy of political liberalism, the S(s)tate should have a minimal function: basically safeguarding the 'sacred' space of the individual by ensuring that the public does not encroach too far onto the territory of life-style choices taken *in private*. This is a major argument for the legalising of abortion and euthanasia and the decriminalisation of certain, self-styled, recreational drugs.

However, such a view of the state's role is superficial. The reality of social life throws up numerous instances where the state is called upon to arbitrate between conflicting claims to freedom or rights (for example, the use of Sundays to shop or as a day of rest for shop-workers, or the use of vehicles against the right to breath clean air). One person's right freely to enjoy a certain activity may well infringe another person's right not to be molested by that activity. The conflict of interests, in such matters as noise pollution, the interpretation of good-neighbourliness and what constitutes cruel sports, is widely acknowledged and legislated for. Naturally, the state also has a responsibility to protect citizens against the abuse of the unscrupulous, in areas such as financial fraud and unsolicited material on the internet. In other words, one of the state's main roles is to make and enforce laws that protect (generally accepted) superior rights against (equally recognised) inferior ones. This has led Ralf Dahrendorf

---

[16] See Andrew Heywood, *Political Ideologies: An Introduction* (Basingstoke: Macmillan, 1992), pp. 26–28.

to stipulate that 'the new liberty . . . is the politics of regulated conflict.'[17]

A minimalist view of the state, which in practice becomes untenable, because of the presence of too large a number of people willing to exploit the system at whatever cost to others, is based largely on a negative view of freedom. This view also underlies the vigorous free-market interpretation of capitalist economic theory associated in recent times with the theories of Friedrich von Hayek and Milton Friedman. Here the contract theory is said to work to perfection. Each individual agrees (implicitly) to trade goods and services in an open market, selling what they have and buying what they need. Hayek argues strenuously that, because a true market economy is spontaneous (i.e. it is not fettered by arbitrary political intervention), it cannot be coercive. Thus, to be disadvantaged in a market society is not a genuine constraint on freedom.[18] Belief in the possibility of free exchange as a natural human process has led extreme liberals to deny that the mechanisms of the market have anything to do with the morality of justice. Thus, Milton Friedman argues that 'most differences of status or position or wealth can be regarded as a product of chance at a far enough remove.'[19]

This kind of argument is based on an interpretation of intention. As limitations on freedom brought about by an unequal distribution of economic power are not intended by the system, there is no question of the economic order as such being held accountable. Accountability only makes sense in the context of individual humans possessing full responsibility for their respective actions. On the other hand, the redistribution of wealth, through the collective power of the state, is coercive. It is the deliberately intended, forced appropriation of what belongs to one person given to another. Arguments put forward for the inviolable rights of private property and the neutrality of a mar-

[17] *The New Liberty: Survival and Justice in a changing world* (London: Routledge & Kegan Paul, 1975), p. 6.

[18] Hayek, *Law, Legislation and Liberty, Vol. II* (London: Routledge & Kegan Paul, 1979), pp. 31–32.

[19] Milton Friedman, *Capitalism and Freedom* (Chicago: University of Chicago Press, 1962), pp. 165–166.

ket economy are highly significant in that it is often assumed, in the Western tradition of political discourse, that political freedoms are dependent upon laissez-faire economic policies.

The ambiguities of freedom

So far, we have dwelt mostly on the classical Western liberal understanding of the meaning of freedom. This view appears to be still in the ascendancy,[20] particularly so in the aftermath of the crumbling of successive communist regimes in Central and Eastern Europe. It is said that these governments collapsed, when they could no longer contain the increasing pressure of the people, attracted by the freedoms and affluence of Western Europe. A joke used to be told in the Czech Republic. 'Why is the sun so happy today? Because it knows that by this evening it will be in the West!' The people spontaneously rose against the oppression of a government (under the auspices of a one party state) that curtailed individual freedoms, administered a stagnant economy and claimed a monopolistic right to rule. The long struggle for genuine self-determination, which had been postponed from 1956 (Hungary) and 1968 (the Czech Republic), was finally won.

Nevertheless, in spite of the near cultic status given to the idea of secular freedom, perhaps the highest position in the sacred pantheon of values, stark realities are largely ignored. Commitment to an ideal with almost religious fervour blinds people, as is often the case with religions, to the adverse consequences of the faith, some of which undermine the very notion of the freedom being served.

There are three main areas, where, I believe, a deeper analysis will show that Western culture is in the midst of a severe crisis, engendered by a virtually unbridgeable gap between expecta-

[20] The justification for regime change in Afghanistan and Iraq was based on the Anglo-American belief that the implantation of the supremely good ends of Western-style elective democracy outweighs the tragically necessary ambiguous means needed to achieve it. (The supposed threat of these regimes to the world community was a political manoeuvre and entirely fictional).

tions of freedom (themselves the product of culture) and the possibility of their realisation.[21]

The question of ends
In one sense the contemporary Western individual is an existentialist at heart. Freedom to choose what one wants to be in the
face of the gut feeling that life is meaningless is itself the only
valid end for humanity. What we are, or will be, is not in any
sense circumscribed by the supposed given nature of life (pre-
ordained by divine will, evolutionary chance, biological fate or
accidental circumstances). Rather, we construct, fashion and
refashion our own image of ourselves by deciding to live in particular ways (life-style choices).

In post-modern thought, the revolt against religion (an institutional interpretation of the allotted order of things) has become a
revolt against all ontologies that claim absolute validity through
time. The result is the refusal of any self-evident truths, which
lay claim upon the thinking and lives of all reasonable people.
Post-modern consciousness thinks in terms of fluctuating images
and (fictional) stories that help us to cope better with the circumstances in which we find ourselves. 'Truth', therefore is
socially produced, historically developed, contingent, plural and
changing. We no longer make choices within a reality already
marked out for us, we choose to create our own reality. Thus, I
may call truth whatever, at any point in time, conveys meaning
on my life.

Two consequences flow from this recently articulated view of
freedom and reality. First, human community and society dis-
solve into fragmented bits and pieces. An abandonment of common beliefs, and the creation of personal values, leads to a
breakdown of communication. We do not share sufficient common understandings of the world to be able to enter into other

[21] Many of the younger generation in the former communist countries of Central
and Eastern Europe are already discovering that the pre-Berlin-wall dream of
liberty and prosperity has faded. Sucked inexorably into the processes of the
global market, they are encountering the severe human disadvantages of current
business practices: neglect of family; personal stress and the lack of time for aesthetic and leisure activities and for exploring spiritual reality.

people's experiences.[22] Secondly, it cannot much matter what we choose to believe and to do, as long as our choice is serious and is pursued with full conviction and commitment.[23] We do not choose any particular course of action because it is intrinsically good or right, or because it is part of a settled over-arching purpose for existence. We choose it because it feels good to us now, and does not appear to produce harmful consequences for others.

The question of means

It is surely a curious paradox, perhaps explained by the severe contradictions induced in the human psyche by the existentialist, post-modern consciousness, that, far from creating a sense of exhilaration, freedom often produces a sense of dread. Erich Fromm explored this conflict many years ago in his celebrated book *The Fear of Freedom*.[24] Thus, for example, a certain obsession with the issue of law and order, which appears largely to treat the symptoms and not the cause of crime, is a response to the fear of lawlessness. Crime springs from the very individual choice to pursue particular ends by violent means (forcibly depriving others of what belongs to them). It leads in society as a whole to the loss of such civil liberties as freedom of movement, information and privacy. It is linked to the insidious threat of intimidation against those who wish to collaborate with law-enforcement agents. It undermines that rare and precious commodity, interpersonal trust, without which freedom is always compromised.

---

[22] Contemporary secular societies are characterised above all by allowing the equal validity of a motley collection of different beliefs and opinions. The inevitable consequence of such a situation is that there is no longer any one collective tradition that binds society together. In the view of many commentators, this is one of the chief reasons for the loss of religious adherence: creedal tolerance leads inescapably to religious indifference and a consequent undiscriminating spiritual pot-pourri.

[23] As in committed co-habiting relationships, whether hetero- or homo-sexual. Freedom is also evident in the loose way in which language is used: commitment can be self-defined to fit individual needs.

[24] (London: Routledge & Kegan Paul, 1960).

There is also, though perhaps less openly articulated, the fear of aloneness. Linked to the more general fear of criminal activities, this may take the specific form of a deep unease about a possible attack on personal possessions. The significance of this fear is an apprehension about losing what is deemed to give substance to life; it is experienced, therefore, as a loss of security. Freedom is forfeited in this case by having to build barriers to protect possessions. So, one fortifies one's house against the intrusion of others. Another kind of anxiety is that of having to take final responsibility for far-reaching decisions in one's own life. Implied in the claim that, to be authentic, the inner self has to be free from unwanted external influences, accountable only to its own desires, is the reality that each person exists as an isolated individual. Freed from the pressure of submitting to the external authority of tradition, custom or convention, the subject is alone in choosing which, of a myriad of options, to follow.

Aloneness, however, is usually experienced as unendurable. Few, if any, people are able to stand as isolated individuals relying wholly on their own resources to cope with life. Thus, most are prepared to barter this idealistic notion of freedom for the reassurance given by submitting to some kind of collective, external 'authority'. Sometimes this 'authority' amounts to a prevalent, fashionable set of assumptions about what is important in life. Beliefs and life-styles are set according to current trends. Anyone who does not share these beliefs is, by definition, old-fashioned. They are deemed to be out of touch, meaning they are dissenters as far as front line opinion is concerned. In this situation, freedom is experienced as a choice between either belonging to the past or being up to the minute. What is important, however, is not the rightness or wrongness of the creeds being espoused but the sense of not looking different from the group that is setting the trend.

Thus, real freedom, which in its secular manifestation rests, as we have seen, on the ability to resist external pressures to conform, may well be compromised for the sake of psychological tranquillity. It is a curious anomaly that those who most strongly demand the outward form of freedom (young people in their struggle to be free from parental directives) most easily succumb to the pressures (and, on reflection, even the tyranny) of fashion. Perhaps conformity to the collective opinion of their peers concerning clothes, music and experiences is a source of the courage needed to exert influence on their parents; 'cool' becomes a synonym for normal *in their world*! Whatever the causes and whatever the rhetoric, the reality of freedom demonstrates that genuine human choice is bound to purpose, community, tradition, responsibility, established identity and right and wrong. Without all these elements in place, language about human rights has no meaning and freedom is self-delusion.

The question of economics
The view that the ideals of capitalism as a system of economic exchange and growth represent the best of all possible, though not necessarily all imaginable, worlds is superficially attractive. Certainly the technological innovation and the selective accumulation of wealth engendered within the system have been phenomenal. However, such a view can only be held plausibly by selecting evidence, which favours the thesis, marginalizes that which does not and ignores or denies adverse consequences.

The ideal of an economic system unfettered by social and political constraints simply jettisons unpalatable realities. We mention and comment briefly on three of them. First, the distribution of resources is not due largely to the mechanisms of an impersonal set of economic laws, under which all individuals are potentially equal, but to a process of violence. The primitive accumulation of wealth is, more often than not, the result of those possessing social power exploiting the misfortunes of the socially weak by restricting their economic freedoms for personal gain. Thus, for example, the ancient prophets of Israel, with divine insight into the social conditions of their times, saw clearly how those who held political power exploited the tax system to raise money for capital building projects. By extending their assets, they increased their power yet further. This process, along with the burden of taxation on the most disadvantaged to finance war, can be observed with ruthless clarity in the reign of king Solomon.[25] Markets do not operate in some kind of sanitised social vacuum. They work according to the manoeuvrings of those with most ability to influence outcomes. Where vested interests clash, those able to manipulate market conditions will almost always succeed. It is for these reasons that the notion of economic justice and economic inequity are not meaningless terms. It would indeed be surprising that economic life alone was unaffected by the old adage that power tends to corrupt.

Secondly, it is a myth to pretend that capital and labour are equivalent factors in the productive process. Capitalism as an economic way of life presupposes that both capital and labour demand a price in the market (either the payment of interest on loans and investment or the payment of wages), as if they were separate and equal entities that somehow come together to increase wealth for everyone's benefit. Capital, however, is another name for surplus-value, which is produced in a manu-facturing process by labour (i.e. human time, power and abili-ties). One is the product of the other. However, in present circumstances and increasingly on a global scale what is created controls those who create it. Thus, freedom to share in the fruits of labour is exchanged for the relatively restricted freedom to sell one's labour for whatever price capital ultimately allows the market to offer.

Thirdly, the freedom of the market is not exercised through the harmonious reconciliation of mutual interests. Rather it operates as a system in which power conflicts with power and is tempo-rally resolved. It has been described as an arrangement in which general 'warfare' at the centre is suspended, but without elimi-nating frequent skirmishes on the periphery. Economic libertari-ans are ingenuous if they pretend that firms and corporations are part of a neutral, spontaneous system, which upholds basic free-doms and rights. To survive they have to act forcefully, often pushing expediency to limits only curbed by the countervailing force of popular morality in cases such as the degradation of the

---

[25] See Helen R. Graham, 'Solomonic Models of Peace' in R. S. Sugirtharajah, *Voices from the Margins* (Maryknoll: Orbis Books, 1991), pp. 214–226.

environment, low wages, sub-human working conditions, ethical investment and industrial espionage.

Christian mission and secular freedom

Whilst acknowledging that the subject of freedom is complex and ambiguous, I have tried to examine some of the characteristics of what appears to be the dominant motif of modern cultures. Meanings are by no means uniform, and yet as a concept freedom has enormous motivating power. It engenders expectations that are written into the warp and woof of the self-identities of modern societies. If a full appreciation of the dynamics of context is a necessary condition for understanding the shape of the Christian community's mission, how should Christians respond to some of the realities we have been describing? Does it have, for example, a more fundamental, comprehensive, realistic, and therefore satisfying, understanding of freedom? Do Christians, individually or in community, practise a different model of freedom?

Mission as communication depends on a shared reality

There are good reasons, both theological and practical, for beginning a discernment of the task of mission, in the context of a secular view of freedom, with the reality of being human. If there is to be some sort of communication between Christian and secular thought, it is necessary, in my opinion, to recover, with appropriate safeguards, the long tradition of 'natural theology'. I recognise that, in the middle years of the twentieth century, 'natural theology' fell into disrepute under the aggressive challenge of 'dialectical theology'. Some are still sceptical. Nevertheless, more recently it has deservedly recovered some of its lost prestige.[26]

Natural theology is realist in its epistemological assumptions.

---

[26] See Jurgen Moltmann, *Experiences in Theology: Ways and Forms of Christian Theology* (London: SCM Press, 2000), chapter 6. However, John Milbank, a representative of the 'radical orthodox' school of theology, remains sceptical: see *Being Reconciled: Ontology and Pardon* (London: Routledge, 2003), pp. 117ff.

It holds that God has created an order of life and being which is objectively there, irrespective of the perspective from which it may be viewed. Human nature is located in an eternal order of being that maintains a consistency not disturbed by either time or the human will. Freedom can only be exercised within this order. Thus, it finds its perfect fulfilment, when used in harmony with the way the world is. Thus, for example, in the field of art, the artist expresses real freedom of expression not by trying to create some kind of personal meaning out of a formless chaos, but by exploring, in a huge variety of different ways, the magnificent diversity of colour, tone, shape and juxtapositions already inherent in creation. Freedom is guaranteed by the almost limitless possibilities of seeing something new and expressing it in a variety of forms.

This interpretation of the possibility of freedom is almost dia-metrically opposed to that found in all kinds of existential phi-losophy. According to the Christian world-view, being precedes becoming.[27] We do not come into the world as pure potentiality, bearing an unshaped nature, which could, in principle, develop in any number of different directions. Attempting to create our own reality out of an unbounded set of prospects, either indi-vidually or as part of a community, is not only idolatry (in theo-logical terms) but also foolishness.[28] We cannot measure freedom by the ability to escape from our human condition. We may, and do, have immense creative capacities, but they can only be exer-cised freely within the actuality of a pre-ordered creation. Were it not for the fact that we human beings share, by nature, a rela-tively stable common reality, communication would at best be haphazard, at worst unattainable.

In contemporary secular understandings of freedom, one can trace a logical path from the assumptions of modernity to those

---

[27] It is arguable also that in the areas of understanding and explanation, being (ontology) precedes knowing (epistemology), thus reversing the famous Cartesian formula, so that it becomes 'I am, therefore I (can) know.'

[28] Paul, the apostle to the Gentile world, explains the tragic condition of a human-ity gone astray in terms of idolatry and folly in Romans 1. 18ff. See J. Andrew Kirk, *The Meaning of Freedom*, op. cit., pp. 204–205. I will return to the thought of this passage, as it addresses a particular contextual moral issue, in chapter 9.

of post-modernity. Kant's famous aphorism 'dare to know' was echoed by an equally emphatic 'dare to be free'. Freedom has been measured by the adventure of discarding the empirically untested beliefs of religion and political philosophies in favour of a new understanding of life, supposedly under the control of careful, rational processes and objective scientific methods. The problem with this view of freedom is that human existence is not like a kind of raw material that can be observed, experimented on and explained dispassionately. We are already part of a long tradition of disputed interpretations of what it means to be human. It is just impossible to discard all these and start afresh, for such a project has already selected just one set of traditions for positive treatment. It is not surprising, therefore, that the modern project, which hoped for one universally acknowledged rational resolution of human life, has irretrievably broken down. By seriously limiting the horizons of human self-consciousness and then dismissing alternative visions, it was a self-contradictory enterprise from the very beginning. There was no chance that it could succeed.

The consequence of the failure of modernity was not to return to a more reliable understanding of freedom, based on the reality of being a creature in an ordered universe. On the contrary, the search for a universally valid rationality that audaciously would set the human race as a whole free was exchanged for a personally chosen decision to be free anyway. Modernity pursued a grand scheme that would unite humanity in a self-evidently rational approach to life. We would, by a patient and collaborative observation of our surroundings, come to know the truth for ourselves, and therefore be free.

Post-modernity is a condition of contemporary existence which proclaims that the grand design has failed. The future for humanity is not mapped out in terms of coming to a universally recognized common understanding (and, thereby, ending history), but in learning to live with and rejoice in multiple differences. Whereas modernity preached intolerance towards ignorance, post-modernity is inclined to dismiss ignorance as a meaningless category, since there are no criteria for judging the truth or falsity of one's own self-knowledge.

We might sum up the fundamental difference between the Christian and secular notions of freedom by stating that a *choice* to be and to live in a certain way and the *freedom* to do so are possibilities of a different *order*. Nevertheless, in spite of secular views of freedom, particularly those surrounding the defence of creedal and cultural plurality, communication still remains open, for, whatever our beliefs and values, we are united in a common humanity. Christian belief and secular thought do not have to pass each other silently in the night.

Taking responsibility for consequences
Within Christian thinking, the message of the prophet possesses three crucial strands: denouncing idolatry and injustice, warning of the consequences of remaining indifferent to coming judgement and announcing the hope of a new creation through God's direct action.[29] Unfortunately, in much 'political theology' the prophetic message is reduced to the first and last strands. As a result, it is often heard as a combination of moralism and utopia.

It is an obvious truism that there is no responsibility without freedom: to be held accountable for certain actions would be unjust, unless a real possibility of acting otherwise existed. However, the reverse (no freedom without responsibility) is not generally accepted in secular culture, for there is a reluctance to calculate the probable costs of freedom as choice.

Nevertheless, there are a number of social activities where calculations have to be made. One of the most obvious in an affluent society, where the population is spoilt for choice, concerns the maintenance of a physically, emotionally and spiritually healthy life-style. Where people indulge in habits that put their health at serious risk (for example, smoking, eating an excess of fatty foods, heavy drinking or engaging in unrestricted sexual practice), society may not be justified in forcefully prohibiting them from their actions. Nevertheless, it would be criminal not to warn them of the dangers their demand for freedom may entail.

[29] I will explore the relevance of the prophetic message to mission in more detail in chapter 8.

Actually, the consequences are more serious than just for the individual concerned. The question has to be raised, although the subject is still largely taboo, as to whether a person who willingly chooses a course of action knowing that it will almost certainly lead to a deterioration of health should expect to receive the same, unconditional medical treatment as a person who is inflicted by illness through no personal fault; or, if they do, should be charged for the costs. On one interpretation of justice, it could be argued that people should receive what is owed to them. In this case, what is owed are the consequences of a deliberately chosen way of life whose negative outcome is easily predictable. To what extent, therefore, should a person, who wittingly risks ill-health, even death, expect to avoid, by costly medical intervention, the consequences of their action?

Such questions and such an argument are dynamite in a morally lax and permissive society. The secular view of freedom is not conducive to proclaiming the moral law that what we sow we will also reap. Such a verdict is dismissed as illiberal, bigoted judgementalism. There is an expectation that, despite our choices, we can escape from the full effect of the consequences, either by good luck or by the forbearance and compassion of others. However, the kindest and most humane response may be to hold people accountable for their choices. At least, by so doing, we respect them as full human beings. Although out of fashion, the notion of guilt has the advantage of treating an individual as a real, full human person, not as an automaton, driven by uncontrollable impulses and desires. One of the long-term consequences of a society that has implicitly embraced a secular world-view is that it becomes transformed into a shame culture. Strictly speaking sin has no meaning, where there is no acknowledgement of the existence of a personal God. Guilt, which is a meaningful concept only within the framework of the reality of sin, also becomes problematic. We are well on the way to a dehumanised society.

The long-term, global effects of irresponsible freedom, whose consequences are also clearly predictable, can be seen, not only in the area of personal life-style (for example, sexually-transmitted diseases), but also in the present world economic order. The message of the prophet is addressed equally to the consequences of foolish decisions taken by individuals and those taken collectively by political, commercial, financial and business institutions. If, in spite of repeated warnings, a society as a whole decides to privilege its own (negative) freedoms over the (positive) freedoms of others in a way that defies elementary principles of justice, then it will reap the just reward for its unjust dealings. Prophets may not cut a popular image in a self-indulgent culture. Experience, however, demonstrates that an unpalatable prediction stands a good chance of coming true. Christian mission has to be seen in terms of authentic prophecy, however unwelcome by the culture.

A fresh look at freedom

For close on a quarter of a millennium, modern people have believed that freedom can emerge in human life and society by a kind of spontaneous generation, once the forces holding it back are abolished.[30] Such a view is based on the serious misconception that what is desirable can be possessed and enjoyed without affecting subsequent freedoms. However, the experience of human frailty, error and perverseness suggests otherwise. In Christian thinking, human wrongdoing is bound up with the misuse of freedom. Because of the prominent value placed on freedom in contemporary society, the stakes are very high. The most fundamental choice of all is to decide (perhaps by default) within what framework of belief one is going to approach life. This is a question, ultimately, of committing oneself to one of two options: either to accept the world as the unmerited *gift* of a bountiful giver with thanksgiving, respect and responsibility in a spirit of service to others or to take it as an entitled *possession* to dispose of according to one's own ends.

Here, however, there is no absolute choice to be free of external restraint, in order to create one's own life. Such a choice, attractive as it may be, is an illusion, for it collides with the real-

---

[30] See John Milbank, *Theology and Social Theory: Beyond Secular Reason* (Oxford: Blackwell, 1990), p. 189.

ity of human existence: created by a personal divine being to function according to certain laws and seriously flawed by the effects of an innate self-centredness. The very possibility of freedom is already severely constrained for all who refuse the summons to walk in the ways of God. The first step towards the recovery of an authentic freedom is to recognise our true condition as human beings. This requires the gift of wisdom, an extra-precious commodity in a world obsessed with information that prizes knowledge of data as the key to career advantage.

By definition, a secular view of freedom misses one of the most essential realities of our being in the world: the belief that humans may choose their mode of life of their own volition is a tragic delusion. It is a fantasy. We come into the world already in a state of unfreedom. The Christian message, to be honest, has to proclaim the bad news that the claim that 'all human beings are born free'[31] is untrue. As long as we do not recognise that freedom is only possible within the reality of our own essential humanity created by God and recreated through Christ, we will remain with our illusions. Freedom is a gift of grace, not an intrinsic right that pertains to human beings as such. There is no philosophy, ideology or religion that can possibly ground a belief in freedom as a natural right.[32] It becomes a genuine possibility when human beings enjoy fellowship with God. When our true humanity is restored to us, freedom becomes a genuine reality. It is Jesus Christ, the only human being who has ever used freedom entirely to sacrifice himself for others, rather than using it to satisfy his own desires, who makes us human again.

Living out the freedom of a restored humanity
What we are saying is that, because we live in a world that has been given a certain order fashioned by God, we can only discover our true selves, when we understand and live by the reality that is. This will entail, certainly, an exploration of the true riches of freedom that God has given, but also the proper limits

---

[31] *The Universal Declaration of Human Rights*, Article 1.
[32] See E. Bucar (ed.), *Does Human Rights Need God?* (Grand Rapids: Eerdmans, 2005).

to freedom. This is not a simple matter. On the one hand, we are surrounded and unquestionably influenced by the kind of culture we have been describing, one that has no way of distinguishing adequately between true and false freedoms. Contemporary society has converted a means to a greater end into the end itself, and experience suggests that there is always trouble stored up for those who confuse means and ends. On the other hand, there are many self-proclaimed interpreters of freedom who would impose their views on others. A society that has lost touch with the source of human well-being is constantly caught between an arbitrary libertarianism - anything is permitted in private as long as it is consensual and does not harm any third party - and the legalistic suppression of freedoms. Unless one has a clear idea of what it means to be human, freedom will clash with freedom, human right with human right.[33]

Living out a true freedom is something to be learnt in the act of following in the way of Christ. As was the case of his earthly life, the first challenge will be to stand against false temptations, the natural urgings to follow the paths of self-indulgence, security and material possessions. Like Christ, resistance can only be achieved through prayer, a constant listening to God's word and the support and encouragement of the Christian community. The truly free are those who have experienced liberation from self-preoccupation brought about through Christ's entirely voluntary death, the ultimate negation of freedom, as the price of restoring freedom to the lost. They will need then to emulate Christ's freedom through the gift of God's grace communicated by the Holy Spirit.

Mission in the way of Christ entails being liberated from a concern for one's own freedom and rights to consider first the well-

---

33 Human rights are not self-evident givens of life. They presuppose a clear acknowledgement of the intrinsic dignity and worth of individual human beings, which in turn presupposes a supra-human source that warrants such a belief. The danger of a theory of 'natural' human rights is that, in the absence of a transcendent point of reference, the state becomes the determinant and arbiter of what it means to be human (for example, in the case of the human foetus and abortion, and chronic disability and euthanasia) and what rights, therefore, are applicable , see *Being Reconciled*, op. cit., p. 97.

being of others. Like so much that God has made in the world, freedom is the by-product of a goal that is much more significant and fundamental. Many of the civil freedoms obtained by ordinary citizens from the inadmissible claims of authoritarian powers are rightly to be defended. Nothing said about the given nature of the created world should be taken as reasons for a politically reactionary imposition of arbitrary, ideologically-inspired norms of conduct. However, it is in God's service that there is perfect freedom to become what we have been created to be. It is, then, the mission of the people of God to discern humbly in all situations the nature of the true freedom and to proclaim it, chiefly by modelling it in their lives, but also through argument and persuasion in every aspect of public life.

CHAPTER 2

———

Mission as Dialogue:
the Case of Secular Belief

The challenge to Christian mission of a thoroughly secularised culture is causing much puzzlement and perplexity. All sectors of the Church in Europe, and increasingly the Church outside Europe, as it seeks to fulfil its cross-cultural missionary calling, are showing great interest and concern. How exactly to address the pervasive influence of secular thinking remains one of the most problematical, unanswered questions of current Christian reflection and practice.

Although Christians concerned about mission should be equipped to appreciate the theoretical assumptions and practical impact of the secularising process, no exploration of this fascinating, crucial and difficult subject can be satisfied with a purely intellectual treatment. In seeking to understand the origins and nature of a secular culture, one is grappling not only with ideas that have provoked massive changes in the way in which contemporary people approach and 'see' reality but also the values that flow from them. Ideas do indeed provide a crucial conceptual framework that underpins practical belief; but it is values that mainly influence the way in which people shape their individual lives and societies construct economic, social and political ends and means. Secular, modern ideas bring with them particular assumptions that lead to distinctive life-styles. In so far as these contradict, at times, a Christian view of what it means to be

truly human they provoke analysis and comment from the perspective of the 'apostolic message of Jesus'.

On the surface, secular ideals appear to have both liberating
and destructive tendencies and consequences. In so far as the
Christian community in mission has to be concerned about the
relationship between the Gospel and specific cultures, it must be
able to develop tools of analysis that allow it to make mature
judgements, from the perspective of its core beliefs, about positive and negative elements in secular culture. Dialogue, as a
means of building relationships of trust between those of different convictions and helping to understand others' points of view,
is generally recognised as an important instrument to further
mutual comprehension and respect. In grasping the meaning,
significance and impact of a secular consciousness, it is crucial to
listen to actual people who are committed to this way of thinking.

The purpose of dialogue

Although interpretations of its implications may vary, it is recognised by most sectors of the church that dialogue is a vital part
of best mission practice. However, the possibility that such dialogue might be extended to people who espouse no clear religious convictions is hardly ever touched upon. There may be
understandable reasons why this should be so. Dialogue has
been pursued, as part of the Christian community's calling,
almost exclusively in relationship to people of religious faith.
Even here, however, the dialogue has been limited largely to the
five generally recognised as 'world' religions – Buddhism,
Hinduism, Islam, Judaism and Sikhism. More recently founded
religions, often offshoots of the parent bodies, are not usually
included. Then, although it is accepted that secular *culture* is a
reality, which affects people living in a certain environment, the
existence of secular *belief* as a recognisable body of rational
thought and personal allegiance is not clear to many.

In this study, I wish to argue (a) that a secular outlook on life
shares many of the same characteristics as religious faith and,

therefore, (b) that Christians should see it as a potential partner in dialogue about fundamental issues in life. In order to justify this viewpoint, I will move from more to less familiar territory, from the notion of dialogue as an integral part of mission to the notion of secular belief as a legitimate partner in an 'inter-faith' conversation. I realise that the use of terms like belief and faith of the secular frame of mind may not be wholly welcome by those who reject, in principle, the claims of all religious bodies. One of the anomalous consequences of the influence of modernity is the perception that the language of faith belongs exclusively to the world of religion. This notion, which is false to experience, needs to be corrected.[1]

I also recognise that different people mean different things by dialogue in the context of inter-religious exchange. At a minimum, it means people belonging to different religious communities coming together to share their convictions about the way the world is and how life can be enhanced for all people. As a working definition, I suggest that the following principles usually motivate and guide the practice of dialogue.

(a) Respect for the dignity and integrity of all human beings. Given that religious belief and practice is central to the lives of the majority of humanity, respect entails taking seriously what other people say matters most to them, irrespective of whether I share their ideas or not.

(b) The need to represent other people's views fairly. It is dishonest and unjust to rely exclusively on outsiders' interpretation of the meaning and implications of a particular faith. Careful listening to practitioners is a precondition for overcoming caricatures and stereotypes.

(c) The need to hear and consider what others say about our beliefs and practices. Convictions, when held intelligently, are open to criticism leading to the possibility of conversion and change. Other people's opinions, however strident, received in a spirit

---

[1] There is a comprehensive discussion of this point in Juan Luis Segundo, *Faith and Ideologies* (London: Sheed & Ward, 1984).

of openness and humility, may help believers root out what is
unacceptable in their creed and practice.

(d) The call to work together in common projects that seek justice
and reconciliation in society. It has been shown that there are
many occasions when people of different faith convictions, and
possibly for different reasons, can agree on certain goals and
strategies concerning issues such as the implementation of
human rights, community development and the overcoming of
community strife.

(e) Mutual witness. For some this is the most controversial aspect
of dialogue. However, there is a sense in which all religions are
'evangelistic' in intent, in that they see themselves as the
guardians of crucial insights into the nature and meaning of life
itself and how it should be conducted, which they have an obligation to share. Christian thinking, to be consistent with its core
beliefs, has to understand dialogue as a mode of evangelism.
Or, perhaps, it would be more appropriate to reverse the idea
and say that authentic evangelism has to be conducted in a dialogical manner, in that its method is patience and gentleness,
rather than aggression, persuasion rather than threat, an expectation of God's working rather than human enterprise and exertion.

The nature of religion

In contemporary missiological thinking, the partners in dialogue
are uniformly considered to be members of religious communities. Thus David Bosch, in his classical treatise on mission,[2]
includes a section on dialogue under the heading, 'Mission as
Witness to Peoples of Other Living Faiths'. It is, I believe, symp-
tomatic of much contemporary missiological thought that Bosch,
having correctly diagnosed that one of 'the two largest unsolved
problems for the Christian church is its relationship to *world
views which offer this-worldly* salvation',[3] does not return to the

[2] *Transforming Mission: Paradigm Shifts in Theology of Mission* (Maryknoll: Orbis
Books, 1991).
[3] Ibid. pp. 476–477.

theme, but concentrates exclusively on the other one, *'other faiths'*.

Although trying to give a definition of religion that fits all categories is notoriously problematical, there are certain common patterns of belief and practice that can be recognised in most cases.[4] The following ingredients may be identified as the most central:

(i) a *message* (comprising certain claims, ideas and obligations) recognised to be valid universally

(ii) an *experience*, relating to the message, which validates it as authentic and relevant for human living

(iii) a *community* committed to and bound by both the message and the experience

(iv) an *historical tradition*, which, although it may change over time, links communities together across time and space

These factors afford a measure of self-identity, a basis for interaction with the world outside the particular community and a means by which other communities can recognise them. We now have to consider the crucial matter as to whether these can be applied, without begging too many questions, to a self-consciously non-religious group of people. Is secular *belief* a meaningful concept or a contradiction in terms?

Between religion and the secular: ideological conviction

There may be an intermediate link between inter-religious dialogue and dialogue with people committed to a secular view of the world, namely ideological belief. The World Council of Churches recognised an association in publishing the report,

---

[4] I have avoided using the terms 'transcendence' and 'sprituality' in this definition for two reason: (a) they tend to multiply ambiguities, in that their own meaning is vague and ambivalent; (b) they do not fit all religious manifestations (for example, Theravada Buddhism), except in a very loosely extended sense. Religion is a word that has to be used to identify certain communities and beliefs, and yet is a category invented to describe phenomena which do not easily fit the designation.

Guidelines on Dialogue with People of Living Faiths and Ideologies.[5] The time of publication was significant. There was an escalating build-up of nuclear arms within NATO countries and the nations of the Warsaw Pact. Two relatively self-confident ideologies, cap-italism and communism, were entering a new and highly per-ilous stage of confrontation. Both ideologies possess convictions, which share common characteristics with religious beliefs, about human nature, the relation of human life to the environment, about worthwhile human goals and how to reach them. They revolve around great motivating values like freedom, justice, rights, welfare, self-determination, participation, democracy, progress and so on. Behind these great themes lies a more or less coherent world-view, which in both cases, is built, to a certain extent, on the Christian vision of reality. Indeed, both ideologies, in their own way, can be legitimately interpreted as secular ver-sions of the Christian hope.

The notion of ideology arose originally as an attempt to sys-tematise the history of ideas.[6] Antoine Destutt de Tracy, who first used the term (in 1797), thought of ideology as a discipline, par-allel to the natural sciences, that would explore the origin, causes and effects of distinct ideas through different historical periods. He shared the modern assumption that disciplined, reasoned scholarship, working from a position of suspended judgement, was best able to organise empirical data in such a way that trust-worthy knowledge would ensue.

In the course of time, ideology became associated with two conflicting ways of interpreting and organising social existence, both indebted to the spirit and method of Hegelian dialectic. Capitalism and Marxism are both ideological in the sense of pos-tulating and defending, if necessary by coercion, only one, pre-determined direction and outcome for history. It is instructive that Marx spoke of the split between pre-history and what he called 'history proper' whilst the modern prophet of liberal capitalism, Francis Fukuyama, speaks about 'the end of history'.[7] Both envisage an historical process, in which the imminent forces

---

[5] (Geneva: WCC Publications, 1979).
[6] D. McLellan, *Ideology* (Milton Keynes: Open University Press, 1995) is an excel-lent survey of the topic.

of history itself will resolve all conflicts. The dialectic process of the struggle between opposing forces will come to an end in the final 'negation of all negations' for one in an entirely cooperative, egalitarian society where the means and ends of the productive process will be brought into harmony for the welfare of all citizens (Marx); for the other in a participatory society, in which each citizen will have an equal opportunity to share in the wealth of society and choose their mode of life, a society without 'masters' and 'slaves' (Fukuyama).

Here one finds two similar ideas, whose merits and defects can be debated and assessed from the perspective of various disciplines: historical studies, sociology, political economics, philosophy and theology. The idea becomes ideology, when it is used by dominant groups in society to move history in the desired and predicted direction. At present capitalism has demonstrated a greater power than communism, though not necessarily a superior understanding of history or human needs. The point to grasp in the context of this discussion is that both ideologies are firmly rooted in a series of beliefs that are neither empirically verifiable nor rationally self-evident. In a real sense they demonstrate a stance of faith based on assumptions held a priori.

Secular belief?

Ideological belief, like that of the various religions, is easily identifiable. It is not difficult to produce a brief summary of the core convictions of both capitalism and communism,[8] showing the main philosophical and methodological assumptions of each and demonstrating the underlying beliefs. Ideologies have arisen out of the secular imagination.[9] There may, therefore, be a pre-

---

[7] *The End of History and the Last Man* (London: Hamish Hamilton, 1992).

[8] We mention these two as the main examples of ideology. There are others – such as nationalism and racism – which would have been included, if our purpose had been to embark on a general discussion of the subject.

[9] It is arguable that they could only flourish in an environment where religious convictions no longer controlled people's perceptions of truth and the good. In part, they became secular substitutes, supplying purposive and motivating functions lost with the demise of religion as the over-arching interpretation of existence.

sumption that this imagination is itself based on a set of affirmations that share similar characteristics to religious and ideological beliefs. Is there, then, such a general category as secular belief, which is equally recognisable? A number of commentators think there is. By way of advancing the discussion, we will explore briefly the analysis given by two writers, representing different religions – Islam and Christianity. The reason for proceeding in this way is that it is arguable that religious commentators have their intellectual senses more attuned to detecting the distinguishing marks of a belief system than those who still adhere to a positivistic interpretation of reality, and who, therefore, see a secular viewpoint as based strictly on scientifically demonstrable evidence.

Professor Nasr, a distinguished Islamic scholar, locates secular belief in the Western humanist tradition that has its origins in the Renaissance.[10] For him the two main characteristics of secular humanism are the revolt against tradition and hierarchy and the claim that the human person is the ultimate measure of all things. According to this view, the human being is an independent earthly being, the only being in the universe whose brain has developed rational, thought processes. This being can no longer accept the myth that there is any other reality, beyond its own experience of the universe and reasoning about it that could supply information about the origin, meaning and purpose of life.

This means that the main alternative explanation of reality, theistic faith based on instruction from a non-human existence, is no longer valid.[11] Thus, for example, the story about humanity being ejected from paradise has to be regarded as a strictly unreal legend about the state of human life. It can be discarded

---

[10] See *Religion and the Order of Nature* (Oxford: OUP, 1996). Whereas, in the main, I give a summary of his argument, in places I expand it with comments of my own.

[11] It is intriguing that some scientists and philosophers, who reject the possibility of an unseen, non-material world, are prepared to speculate about parallel universes. By definition, such universes would be undetectable, wholly unavailable to human observation. Could it be that such conjecture fulfils an unconscious longing for there to be something more real than a universe that has come into being and evolved by blind chance and is destined, according to the second law of thermodynamics, for extinction?

along with the humiliating doctrine of original sin and human corruption. Thus, where Christians state that the present situation of human beings is in many ways abnormal, because they have decided to reject God's purposes for life, secular humanists affirm that present reality is normal.

However, in spite of seeking to live in the bold new world of their own creation, secular humanists are driven ultimately to a radical scepticism concerning conclusive knowledge about any aspect of reality. It is as if human intellectual endeavour was being driven by the slogan, 'systematic doubt is the beginning of wisdom'. It is advisable to approach all claims to knowledge and understanding, all explanations of the meaning of existence, all affirmations about moral virtues and values with an appropriate dose of suspicion. The loss of belief in a world-order that is benevolent, despite all appearances, has given rise to incredulity and mistrust about any conviction. There is no ultimate source of trust in the universe, no assurance that truth will be vindicated finally by one who is the truth. The present secular mood (in its post-modern phase), therefore, tends to cynicism, based on the supposition that ideas, beliefs, policies and strategies simply serve vested interests.

At the same time, and perhaps partly in compensation for the doubt about grandiose schemes of belief, modern secular people have rediscovered, over against the long Christian tradition of asceticism, pleasure as the goal of existence. Seeing that the body is the sole possession of the individual to whom it belongs and will one day disintegrate into oblivion, it may be gratified today. There are no limits, other than the ones we set for ourselves, to how we may entertain ourselves with the amusements that this world offers in abundance. One of the most significant signs of the triumph of secularism in the West is the reinstatement of the old Epicurean philosophy, 'let us eat and drink (and have sex), for tomorrow we die'.[12] Such a conclusion can be logically deduced from the expectation that nothing exists beyond this world. If there is no final moral reckoning, no absolute standards

[12] An aphorism quoted by the Apostle Paul in I Corinthians 15:32, taken initially from Isa. 22:13, but almost certainly echoing also a contemporary, popular Epicurean saying.

of right and wrong to which we are accountable, no prospect of judgement, a hedonistic life-style seems to make good sense. As long as we keep within the bounds of present, legally permitted behaviour, and accepting the premise that laws are there, if not to be broken, at least to be changed, we are accountable to ourselves alone for our choices.

For secular humanists, then, there are no external bounds that might confine human beings in their outlook and activities. There is no given form to life, no divine agency, no cosmic laws. Human beings, therefore, possess no inherent being. They are as they become through their own transforming action on the natural environment, which is there as an object to be used and moulded to their desires. There is no longer any bridge to God, or another world, for such an hypothesis is no longer credible. The human being *is* the creator, alone in the universe to create his or her own forms and meanings. Such a being now acts out the heroic act of defiance, summed up in the celebrated saying of the philosopher Nietzsche:

> Once, you said 'God' when you gazed upon distant seas; but now I have taught you to say 'superman'. Let your will say: the superman shall be the meaning of the earth! I beseech you, my brothers, remain faithful to the earth, and do not believe those who speak to you of otherworldly hopes![13]

This explanation of the meaning of the secular is, in reality, an interpretation of secularism, i.e. a doctrine, which denies that there can be any reality beyond the material world, and which promotes an anti-religious view of life.

Colin Gunton, in the 1992 Bampton Lectures,[14] uses broad concepts to characterise modern, secular reality. The first is *disengagement*. By this he means the separation of human beings from one another and from the external world: 'the key is in the word *instrumental*: we use the other as an instrument, as the mere

---

[13] *Thus Spoke Zarathustra* in Walter Kaufmann (translator and editor), *Basic Writings of Nietzsche* (New York: The Modern Library, 1968).

[14] Published under the title, *The One, the Three and the Many: God, Creation and the Culture of Modernity* (Cambridge: CUP, 1993).

means for realizing our will, and not in some way integral to our being. It has its heart in the technocratic attitude; the view that the world is there to do with exactly as we choose.'[15] Another way of expressing the same thought is by saying that human beings have been compressed into an essentially material view of life. Humans, alongside other animate and inanimate bodies, are viewed strictly as objects of our desires and will. They tend to become reduced in our vision of reality to articles, items or devices. This is patently obvious, for example, in the way we often treat children: not only in the highly exploitative porno- graphic industry, their inclusion in the military and use as cheap labour in some countries, but also in the way parents play out their own ambitions through their offspring, or even see them as accessories to their self-constructed image of themselves.

The second word is *displacement*. God has been displaced in modern societies as the focus for the unity and meaning of being: 'what do I mean by that? Chiefly that the functions attributed to God have not been abolished, but shifted – relocated, as they say . . . When the unifying will of God becomes redundant . . . the focus of the unity of things becomes the unifying rational mind.'[16] On the principle that the human mind abhors a vacuum, the existence of the deity as a necessary and sufficient explana- tion of our experience of reality is replaced by another assump- tion. The value and purpose of life can be worked out and guaranteed by the collective wisdom of humankind constructing its own philosophy.

The third word is *this-worldliness*. The secular affirms the pri- ority of 'time over eternity, space over infinity'. We are conscious of the passing of time, but we affirm the importance of the pres- ent by throwing off the dead hand of the past. Belief in provi- dence or fate gives way to belief in the efficacy of human agency and will. This is the process that is often referred to as the *disen- chantment* or the *desacrilisation* of the world: i.e., the removal of any reference to a causal agent beyond the imminent processes at work in the natural world. This interpretation of life exacts a

[15] Ibid. p. 14.
[16] Ibid. p. 28.

high cost for human experience. It is hard, for example, to be inspired by the magnificent complexity of the universe to wonder and awe, if we believe that it is no more than the effect of an entirely haphazard process. Likewise, a thoroughly secular view of things does not allow for the notion of the holy in life.

There is much in these two accounts of the secular, which agree. The question remains, however, as to whether the characteristics amount in any way to a recognisable set of separate beliefs, with which a Christian might engage in a dialogical missionary spirit. One difficulty is that, until the dialogue is under way, we cannot be sure we have represented the beliefs fairly. The religious mind, understandably from its point of view, is prone to criticise secular thought sharply. The issue then is to identify concrete people, who are glad to be known as truly secular people and who are willing to expound and witness to their convictions in the context of a frank conversation with Christian believers. Then, in the course of the dialogue, perceptions can change.

Hall and Gieben, writing out of a religiously uncommitted stance, list the following key ideas as making up the secular paradigm – 'a set of interconnected ideas, values, principles and facts which provide both images of the natural and social world and a way of thinking about it'.

(a) Reason – understood as thought based on innate ideas independent of experience, demonstrable to any person employing their cognitive faculties properly
(b) Empiricism – all thought and knowledge about both the natural and social worlds is based on empirical facts, discoverable by the experimental methods of science
(c) Progress – the natural and social conditions of human beings are improved by the application of science and reason to the solving of problems, holding out the promise of an expanding level of happiness and well-being for the population as a whole
(d) Toleration – people's beliefs should never be a sufficient reason for excluding them from full participation in civic and economic life or oppressing them
(e) Individualism – individual reason and conscience is not subject

to a higher authority; society is basically the product of the
thought and action of large numbers of individuals

(f) Relativism – there is no single norm derivable from religion,
history or culture, which provides a standard of perfection for
judging others.[17]

Though certainly open to debate about details, I think there is
enough evidence to suggest that a set of beliefs, which can meaningfully be called secular, exist. At the risk of over-simplification,
and by way of summarising the discussion so far, I would suggest that the following elements constitute the essential compo-
nents of secular belief. Firstly, there is the conviction that
religious beliefs and practices have no place in the public life of
society but should be confined to the realm of personal, private
activities. It is typical of a secular mind-set, one that often
influences even religious believers, to state that religious belief is
an intensely intimate affair. As once famously articulated, it is
what one does with one's solitude. Religious practice is seen as a
leisure pursuit, with presumed therapeutic value for certain
types of people in particular circumstances. The secular view is
antipathetic to any notion of the public truth of religious claims.
This may be one reason why 'fundamentalisms', with their links
to the media, political policy and power, receive such a terrible
press. In the last analysis, they are seen not so much as irrational
creeds as rival centres of influence.

Secondly, morality should be seen as independent of religious
belief.[18] There are three senses in which this is deemed to be true:
a non-religious person can lead a life of moral integrity of equal
or greater coherence than a religious person; there are perfectly
plausible ways of discovering right moral values without
recourse to the hypothesis of a divine being; religion is no guarantee of high standards of ethical probity among its followers.
Speaking generally, a secular view of right and wrong is

---

[17] *Formations of Modernity* (Cambridge: Polity Press, 1992), pp. 18ff.

[18] Among others, Michael Martin, *Atheism, Morality and Meaning* (Amherst, NY:
Prometheus Books, 2002) and A.C. Grayling, *What is Good? The Search for the Best
Way to Live* (London: Wiedenfeld & Nicolson, 2003) argue passionately for this
point of view.

deducible from a set of innate, self-evident values, whose merit is judged by the consequences that flow from them. They are to be implemented through a reciprocal care (altruism) for the welfare of the other.

Thirdly, and perhaps this penetrates closest to the heart of the secular attitude, the quality of one's life does not depend on meeting any presumed spiritual needs. Human flourishing, to use a term favoured in recent years, can be achieved whether, or not, a person practices any religion that points to a reality beyond themselves and the universe. The claim, at least, is made that a non-religious person can enjoy a depth of quality of life equal, and often superior, to that of a religious believer.

Secular belief and missionary dialogue

Even if we grant that secular beliefs comprise an identifiable set of convictions that form the everyday horizon of irreligious people (those not involved in any cultic practice nor who appeal to religious belief as the foundation for their goals in life or behaviour), the problem of dialogue as a Christian missionary imperative remains. The gap between 'the apostolic message of Jesus Christ' and secular consciousness seems to be too great, and increasing, for any meaningful contact to be made. It is, seemingly, a gap much greater than that which exists between Christian faith and the world religions. Moreover, and this is a crucial point, there seems to be no external threat or other strong incentive that might drive secular people to wish to engage in dialogue with Christians, unless it be the perceived dangers posed by various forms of 'fundamentalism'.[19] However, interpreting this latter as a problem common to both parties begs a number of questions; not least there is the often inaccurate por-

---

[19] Some people might suggest that serious threats to the environment's ability to sustain life, or the desparate situation of the world's poor, could be issues that would bring Christians and secular believers into dialogue. I suspect, however, that, although these problems provoke much debate about the means of their solution, they do not normally lead to a serious conversation about the ultimate questions of life and death.

trayal by secularists of some religious groups' fundamental beliefs and intentions.

I suspect that there is a mood in many Western societies of mutual suspicion and blame that makes dialogue between the two sides extremely difficult. Curiously, in spite of the much-heralded collapse of modernity and the rise and dominance of a thoroughly relativistic and pluralist approach to difference, religious belief is increasingly being attacked, ridiculed and distorted by secular people.[20] For some strange and contradictory reason, beliefs that are dismissed as intellectually absurd and morally bankrupt, on the very edge of extinction, engender a passionate hatred in the hearts of some people. One may wonder, therefore, whether the antipathy is provoked to a certain extent by the kind of posturing that springs from a deep-seated, only partially conscious unease that perhaps the Christian world-view may be true after all.

Nevertheless, for Christians, despite the unpromising environment, a significant mutual dialogue is not only a meaningful idea, but an urgent calling. The signs that societies are gradually, but inescapably, losing any sense of common vision and becoming little more than an aggregate of isolated people, who have lost trust in public institutions and in people's word as their bond, should alarm anyone concerned about human well-being. An increase in sophisticated, often internationalised and violent crime and the growth of gratuitous violence in the promotion of some cause, or as the outcome of an amoral outlook on life, should disturb all people who care about the inviolability of the human person. Seeing that religious and secular people tend to accuse one another for holding opinions which make these facets of life more probable, perhaps the time for serious talking has arrived.

I cannot speak for secular-inclined people. However, for Christians the following elements seem to be crucial in approaching an open, critical and honest dialogue. First, to

[20] The many misrepresentations of Christian belief in the two books cited in note 18 are examples of this point. Similar generalisations and stereotypes are quite frequently made about the Christian religion in leading articles and programmes in the media.

understand the secular mind-set, Christians should immerse themselves in the thought forms of secular protagonists through their writings or through direct contact with individuals or groups. Understanding will entail the sensitive task of evaluating both the strong and weak points, taking into account the obvious, but often unacknowledged fact, that a secular view of life implies a faith-commitment.[21] I take it to be clear from experience that dialogue proceeds most fruitfully, when people on both sides of a conversation are confident in their own belief.

Secondly, in probing the assumptions that lie beneath the surface, a Christian may wish to explore ways in which the secular creed is unable to fulfil its own ideals. For example, there exist some fundamental ambiguities, if not contradictions, in the rather superficial and glib notion of toleration. These are plain, once one realises that even the most liberal of societies place limitations on the extent to which certain beliefs and actions can be allowed. As examples, we might cite racist attitudes and paedophilia on the internet. Likewise, as explored in the previous chapter, there are inherent limitations to the idea of human rights, most notably in the difficulty of giving any unambiguous theoretical grounding for the notion, and in the clash in practice of different rights. Nevertheless, toleration of diverse attitudes, values and life-styles and the appeal to individual rights as a means of protecting them seem to define the highest aspirations of a civilised, liberal society from a secular viewpoint. Some people, in the same vein, are now speaking of multiculturalism as the 'new culture', i.e. that which defines the core value of a multi-ethnic society.

Experience strongly suggests that, in the drive for human autonomy, authentic humanness is easily lost, and in the pursuit of individual self-fulfilment, the ideals of service and solidarity suffer. Perhaps, even more telling, is the observation that many of the ideals still abroad in a secularised society have essential

---

[21] By the use of this terminology, I do not imply any belief in the existence or importance of a non-material reality. I employ it, rather, to point to the non-empirically veriable and non-axiomatic assumptions that have to be made about reality for any thought to get off the ground.

Christian roots. A humanist ethic, if it wishes still to support the reality of moral absolutes, and not slide into the ethic of the strongest or most persuasive, has to postulate, as a point of reference for moral judgement, some kind of hypothetical, absolute 'being' with 'god-like' qualities.[22] It would appear that the secular humanist is postulating an ethic, *as if* God existed.

Thirdly, a Christian will gently but firmly point out the many inadequacies of the secular account of life. What perhaps is most disturbing about the secular outlook is its highly restricted view of reality. In its zeal to combat the ideological use of religion, it has dismissed whole dimensions of life. However, these are precisely those facets that have the greatest power to explain the deeper levels of experience. For example, whatever purpose we may give to life will be arbitrary, if life does not possess an intrinsic meaning. Our own personal choice of purpose will also threaten our self-assurance, on the grounds that we *alone* have adopted it and, as one individual in an immense universe, are highly likely to get it wrong.

Moreover, the view that human beings have evolved by chance in a meaningless cosmos cannot be equal to the view that human beings are the outcome of the creation of a personal, infinitely great and perfectly good being. If there is no personal beginning to life, no purposive order and design in the universe and no existence beyond death, surely human imaginings, creativities and proposals are without foundation, consequence or ultimate worth.[23] Surely, a completely fortuitous set of circumstances, whereby humans have supposedly developed larger and more complex brains than other mammals, is no basis for

---

[22] Called by Michael Martin 'the Ideal Observer,' op. cit., *passim* (note the capital letters!).

[23] Martin argues that neither the denial of intrinsic moral values or of life beyond death amounts to an affirmation that 'nothing matters.' However, his conclusion that life has meaning 'if as a whole it is good for the person who leads it' begs three fundamental questions. First, how can we make sense of good, when it is defined in such a subjective way? Secondly, what is it that connects good and meaning? Is it not possible to feel good (psychologically satisfied) about some matter and yet hold that life is fundamentally absurd? Thirdly, is it not true that life can only be good for a person if it has intrinsic meaning? Without basic purpose, good loses its value.

according them greater worth than other living species. Since when did size amount to a sufficient reason for granting an entity greater respect?[24] Human rights, which can only make sense if there is an intrinsic order of things, are devoid of a theoretical basis. They become impossible to articulate, if values are relative to time and place, and all cultures of equal worth. However, although these notions are the logical conclusion of a secular world-view, most of them have implications that human beings would find themselves unable to live with.

Finally, and much more difficult than the theoretical debate about the basic presuppositions for knowledge, understanding and wisdom, Christians will have to demonstrate, by means of their practical display of care, compassion and a life of utmost integrity in the community, how their faith in Jesus Christ, as the one saviour of the world, brings meaning, transformation and hope into daily living. Dialogue is, undoubtedly, about a robust exchange of views concerning the most valuable and pressing aspects of life. It is predicated on the supposition that the parties to the dialogue share a similar understanding of rationality, otherwise intellectual engagement will be impossible.[25] Part of the case that Christians will want to press is that dialogue itself and a consistent match between beliefs and practical living are only possible on the premise that the Christian faith is true.

Conclusion

In this brief discussion, we have presented the case for considering that a secular outlook on life represents a coherent body of belief, which shapes the way many people respond to the world and order their individual lives. There are a number of theories

[24] On a strictly naturalist view of human origins, why would not a computer that can regularly defeat the top international grandmaster at chess be worthy of greater consideration? In terms of problem-solving rationality it has evolved beyond human capacities.

[25] Dialogue will, unfortunately, be ruled out by those, both Christians and secularists, who continue to promote the absurd myth that faith and reason are incompatible entities. Roger Trigg, *Rationality and Religion* (Oxford: Blackwell, 1998) explodes the various fallacies that underlie this viewpoint, see chapters 1, 4, 7 and 9.

as to how this system of beliefs has entered into the cultural consciousness of certain nations; we will consider some of them in
the next chapter. Our purpose here has been to establish the principle that dialogue as an integral aspect of Christian mission
should be extended from an inter-religious conversation to one
which includes people who are committed to a non-religious
interpretation of existence. I have argued elsewhere that in
highly secular contexts (like Europe, East and West), dialogue
with secular people is a greater missionary imperative than with
adherents of any of the major religions.[26]

> The decisive datum, I believe, is the tacit acceptance of a
> secular worldview and life-form by the overwhelming
> majority of the inhabitants of this part of the world (Europe).
> If this is the case, the main challenge to Christian mission in
> this situation has to be contemporary secularity and
> secularism, not multireligiosity . . . I am arguing that in the
> Western world there is a missiological presumption in favour
> of engaging first with a reality shaped by secular
> assumptions.[27]

I find that in many Christian circles today this point is not taken
with the seriousness that it merits. I am surprised how many
Christian analysts of contemporary Western culture believe that
we are experiencing a decisive break with the hard secular
assumptions of the last forty, or so, years and moving into a new
era much more receptive to spiritual experience and values. I
suspect that the reason may be that some have failed to appreciate sufficiently that the search for inner healing, integration and
equilibrium, through the medium of a countless variety of therapies, often designated collectively as the 'turn to spirituality', is
quite compatible with a basic secular orientation to life.

It is quite possible that while religious interest is expanding,

---

[26] See J. Andrew Kirk, 'Christian Mission in Multifaith Situations' in Viggo
Mortensen (ed.), *Theology and the Religions: a Dialogue* (Grand Rapids: Eerdmans,
2003), pp. 153–163.
[27] Ibid. p. 153.

secular values are also increasing. It is precisely a unique characteristic of the way Western societies have developed that secularity and spirituality can coexist within the same person, so that the embracing of some 'spiritual' practices does not indicate necessarily a rejection of fundamental secular values.[28]

In the next chapter, I will attempt to give an account of why I believe this, seemingly contradictory, combination is possible, some of the ways in which it manifests itself and how Christian mission might be carried out in response.

[26] Ibid, p. 154.

CHAPTER 3

The Calling of Mission in a Post-Christian Environment

I have begun to explore aspects of the challenge to Christian mission of secular assumptions about life. In particular, I have examined something of the intellectual and emotional energy invested in contemporary ideas of freedom, and evaluated these in the light of a Christian understanding. I have also argued that the secular outlook on life constitutes a system of belief, which in many essentials is comparable to religious convictions. One of my principal conclusions is that *freedom*, as a major personal and social value, and *secular belief*, as a fundamental, theoretical stance for viewing reality, together form the bedrock of accepted discourse in Western cultures. In all sorts of ways they now constitute the overarching canopy, which has taken over the role of Christianity's 'sacred canopy', of providing a framework for deciding what is important and what is acceptable in human affairs. This is true, whether or not personal adherence to the Christian faith is falling, rising or remaining more or less stable. The general lack of regard in Europe not only for the church as an institution but also for the claims of Christianity, as the tacitly agreed explanation for existence, means that the cultural environment is now largely post-Christian.[1]

---

[1] See Callum Brown, *The Death of Christian Britain* (London: Routledge, 2001); Grace Davie, *Religion in Modern Europe: A Memory Mutates* (Oxford: OUP, 2000).

The impact of culture on Christian mission

An analysis of the position of Christian faith within national communities has led some Christians to wonder whether evangelism, leading to membership of the church, is any longer either feasible or desirable. Mission, which in some circles used to be almost identified with evangelism, is now almost completely disassociated from it. It is now aligned, more or less, with service to the community and ethical pronouncements and action in the political sphere, referred to as its prophetic ministry. Such a limited understanding of mission appears to take its cue partly from the surrounding culture, in particular from an emphasis on the multi-religious nature of contemporary societies,[2] and partly from a misunderstanding of the nature of evangelism. In the latter case, evangelism has been mistakenly identified with certain tactics and techniques, which might appear to some rather aggressive and confrontational. However, one suspects that for some Christians the basic cause of hesitancy about evangelism is due to uncertainty about the truth of the message of Jesus Christ in the light of so many competing claims to truth.

The unsympathetic cultural environment for evangelism and a loss of conviction (or loss of nerve) about the evangelistic mandate create a doubly difficult climate in which the church has to consider its mission calling. After many years of good theological debate, the Christian community as a whole endorses the notion that the church is, by nature, missionary.[3] The time has surely come, specifically in the post-Christian environment of Europe, to argue forcefully again that the church is also, by definition, evangelistic. Such a belief does not condone everything that is done in the name of evangelism. There are solid criteria for judging good and bad practice. However, the impor-

---

[2] I will explore the main reasons why some sectors of the church believe that the evangelism of people of religious faith is inappropriate in chapter 5.

[3] See *Ad Gentes*, 2 (Documents of the Second Vatican Council); David Bosch, *Transforming Mission*, p. 372. However, it is not yet evident that this consensus has begun seriously to transform the thinking and practice of the majority of local churches in nations with a long Christian presence. This may be due in large part to the 'pastoral drag,' i.e. the extreme difficulty of reversing the centuries-long perception that the task of the church is to minister to the pastoral and religious needs of its members and parishioners.

tant point is to concede that mission, envisaged as service to the community and prophetic witness, without evangelism, is like a two-legged stool, inherently unstable and unserviceable.

Evangelism as a defining term of the Church's witness

Unless the Church were to abandon its creeds, it is liturgically committed to confessing its own being as 'catholic' and 'apostolic'. Both terms imply its essentially evangelistic nature. Catholic means universal, and universal means all peoples and every culture. Apostolic means grounded on, abiding by and communicating the apostolic message concerning Jesus Christ. The church could not be part of the life of all nations, unless Christians take the Gospel message to the ends of the world, baptise those who believe and form them into a community in fellowship with the church elsewhere. Being apostolic implies, at the least, following the example of the apostles, sent by Jesus Christ to witness to him as the one saviour of the world.

Given that the task of evangelism in a post-Christian environment is tough, Christians need to remind themselves constantly of the reasons why evangelism is a defining part of mission. Not to take it seriously implies a quite confused understanding of what the core faith means. Foremost, perhaps, is the conviction that God has spoken and acted in the world in a decisive way for the liberation of the whole of humanity from the scourge and consequences of sin and evil. The reality of Christ's finished work of atonement in his death and resurrection is understood by Christians to be public truth about God's changed relationship to the world.[4] It also becomes true for every person, when he or she accepts Christ's work as valid for them.

---

[4] The phrase 'public truth' has been used frequently by Lesslie Newbigin, see *Truth to Tell: the Gospel as Public Truth* (Grand Rapids: Eerdmans, 1991); Paul Weston, 'Gospel, Mission and Culture: The Contribution of Lesslie Newbigin' in David Peterson (ed.), *Witness to the World* (Carlisle: Paternoster Press, 1999), pp. 51–52. It refers to the observation that certain events in history constitute decisive acts of God for dealing with the problem of human sin and misery, that they are recorded in stories and commentaries in most people's own languages and in the open 'letters' of Christian lives, and that what they represent is universally true,

Springing from God's action on their behalf, Christians wish to express their gratitude for the gift of being liberated from a life of futility, falsehood and frustration, by telling others that they too can receive the same gift. Love of one's neighbour implies the responsibility and joy of sharing the best news that anyone could hear.[5] Finally, there are both temporal and eternal consequences of not responding to God's gracious offer of forgiveness and new life: the impossibility of experiencing a full restoration of one's humanity, and permanent separation from the source of life and being.

Without having to decide priorities in mission, it is necessary again in a post-Christian environment to reassert the indispensable calling of the Church to tell the story of salvation in Christ and invite all to respond personally by offering their lives to Christ. It is true that Christians have to think exceptionally creatively in redefining the means they use to 're-evangelise' peoples no longer conscious of the Christian heritage of their cultures. The characteristic stance in evangelism will be to act in 'bold humility': bold, because of a right confidence in the truth of the Gospel; humility, because the message is received as a gift to be passed on, not a human invention.[6] The church's inescapable call to evangelism is to be carried out as an integral part of the wider dimensions of mission: serving the needs of the community, helping to resolve conflict, working for justice for the excluded, bringing comfort and healing to those who are suffering.

The Characteristics of a Post-Christian Environment
Alongside the secular beliefs, values and lifestyles that we have explored in the previous chapters, two further aspects of a post-Christian situation can be considered.

as much for whole societies as for individuals. As Paul, the apostle, declared to the ruling power of his day, 'What I am saying is true and reasonable. The king is familiar with these things . . . I am convinced that none of this has escaped his notice, because it was not done in a corner' (Acts 26. 26).

[5] See J. Scott Jones, *The Evangelistic Love of God and Neighbour: A Theology of Witness and Discipleship* (Nashville: Abingdon Press, 2003).

[6] See Willem Saayman and Klippies Kritzinger (eds.), *Mission in Bold Humility: David Bosch's Work Considered* (Maryknoll: Orbis Books, 1996).

The end of Christian influence

It is not an exaggeration to say that the majority of people in Europe conduct their everyday lives as if God did not exist. This reality holds irrespective of what people may claim in surveys about religious beliefs. When a question is phrased in terms of 'do you believe in God?' it still usually evokes a positive response. This is because it is understood as a theoretical question, which is not recognised as impinging directly upon a person's core beliefs and values. Were the question to be, 'What difference does God make to the way you bring up your children?' Or, 'how does God influence the way you do your job?' I suspect that an honest answer in most cases would be, 'He doesn't.'

However, evidence of surveys also suggests that God is recognised and invoked at times of extreme stress, sorrow and loss. In a curious way, this experience becomes a kind of 'God-of-the-gaps'. When in trouble, when other resources do not give the support necessary to cope with situations of crisis, people turn to God to try to make sense of pain and grief. Here there is an anomaly, a kind of reverse of what one might rationally expect. Where the innocent suffer, either at the hands of violent people, or as the consequence of unexpected and overwhelming forces of nature, or through the transmission of contagious diseases or genetically inherited traits, intellectually the appropriate response might seem to be to declare the non-existence of God, or at least of a God who cares and is compassionate. Strangely, however, where there is a major calamity (like the Indian Ocean tsunami that struck at the end of 2004), people often turn to spokespersons of faith for an explanation. These kinds of events are rare in wealthy nations that have in place careful health and safety control systems and sophisticated medical practices to deal with unexpected traumas. For most people, most of the time, scientific procedures (including counselling techniques) take the sting out of suffering. In the normal course of affairs, God is rather redundant!

The loss of Christian influence is also marked by the ways in which the Christian God is refused admission to the public square. By this is meant the refusal to entertain even the possibility that political, social and economic affairs could be better clarified, explained and changed by recourse to a tradition of discourse that claims that God has spoken intelligibly and persuasively about such matters. Indeed, faith-language brought into the public domain, in such areas as medical ethics, values in education, business ethics, moral standards in broadcasting is hugely embarrassing to many people. There is a tacit convention that public affairs are no business of God (if God exists). So, God is kept at the safe distance of private opinion and voluntary associations.[7]

Contemporary societies are built on many core beliefs and values, whether explicit or implicit. Explicitly, there is a consensus that particular claims about God cannot be considered true, in the sense of being universally valid, because there is no way of producing evidence that could command acceptance by the majority. Society is intrinsically unable to decide between conflicting truth-claims about a non-empirical reality. Whereas Christianity is identified in public consciousness with a belief system that has to be self-assured, the mood of contemporary Western society is uncertainty and a cynical suspicion of the claims and motives of all who profess to know the truth. In a climate of moral and cultural relativism, the language of 'good', 'better' and 'best' is considered undemocratic and repressive. There is a clear repudiation of what some philosophers call binary opposites, i.e. a clear distinction between notions such as sanity and insanity, normality and deviancy. Yet such distinctions, within a Christian view of the world, signal a clear-cut difference between what is authentic to human existence and what is flawed.

Finally, there is a deep-seated, implicit belief that the Christian faith is discredited when it comes to providing the most valid interpretation of reality, a superior purpose to live for, the most cogent moral principles appropriate to a technologically

---

[7] However, there are occasions, when governments will turn to religious leaders for the support of a particular policy. This is particularly true in relation to new legislation designed to meet the threat of terrorism. Also, in some nations, the value of faith communities as a source of 'social capital' is recognised through the educational curriculum of schools in the public sector.

sophisticated and well-informed society and an unparalleled hope for the future. The instinctive reaction to these issues is to assume that Christianity does not measure up to the challenges of the ultra-modern world. In particular, many people do not make a connection between belonging to a Christian community and the answers to these questions. Such participation is not a meaningful priority for their lives.

The return of pre-Christian paganism

One of the features of European society today is that, although historically the notion of paganism has had a deeply negative connotation, now a growing number of people wear the badge with some pride. Paganism is presented by some people as the original religion of the European peoples, usurped it might be said by the alien incomer, Christianity. So, rediscovering the elements of pagan religion is the equivalent of returning to the roots of the continent's history and culture. Moreover, paganism in its many forms represents the oldest, and therefore probably the most venerable, form of religious belief and practice.[8]

Although not directly related, the exponential growth of alternative spiritualities, often connected in some way to the natural world, is a manifestation of a search for spiritual fulfilment and values that are no longer centred on a monotheistic creed.[9] Here, a whole raft of techniques are offered, like weekend retreats for meditation, that are designed to bring inner healing through a search for harmony between human life and the forces of the natural world.

The framework is effectively naturalistic. Claims are not generally made for any ultimate reality beyond the universe. Human beings are deemed to be alone, and need, therefore, to

---

[8] Paganism is a term that refers to a broad range of religious traditions that venerate the sustaining powers of the natural world: see C.H. Partridge, 'Paganism' in Christopher Partridge (ed.), *Dictionary of Contemporary Religion in the Western World* (Leicester: IVP, 2002), pp. 321–327.

[9] See John Drane, *Jesus and the Gods of the New Age: Communicating Christ in Today's Spiritual Supermarket* (Oxford: Lion Publishing, 2001); *Do Christians Know How to be Spiritual? The Rise of New Spirituality and the Mission of the Church* (London: Darton, Longman & Todd, 2005).

find resources within themselves, individually and collectively, to solve the problems of stress, violence, anxiety, absurdity, and the triviality of a life centred on consumption and pleasure. Part of the problem is located in counteracting the materialist values that drive the global economic machine and suck people into believing that these are the measure of the good life and the generator of happiness.

One of the outcomes of the way of life that the middle classes of the rich, industrialised nations expect to enjoy is the destruction of the natural world. So, environmentalism has become, in some quarters, a kind of successor to Marxism as an attempt to explain and overcome a fundamental problem of human alienation. Christianity is seen as one of the factors that has led to an instrumentalist view of nature, in that it is portrayed (erroneously) as teaching that the human community is justified in exploiting natural resources for its own enjoyment.[10]

A rediscovery of the significance of feminine qualities in human nature also links into this concern with the environment. Thus, a concern for the body, the physical and the practical is contrasted with the presumed masculine qualities of reason and the theoretical. The female persona invests more time and energy in building relationships, nurturing the weak and the vulnerable, defusing confrontational stances, deconstructing hierarchical attitudes and structures and investing in people, rather than in ideas, projects, schemes and plans. Again, Christianity (wrongly) is linked with patriarchy, hierarchy, rationalism, aggression and intolerance. It is judged to belong to another age and another world.

The outcome of the mood of contemporary society is not so much to repudiate the one God who has 'sat above' and directed the history of the Western nations, but to demote him and place alongside any number of other 'gods', according to individual preferences. These gods are characterised by their indulgence and tolerance of the quirks and misdemeanours of ordinary, frail citizens. Therefore, the overwhelming mood of Western

[10] See J. Andrew Kirk, *What is Mission?*, chapter 9, 'Care of the Environment;' D. Wilkinson, *The Message of Creation* (Leicester: IVP, 2002), pp. 41–43.

culture is to allow diverse religions equal recognition, as long as they pursue their activities in peace and do not seek to gain power and influence in public life. In a multi-cultural, religiously plural world, the Christian faith can no longer expect any privileges.

The effect of the post-Christian environment on the Church
Ethical values are divorced from the Church's teaching
The opinion of the Church on most of the moral questions of the moment is no longer taken as decisive in shaping society's response. Today, there is an emphasis on the moral equivalence of the best of good humanist behaviour. Religion is no longer viewed as a guarantee of ethical integrity. The non-religious person, it is generally assumed, is as able to discern and lead a good life as one who is a religious believer.

A kind of secular consensus is being built that human beings can appeal to self-evident moral values as a guide to legislation and normal human practice. The 'golden rule' in its negative form – do not do to others what you would not accept their doing to you – underlies much morality. It is pragmatic and consequentialist in its orientation: any action should be permitted as long as it does not bring harm and suffering to others. This, as we have seen, is also reinforced by strong appeals to natural rights and justice, as if after all there is a hidden code of conduct built into the fabric of the universe.

The problem for the Church, in the shift of moral consciousness towards a *laissez-faire* attitude accompanied by a sustained attack on the 'Divine Command Theory' of ethical norms,[11] is its inescapable need to defend the notion of *intrinsic* right and wrong. Thus, where the Church appeals to principles of normative behaviour that do not depend upon social trends, consensus thinking or personal desire, in areas like marriage and divorce, human sexuality, gambling, human fertilisation, embryo experi-

---

[11] For a brief account of this foundation for ethics, see Janine Marie Idziak, 'Divine Command Ethics' in Philip L. Quinn and Charles Taliaferro, *A Companion to the Philosophy of Religion* (Oxford: Blackwell, 1999), pp. 453–459; also, Richard Mouw, *The God who Commands* (Notre Dame: University of Notre Dame Press, 1990).

mentation, mercy killing and physical self-abuse, its views are likely to be rejected as unduly dogmatic, arbitrary and oppressive.

The Church seeks to uphold the reality of a given moral order: the good is what fits the way God has created us and that, consequently, maximises human flourishing to the greatest possible degree. A post-Christian world, on the other hand, believes that morality is changing, and can be discovered through experimentation. In a plural society, it is assumed, where people are committed to a variety of value-systems, it is important to recognise that the most that can be expected is a minimum consensus and a maximum tolerance of other people's choices. With basic assumptions so far apart, the Church has a major task to persuade the community that its views on first order ethical issues are based on a sound, well-tested tradition and, for that reason, work for human well-being in all its dimensions.

Another aspect of the present climate is the belief, with regard to some controversial questions, that empirical research can determine the right ethical decisions.[12] Thus, in the cases of adoption by a single parent or the state's official recognition of same-sex unions, it is argued that well-controlled observation and monitoring of the outcomes can demonstrate the ethical acceptability of both practices. This conclusion is based on the utilitarian principle of no-harm. The principal actors in each case are better off for the altered relationship they enjoy, and no one else is worse off.

Finally, the immense changes that have been taking place in the way society views moral values also affects the way many people view their relationship to the Christian faith. It is quite commonplace for non-Christians to equate religious belief with moral action. Thus, if such people are content with their own morality, or at least think that it is conducted at a level similar to that of Christians, it would be logical to conclude that they have no need of religion.

---

[12] This view comes close to identifying the existing situation ('is') with an ethical imperative ('ought'), or at least with ethical permission.

Contextual confusion within the Churches
Given the secularising process that we highlighted in the first
two chapters and the return to pre-Christian religions and spiritualities touched on here, the Church faces big questions about
how to communicate a message that has now become strange in
the land. What really are the essentials and the inessentials?
What are the most crucial points of contact? How much of the
baggage of beliefs, customs and traditions must be retained, and
how much can be jettisoned or adapted to changing circumstances without losing the heart of the matter? What does faithfulness to the Gospel of Jesus Christ truly mean? Or, how do we
know if we are really defending the indefensible? These are crucial, defining questions for Christians eager to rediscover a
meaningful missionary engagement with today's varied cultures. Agreement is not easy to reach.

On one side of this passionate debate stand the 'conservatives'.
This group believes that, whatever the circumstances, the
Church must witness to its unchanging, divine nature. There is
no good reason to change its liturgy or structures, or seek to find
contemporary language to convey its message. The message is
eternal. It is, therefore, also always contemporary. In the midst of
rapid change and confusion, the good news is that there are
absolute standards, objective truth and a pre-ordained reality
that do not shift. The proverb is sometimes repeated that 'those
who get married to one generation will be divorced by the next'.
Faith transcends fashion. It offers a point of great stability from
which the passing fads of modern or post-modern thought can
be properly analysed. Adaptation is futile. It represents a loss of
nerve. Moreover, statistically speaking, only 'conservative'
churches seem to be growing.

On the other side stand the 'radicals'. They hold the view that
as the Christian community engages with a world in perpetual
flux so the message itself changes. There is only a bare minimum
given, enough to convey a sufficient identity with the tradition
through history. To this is added, in every generation, what can
be discovered of the reality of the Spirit in the struggles of every-

day life. The message does not come pre-packaged in certain linguistic formulae valid in all situations, it is discerned as the Church listens to the word of its founder present in solidarity with suffering and excluded people.

According to this view, the Church has generally been compromised by sticking with a pre-modern world-view (for example, the existence of miracles), which has had the effect of diminishing the scope of God's acting by creating a 'trouble-shooter' God-of-the-gaps.[13] Also, it tends to make a fool of itself by confusing culturally-bound theological and ethical views with eternal, revealed truth. The classical case would be the way that the presence and ministry of women in church and society has been handled. According to the radical position, it is only a matter of time before the Church, as a whole, will accede to the increasingly accepted reality of homosexual 'orientation'.[14] According to its history, it has always lagged behind the most progressive views by at least one generation. It has then had to run to catch up!

The Church as a commercial organisation

It is not surprising that in a society heavily influenced by market values, the church should be viewed as one more organisation that seeks to offer goods and services in a competitive environment. Thus, the belief systems and practises of the Christian faith are seen as interesting alternatives in an open market system. They are in competition with old and new spiritualities, therapies, counselling advice and techniques, approaches to healing and contemplative practices, all designed in different ways to bring personal and social harmony to their practitioners. What the church offers is judged on pragmatic grounds; its value is functional. Does it meet 'felt' needs? Does it work for me? Thus,

[13] This expression conveys the idea that God's existence is dependent on being the explanation for an ever diminishing set of problems that the natural sciences have not yet been able to fathom out. God may be likened to a kind of cosmic technician, called into to repair our faulty systems, when the DIY attempts all fail.

[14] I will explain, in chapter 9, why acceptance by the Church of homosexual inclination and practice would not be of the same order as that of its affirmation of the gender equality of ministries.

to be successful, the church has to adapt itself to the market out-look. It needs to package its goods attractively, advertise itself, discover a niche market and outperform its rivals! In accordance with this environment, it is unsurprising that precisely those churches considered most successful (growing numerically) are the ones whose promotion strategies have been able to attract the most customers.

Behind this attitude lies an instrumentalist understanding of truth. A post-modern generation has no patience with what it considers an abstract view – truth is whatever conforms to the reality of what is – because it is not sure that in the realm of ideas, values and norms of wholesome living, there is such a thing as reality; or, perhaps, there are many realities. Thus, there is no way of judging whether different religions or spiritualities are true in some absolute sense. They are probably equally true (helpful), in so far as some people will find one, and some another, to be valid and meaningful paths to wholeness for them. Without exaggerating too much, selecting a religion to follow is like choosing a car. First, we decide what is affordable (the cost should not be too burdensome). Then, we work out what are the features we need – petrol or diesel, manual or automatic, saloon or estate, five or seven seats, etc. Finally, we weigh up the merits and disadvantages of the various models and ranges on offer, probably consulting the latest expert opinions and reports in the press. Some analysts of contemporary religion in Europe urge the churches, as in the USA, to be bolder in advertising their wares:

> If a free market in European religion were allowed to emerge, there is no reason why the religious institutions in this part of the world should not flourish in the same way as their American counterparts. Secularisation in Europe is caused by deficiency in religious supply, not in demand.[15]

However, others rejoin that the social situation in Europe is so

---

[15] See Grace Davie, *Europe the Exceptional Case: Parameters of Faith in the Modern World* (London: Darton, Longman & Todd, 2002), p. 43.

different from that of the United States that such a strategy is unlikely to bear much fruit:

> Most Europeans look at their churches with benign benevolence – they are useful institutions, which the great majority in the population are likely to need at one time or another in their lives (not least at the time of a death[16]). It simply does not occur to most of them that the churches will or might cease to exist but for their active participation. It is this attitude of mind which is both central to the understanding of European religion and extremely difficult to eradicate . . . It is not that the market isn't there . . .; it is simply that the market doesn't work given the prevailing attitudes of large numbers in the population.[17]

My own opinion is that the second view is right in terms of being able to attract more participants through more focused advertising, but for the wrong reason. I suspect that the reason why a sustained and clever marketing strategy would produce few results is that the majority of populations in Europe have basically rejected the brand. Therefore, the church will not succeed by re-imaging the brand. It may have to wait one more generation before it can genuinely present Christian faith as an entirely new brand, by then entirely unknown!

The church is also competing with an increasing variety of recreational activities. This means that those who are still attracted in some way to the activities of the church will avail themselves of them, as long as they fit in with other commitments they have taken on. Thus, in so far as churches continue to insist on having their main weekly activity on a Sunday morning, many will feel excluded. Among families with young children, there is a great premium put on satisfying the imagined needs of their offspring, particularly sports of all kinds; these are often arranged for Sunday mornings. In a situation where many children live

---

[16] May it be a matter of time before funerals in church, like baptisms and weddings, dwindle to only an occasional visit? Then, 'dispatched' will go the same way as 'hatched' and 'matched.'

[17] Davie, op. cit., p. 44.

apart from one of their parents, Sunday may well be the day when they travel to be with the other one. Also, Sunday morning is regarded by many as the only day of the week when it is permitted to rise late with a good conscience.

So, today's generation divides its time among different pursuits which either exclude, or give a low priority to, church events that take place on a Sunday morning: worship and Sunday schools. It is not too late to declare (whisper who dares) that it is culturally perverse to concentrate church activities on Sunday mornings. Given that every day is 'holy to the Lord', there seems to be no good reason, apart from the weight of tradition, against moving activities to times in the week more likely to be suitable for actual people. It would be difficult to argue, I think, that such a suggestion directly compromises the Gospel and Christian discipleship.

Christian identity no longer depends on territory

It is a salient and not surprising fact that all churches that have functioned in some way as national churches have practised the baptism of infants. The converse is also true: churches not practising infant baptism have never existed as national churches. At the time of the Reformation, when national churches were coming into existence on the principle of *cuius regio, eius religio* (whichever the realm, that the religion),[18] the question of baptism was a political option. The baptism of babies into the church of the realm was a signal of national belonging. Refusal could be treated as if it were treason: the dissenter broke the unity of the national community.

Today, the situation could not be more different. In many nations, even with the remnants of a state church, there has been a huge decline in infant baptisms. Parents no longer see any necessity in having their child christened or 'christianised'. There is no longer any pressure to secure a national identity by

---

[18] The Latin tag expressed the fact that particular geographical regions where likely to adopt the confession (Catholic, Lutheran, Calvinist) of their principal ruler.

having the baby baptised (or a personal identity by ceremonially naming it). The church is no longer co-extensive with a particular territory. A post-Christian society is marked by ceasing to identify any given territory with a particular creed.[19]

Moreover, in so far as baptism is properly understood by parents, it could appear to give a finality to the confession of one faith, a situation that clearly militates against the post-modern tendency to 'serialise' experience. The relationship between faith-convictions and life-style has been decisively reversed. The former are now considered important in so far as they service the latter. They can be held just as long as they fit the mood. Christian baptism is a sign of the willingness to dedicate the whole of one's life to being a disciple of Jesus Christ. The child (or adult) is signed on the forehead with the cross, with the prayer that s/he will remain Christ's faithful soldier and servant to *the end of life*. Such a definitive dedication in the setting of a solemn ritual negates the principle, often poorly thought out, but nevertheless frequently articulated, that it denies the freedom of the child to make its own choice whether, or not, to adhere to the Christian faith.

Such is the confusion with which a post-Christian society engages with the question of faith that baptism can be seen superstitiously as a kind of protection against possible (unpredictable) misadventures and, yet, as not comparable to the common vaccinations which a child receives. The reason is that, in the latter case, their benefit in minimising the threat of serious illness is demonstrated medically (i.e. scientifically). In the former case, no harm is done, and one lives in hope!

It should not be imagined that these trends are all necessarily negative. The Christian community desperately needs the gifts of discernment, the ability to read wisely and competently the 'signs of the times'. It needs to understand with empathy what people believe and why, and how this affects the decisions they take. Its task is to recognise changing patterns of behaviour,

---

[19] There are some exceptions: the baptism of babies is still practised extensively in Russia, Poland and the Nordic countries, see J. Luxmoore, 'New Myths for Old: Proselytism and Transition in Post-Communist Europe, *The Journal of Ecumenical Studies*, Vol. 36, 1/2, 1999, pp. 43–65.

without jumping too quickly to condemnation, in order that it might present the good news of the Gospel as a surprising message of grace, liberation and hope to each generation.

The calling of mission
A unique situation
The church in Europe finds itself today in a novel situation. There are no historical precedents that might help to guide it in its present mission calling. For the first time ever, it has to bear its witness to Jesus Christ in a post-Christian environment. A society which once embraced the Christian faith, at least culturally, but has now become indifferent to its spiritual heritage, is not fertile ground for planting the seed of the Gospel. Ignorance of both the content of the faith and the impact that it has made on social history is widespread. Some sectors of the population are embracing beliefs and practises reminiscent of societies prior to the evangelisation of Europe.

Nevertheless, history cannot be reversed. Unfortunately, perhaps, Christianity is not the novelty that it once was in the days of pioneer mission. What we see today increasingly is the kind of distorted cultural memory and misinformation that leads to a caricature of the faith. Quite often this is exacerbated in the media, when highly idiosyncratic interpretations of the faith are given prominence on the grounds, presumably, that heterodoxy is much more exciting than orthodoxy!

Reinventing the church
What, then, are the paths the church could take that would help it to adopt a more authentic expression of its faith in the reality of a post-Christian environment? First and foremost, it needs to rediscover its missionary nature and calling. Although the Church now exists in unfamiliar territory, it has to attempt to grasp the reality of the situation as an advantage. The whole long history of Christendom, in which the Church has been accorded a special place within the state and the Christian religion a privileged role in education and in shaping the morality of nations,

is finally at an end. Maybe the Church (particularly established churches) needs to recognise the inevitable by celebrating, in this sense, the burial of the past. This will enable it to free itself psychologically from a debilitating wistfulness for what has been, in the expectation of what could be in resurrection to a new vision.

Now the Church has a wonderful opportunity to reinvent itself again as a truly catholic and apostolic community, free from the burdens of false prospects, to reflect on its essential nature and calling. Fortunately, this is already beginning to happen in broad movements such as the call to be a missional church. Although quite diverse in its many manifestations (base-community, cell church, missionary congregation, network church), these new visions share a number of common characteristics. Foremost is their concern not to maintain their traditional life at any cost. The motivating drive is to reach out to non-Christian neighbours and friends, not to spend all energies on serving already existing adherents.

Thus, secondly, the form of church life is consciously subordinated to the overriding obligation to tell out the story of Jesus Christ, the only Son of God. There can be little doubt that many outsiders view the church (however unjustly) as an institution preoccupied with its own survival. It has, therefore, to show its desire and ability to adapt and change, so that it becomes a community 'for others'. Otherwise, sadly, it will die, and deservedly so. Thirdly, given the nature of the changing culture, the missional church is dedicated to expressing an authentic pattern of community life. In a fragmented and self-regarding generation, where many young people do not experience the stability and security of a protective family environment, where people of all ages find it ever more difficult to build long-lasting relationships of trust and support, the church has a wonderful opportunity to be that reliable family, which many have never known.

Finally, this kind of church seeks to model a different way of living. With respect to the normally accepted values of a consumer-culture, the Christian community will attempt to emphasise a vision of life in which simplicity, frugality and sharing are the chief virtues. With respect to a culture which finds it increasingly difficult to control violence as the first resort in settling disputes, the missional church consciously practises and commends non-violent strategies for overcoming conflict.[20]

Death and resurrection

What we are talking about here is a paradigm shift of mentality for an institution that has operated for so very long according to a different understanding of its place in the world. Death and resurrection is not an exaggerated language to describe the process through which the church in Europe will need to go to rediscover its missionary vocation. It will be traumatic for the church to give up willingly the power and status that it has enjoyed in European society for so many generations. For those who maintain that salvation is in Christ alone, coming to terms with a culture that is indifferent to religious differences will be particularly hard. The Christian faith will have no special advantages. Henceforth, it will have to rely wholly on the truth of its message, the transformed life of its members and the promises of God. Death implies a process by which the church loses all preoccupation with itself. Survival as such is not a Christian virtue. Many forms of church life should be extinguished, so that more adequate ones may emerge, not compromised by the past. The church is a pilgrim people, travelling towards a defined destination, which is the completion of God's reign on earth, as in heaven. As never before, it has to distinguish between the elements vital for the journey and the unnecessary baggage it has accumulated along the way. If the people of God mean business in a post-Christian environment, they have to know the difference between the essential and inessential elements of a missionary church.

Quality assurance

From time to time, a local church would be advised to undertake a mission audit, a kind of inspection of its life and achievements judged against its own mission statement. The following criteria

---

[20] This aspect of mission will be expanded upon in chapters 6 and 7.

for appraising the missionary effectiveness of a Christian community could be used. Firstly, how well does it *engage with its context*? Does it know the different kinds of people who live in its neighbourhood? Does it know the range of beliefs and life-styles that are represented? Does it know about any particular social or economic pressures that are characteristic of the local situation? If located in a multi-religious and multi-ethnic area, how aware is it of the situation of the different groups?

Secondly, how well does it *identify with its context*? In what ways is the church seeking to serve the needs of its community? Is it engaged in specific projects? If so, how does it monitor their usefulness? Are there special opportunities that the church might take hold of, such as instances of compassionate service not being undertaken by any other agency? The watching world challenges the church to demonstrate in practice that the Gospel is the good news that Christians claim.

Thirdly, how well does it *communicate with its context*? Is the church reviewing the efficacy of its attempts to transmit the good news of Jesus Christ within its neighbourhood? How aware is it of the distance between the Gospel message and the beliefs and values of most citizens today? Has it really taken on board the fact that the vast majority of people living in Europe now are no longer lapsed Christian believers, or even the un-churched, in the sense that belonging to the church would still be culturally appropriate. Neither Christian belief or moral values nor belonging to a faith community are remotely within their horizon. There is little or no residue of a common language that could form a bridge between the Jesus story and their own stories. The church often gives the impression that it is content to minister to an ever-dwindling population. Christians have to learn how to make the unchanging message of salvation in Christ meaningful to generations preoccupied with quite other concerns.

If the message is good news, the church has constantly to learn in what ways it is good news in specific circumstances. This does not mean having to adapt the message to fit an alien world-view. Many Christians in the post-Christian West have already panicked unnecessarily in the face of resistance, ridicule, misrepresentation and indifference. They have adjusted and accommodated the faith to such an extent that its heart has been plucked out. The emasculated message that results is little more than an echo of the current secular outlook dressed up with religious language.[21] The language of meaning, liberation and hope, when understood in the realist terms of objective change from a mode of existence under the sign of death and destruction to one characterised by new life and humanity restored, may be the most powerful for our generation of doubters and sceptics.

Conclusion

There can be no guarantee that the Christian faith will persist in the post-Christian environment of the ultra-developed nations of the world. There will be little chance of maintaining a meaningful presence, if the church dwells on its sense of loss. Adjusting to an environment, where the Christian faith is no longer held in esteem, where many people create their own 'spiritual' agendas, where most people believe that religious truth is defined by its pragmatic value and that it makes little difference whether one believes one set of religious claims rather than another, will be painful and distressing.

In particular, as a number of laws will increasingly reflect pagan, rather than Christian, values – for example, what it means to be human,[22] the nature of marriage and gender identity – so Christians will grieve over the effects of godlessness. We will experience more and more the feeling of being aliens in a strange land. We will have to learn to live as a minority, with the possi-

---

[21] In chapter 9, I explore one fraught moral issue, which illustrates exceptionally well the clash between the Gospel and contemporary thought.

[22] In the discussion about reasons for terminating pregnancies, deformed foetuses are now generally considered a good reason for abortion. The implication is that being human is defined by something external to the living organism in the womb, namely quality of life, not something intrinsic to the being conceived, namely the image of God. In the first case, protection will depend upon a particular society's subjective evaluation of worth. In the second case, value is inherent to the young embryo. It cannot be either given or taken away on the whim of moral philosophers, the medical profession, counsellors, social analysts, legislators, or anyone else.

bility of being the subjects of a progressively hostile attitude that could even lead to persecution, or at the least to the imposition of discriminatory sanctions.

At the same time, the irreversible changes that are taking place can prove to be a magnificent opportunity for the church to reassess its calling, review its activities, renew its hope, reconsider its relationship to the society and culture which actually exists and overcome every temptation to nostalgia for an irretrievable past.

CHAPTER 4

Vindicating Scripture in a Pluralist Culture

To speak of Jesus Christ as good news for a generation brought up in a post-Christian environment is problematical. The main access to Jesus Christ is the text of the New Testament. For those who believe that Christ alone can restore fellowship with God and other people, the New Testament is an authoritative text. Its portrayal of a unique story of liberation and hope rings true to their experience. The more they are guided by its wisdom, the more they are convinced by its affirmations. However, for those inclined to doubt Christians' claims, the text has no particular advantage or merit. Non-Christians see no good reason for sharing Christian assumptions about this particular set of writings.

The place of the Bible in the culture of the West has changed dramatically since about the mid-nineteenth century. For nearly eighteen hundred years, the Christian Church has held a nearly unanimous view on the nature of the Bible. In summary, whatever the Bible unmistakably affirms to be true has been regarded as coming from God by the inspiration of God's Spirit. As it has the creator of the universe's authority behind it, it can be accepted as an utterly trustworthy account of reality. There are many matters concerning human nature only revealed in this text. If we did not have it to hand, our knowledge of life would be greatly diminished. Those who have believed and acted on the truth of the message have never been misled or disappointed. With notable exceptions,[1] the general population within the heartlands of the Christian faith did not question this view.

Nevertheless, within the last 150 years or so, principally in academic circles, doubt and suspicion has been applied as an intellectual approach to the biblical text. The Bible has often been treated as if it were already guilty (of falsifying history in the interests of religious propaganda), until proved innocent. The burden of proof has been switched quite dramatically from the presumed accuracy and dependability of the text to its presumed bias and even self-promotion. Anyone, therefore, wishing to argue that the text's affirmations about God, sin and salvation are true for all people, will have to deal with the suspicion that their reasoning is based on special-pleading and circular argumentation.

In order to demonstrate that, despite massive shifts in the intellectual climate, the Bible can still be trusted to provide true knowledge, it is necessary first to confront the main problems that arise when a particular community regard a historical text as having a special prerogative in the affairs of humanity. It should be noted that all religions, which regard certain texts as having a special sacred quality, face similar objections. However, as philosophical scepticism has so strongly influenced modern Western thought, and the Bible is the sacred Scripture of that community which has developed, until recently, most strongly in Europe, the attack on the integrity of the Christian Scripture has been the fiercest. Four themes constantly recur in considering reservations and incredulity towards the validity of the biblical message.

Historical development

On the whole, contemporary people are reluctant to accept at face value a message formulated two to three thousand years ago. There are two major, related difficulties. In the first place, we live in a culture impregnated with a belief in progress. One

[1] Especially among some philosophers since the 17th century, see Michael Hunter and David Wootton, *Atheism from the Reformation to the Enlightenment* (Oxford: Clarendon Press, 1992); W. Warren Wagner, *The Secular Mind: Transformation of Faith in Modern Europe* (New York: Holmes & Meier, 1982).

aspect of what is implicitly considered a linear development from a lower to a higher consciousness is trust in the power of rational thought, based on critical intelligence, to sort out genuine from spurious propositions. Following the indisputable achievements of the scientific endeavour, founded on a public process of empirical research, hypothesis and demonstration, humanity has crossed an intellectual boundary which can never be surrendered. As far as knowledge is concerned, we now live in a period of history that is qualitatively different from any previous ones.

Adherence to the notion that history records an intellectual ascent from the primitive to the sophisticated militates directly against trusting statements about the world written long ago and far away. Is it not almost certain that, because knowledge and understanding is cumulative, later generations will discover by observation, logical thought and critical interaction with the past truths hidden from our ancestors? As we have inherited a treasury of accumulated insights from the great thinkers and experimenters of the past, we are much more likely to be able to distinguish truth from error and right from wrong. Whatever comes later has, prima facie, a better claim to accuracy. The claims of an ancient text must, therefore, be subjected to the same proven methods of critical reflection and assessment as applied to any other text. The claim that the Bible contains a sacred and unique message is not a special reason why it should be exempt.

Secondly, contemporary society is so utterly different and remote from the world of the Bible that we should not expect it to be able to provide answers to our questions. Our whole perception of the world, the way we live, think and organise ourselves is too discontinuous with that context for us to be able to relate its interpretation of the world to our situation. It is, surely, anachronistic to expect an ancient text to be able to speak meaningfully to such a different environment. It may be an interesting historical exercise to try to understand the ways in which the Christian faith appealed to so many in the Mediterranean world of the Roman Empire. However, history has decisively moved on. Today's generation needs fresh resources to interpret life and enable human flourishing.

In short, there is a *temporal* chasm. The Bible is pre-modern and, therefore, pre-critical. Its word is limited by its temporal location.

Pluralism

Modern societies now accept that they will be culturally, ethnically and religiously cosmopolitan. People who adhere to a bewildering variety of religious beliefs, and none, live next door to one another. They meet in supermarkets, offices, on factory assembly lines, on sports fields, in queues at airports and elsewhere. They have their own convictions about the ultimate meaning of life. Many of them are fervent practitioners of their respective faiths. Why, then, given this amazing plurality of religious commitments, should we consider one particular religious book to have a greater claim to be believed than others? There are many other holy books – the Qur'an, the Hindu Vedas, the writings of the Buddha, the Book of Mormon. Why, then, should anyone prefer one to another? Is it not unfair, arrogant and intolerant to regard the Bible as in some sense a special, unique disclosure of God's ways with humanity? As such a claim implicitly questions the beliefs of other ethnic groups and considers them inferior, is it not even sectarian and racist?

One can imagine a situation where the logic of this line of questioning would prohibit Christians by law from comparing other Scriptures unfavourably with their own or dismissing other religious beliefs as ludicrous, harmful and unacceptable. Liberal societies possess a whole armoury of linguistic niceties with which to berate those who do not conform to current understandings of tolerance: discrimination, bigotry, narrow-mindedness, incitement to hatred, gratuitous offence and defamation of character. To make claims for the superiority of one book is the religious equivalent of political and cultural imperialism: the imposition of one way of viewing the world on other allegedly less developed peoples in the name of a superior civilisation.

Such a strategy, so it is reasoned, springs from the ghetto mentality of a community restricted in its contact with other communities, and from its dogmatic refusal to discover the riches of other religious traditions. It adopts the well-known political ploy of bolstering its own power, prestige and position by making unfavourable comparisons between its own beliefs and those of people it desires to discredit. Moreover, if judged by the pragmatic criterion for truth, other beliefs work just as well for their adherents as does Christianity for Christians. Why, then, pretend that the former are insufficient or even distorted?

In short, there is a *geographical* chasm. The Bible belongs essentially to Western culture just as Christianity is a Western faith. In addition, it now belongs only to a minority of the white population of European nations. In places, where other faith traditions have shaped history and habits of thought and life, it is an alien book.

Truth is individual and private

Given that in a post-modern ambience many people are searching again for a stable meaning and purpose beyond the ephemeral trivialities of a hedonistic, consumer-led, existence, some may now be willing to consider that the Bible could have some interesting religious insights into the nature of our existence. However, this new quest for a spiritual dimension to life does not lead automatically to an acceptance of the Bible's claim that Jesus Christ alone is the way, the truth and life, equally for all people.

Such an unequivocal view has to be unacceptable, for the obvious reason that this kind of truth claim, intrinsically closed to scientific methods of independent research based on experimentation and verification, remains purely speculative. It does not constitute public knowledge, evaluated by universally accepted criteria of assessment. It is a matter of private opinion and individual experience. There are, apparently, no objective means of testing this type of claim. At most it may inspire personal belief and action, but cannot have any binding force on public human life or the consciences of others. Its value lies in its ability to motivate individuals to lead a wholesome life and overcome their personal problems.

Therefore, it is quite meaningless to talk of Jesus Christ being true good news for a whole population. At the most, the message of the Christian Scripture offers some signposts for some people's spiritual journeys. It is one aid on the way. It does not represent either the definitive map of the journey or the destination.

In short, there is a chasm between notions of *public* and *private* truth. The former has to be able intrinsically to convince any right thinking person of its correctness. There have to be incontestable criteria in place that lead to assured judgements. The latter do not have to pass such a rigorous test. Basically, to count as truth, it is sufficient if a person or group has some rational justification to believe a proposition, is not obviously deceived or defrauded and allows the belief to shape their daily practice.

The lure of freedom
So far, we have briefly introduced objections from the perspectives of history, culture, religion, experience and science, to the proposition that the Bible possesses a supreme authority unmatched by any other historical text. These are formidable onslaughts on the absolute value of the Bible's teaching.

Ultimately, they are all based on the observation, we explored in chapter 1, that modern human beings are reluctant to submit to any authority they consider liable to overrule their own critical reason. Given the devastating destruction brought by unchallengeable ideological and religious totalitarianisms of recent times, it is imperative that human beings remain free from the imposition of ideas, so that they can discover for themselves the meaning and value of life in their own way. Freedom is rightly regarded as a high cultural value that has to be protected against the encroachment of devious propaganda, cunning publicity, unscrupulous persuasion or even the threat of emotional or physical coercion.

This modern outlook creates a fundamental problem for the Bible, as it claims to be an external source of truth from another world, unreachable by personal or collective exploration. This claim does not fit modern categories, for the alleged truth cannot be discovered by human endeavour, but is given prior to any human interest in knowing it. Moreover, there is no way of recognising its truth-value that commands universal assent. Assuming that the Bible speaks about a reality that can be experienced by any human being who wishes to know it personally, there are no agreed criteria that would demonstrate the validity of the experience. In this sense, knowledge of reality that comes from the Bible is different in character from the knowledge that comes through investigation of the natural world.

Nevertheless, although it is apparently much easier to accept the data that comes from scientific research than that given in divine revelation, it is doubtful whether the former is truly 'knowledge'. What the sciences provide in abundance is information. In magnificent detail, science apprises us of the facts of the physical universe. However, without some kind of meaningful framework in which the data makes sense, human beings can do little more than accumulate information. In the last resort, fascinating though this kind of 'knowledge' may be, in comparison with a convincing explanation of why it is important, it is little more than a trivial pursuit.

Human beings do not function on the basis of the mechanics of existence, but according to an adequate theory that makes sense of the whole of experience. Thus, for example, in the light of a huge natural disaster, like the tsunami that struck South East Asia at the end of 2004, much of contemporary life in the affluent, secular nations of the West, driven by the pleasure principle, facilitated by an extraordinary accumulation of technical knowledge, seems extraordinarily banal and insignificant. Moreover, people are not satisfied with a purely natural explanation of this kind of calamity, in terms of the movement of tectonic plates; they wish to know whether there is a deeper significance. In seeking answers to the more profound questions, they do not turn to scientists, as such, but people who believe in God.

Of course, every human being is bound by conscience not to submit to an external authority, simply because told to do so. The freedoms gained, after huge political and social struggles, entail the right and responsibility to question and test any self-proclaimed authorities. As we shall argue, the Bible has itself been instrumental in winning the freedom not to conform. However, the question of authority is more subtle in practice than a rather libertarian notion of human autonomy would allow. Disputing authority is not a matter of throwing off all external constraints, but rather choosing which authority one is going to give credence to.

So, one may reject the authority of the Bible, but only on the basis of having accepted another authority in its place. Critical methods are employed from some vantage point that, ultimately, has made itself immune from criticism. They are taken, on trust, as self-evident. Otherwise, there would be no way of avoiding a persistent scepticism about any matter.

Nevertheless, there is a *conceptual* chasm between a commonsense and faith-based view of the way authority functions in human communities. It is hard to convince people who have imbibed a secular notion of freedom that the only ultimate guarantee of human liberty is submission to 'the truth as it is in Jesus Christ'.

A modern approach to the Bible
A whole range of 'critical' ideas about the reliability of the Bible has grown up in this kind of unsympathetic climate. Not only those hostile to the Christian faith, but also Church leaders and theologians have come to the conclusion that many episodes in the Bible purporting to be historical are inaccurate and no more than pious legends. Moreover, the Bible is said to contradict itself at a number of points, not just about trivial issues but major concerns like the relationship between men and women in creation.

A number of its assumptions are said to be outmoded: for example, obedience to the state; same-gender relationships,[2] and the claim that Jesus Christ alone is the way to God.[3]

People who hold to these sceptical views about the Bible assume that critical scholarship has duly established them as valid. Anyone, therefore, who sustains another opinion has to be an intellectual dinosaur. Those who wish to argue for the historical reliability of the biblical narratives, the unity (as well as the diversity) of its message, its teaching about gender, marriage and the family and the exclusivity of Christ's act of atonement may well be tarred with the brush of 'fundamentalist', one of the severest terms of abuse the 'enlightened' elite employ.

As a result of the self-styled 'critical' approach to the Bible (and this is crucial), many scholars and others believe that they have permission to pick and choose what to accept and believe. Imagining that the text of the Scripture is like a greengrocer's stall, it is legitimate to help oneself to bananas, mangos, carrots, asparagus and apples, but reject turnips, grapefruit, papaya, broccoli and cabbage.[4] The criterion of acceptability is either one's own taste and experience or what is currently fashionable to eat.

Attractive though this approach might appear in a thoroughly mistrustful environment, there are serious problems. If the message of Scripture is only deemed true in so far as it confirms our preconceptions, we are using the text mainly to consolidate ideas and views that we hold on other grounds. Then the text simply echoes back to us only what we are prepared to hear. With this approach it is hard to see how one can avoid a series of arbitrary decisions regarding Scripture as the rule of faith. The standard by which we judge the admissibility of the Bible's teaching is

---

[2] This controversial subject as an issue for Christian mission will be explored in chapter 9.

[3] The place of Jesus Christ in a missiological approach to religions will be tackled in chapter 5.

[4] The choice of particular fruit and vegetables in each list is purely arbitrary! The selection is made simply to illustrate the point of personal preference. The lists could be entirely different, as in the case of what to accept and reject of the Bible's teaching.

taken from whatever happens to be the cultural consensus of that group of society with which we identify. The text loses its prophetic and counter-cultural power.[5]

So, even within Christian circles, it is often assumed that the Bible contains God's word here and there. According to a common view, it represents the various writers' and compilers' imperfect grasp of God. It is a fallible witness to a greater truth of God that always lies beyond the text. It can become God's word for us, if and when we recognise it to be so. A discussion of the nature and authority of the Bible gives a clear view of how human consciousness and imagination is exalted for some Christians as the final arbiter in all matters of faith and action.

Upholding the Scripture Principle

In defending and promoting the supreme authority of Scripture in all human affairs, there is no desire to undermine the need for a strong intellectual examination of the basis of faith. There is no merit at all in behaving like ostriches! Many Christians, sadly, by not facing and resolving the powerful criticisms made of their beliefs, have made a shipwreck of their faith. Many contemporary sceptics once held orthodox Christian beliefs. Had they wrestled with the issues early enough in their spiritual pilgrimage, rather than perhaps accepting too naively what others pressed them to believe, they might have won through their legitimate doubts to a place of greater confidence.

So, the answer to the kind of one-sided intellectualism that is characteristic of the modern and post-modern mind is not anti-intellectualism. It is quite fatal to attempt to divorce faith and spiritual experience from sober rational analysis. A thoughtful response will not reject dispute but accept the challenges, from wherever they come. Adopting an authentically rational approach will ensure that a critical method is properly critical by questioning its own basis and assumptions.

[5] In this context, there is a massive difference, often misunderstood by both protagonists and opponents, between a liberal theology of the affluent Western world and a liberation theology emanating from the world of the excluded poor. We will explore the implications of this distinction further in chapter 8.

A genuinely rigorous intellectual approach to the place of the Bible in contemporary Western culture will refuse the label pre-modern, modern or post-modern as inappropriate historical categories for questioning the proposition that the Bible, as always, remains God's unique and authoritative word. Rather, it will propose its own reasons for judging the claim still to be credible and valid.

The Bible's claims for itself, just in case they might be true, should be considered with an open mind
The approach to belief made famous by Pascal in his celebrated wager still merits consideration.[6] Given that there are no conclusive rational arguments for either belief or disbelief, it is wiser to gamble on the truth of the claims of faith than on their falsehood. This policy involves success, if faith is true, and no significant loss, if it is false. In other words, if it were shown to be true, it would be disastrous to reject it. But even if it is open to dispute, so noble are its sentiments that everyone would gain by observing them.

As Pascal rightly surmised, there is no wholly neutral ground from which the truth of the Bible's message may be dispassionately evaluated. Any critical theory always works from the perspective of faith. One set of beliefs can only be judged on the basis of theoretical assumptions, behind which are another set of beliefs. This is the nature of rational thought. So, one particular truth-claim will either impress or fail to persuade according to what other truth-claims have already been taken on board.

It is true that Pascal's particular wager will fail in the case of those who are convinced that reason can demonstrate the non-existence of God and those who believe that the chief end of existence is to maximise personal pleasure, regardless of the

---

[6] It is found in Blaise Pascal, *Pensees* (translated by A. Krailsheimer) (Harmondsworth: Penguin, 1980), # 418; see also N. Rescher, *Pascal's Wager* (Notre Dame: University of Notre Dame Press, 1985); Stephen T. Davis, *God, Reason and Theistic Proofs* (Edinburgh: Edinburgh University Press, 1997), pp. 156–166.

consequences.[7] However, in both these instances, people have to propose their own wager: either that human reason is powerful enough to prove the greatest negative of all time (that there cannot be a God), or that there is no personal responsibility attached to the predictable results of actions. For any sane (rational) person, Pascal's wager would seem to be a much sounder bet.

Now, the message of the Bible is of a type that demands either acceptance or rejection. It speaks clearly about the final destiny of human beings, either in the full completion of life in God's presence or in the despair of an existence separated from the only source of true happiness. Human beings are compelled to choose either a life centred on the one true God or on other pursuits: 'no one can serve two masters' (Matt. 6:24). Both the Bible and experience suggest that many people naturally choose to follow their own desires. In their own minds, their attitude to God may be non-committal. In reality, however, a careless attitude amounts to rejection, because God by definition expects our unconditional subjection to his will.

Ultimately, the truth about which the Bible speaks is not just an elegant, theoretical system of doctrine, like a catechism that can be believed as an abstract system. Rather, it is the answer to both the profoundest and simplest questions about the meaning and practicalities of existence. It also makes a demand upon the conscience and wills of individuals.

Although the offer of the fullness of life in union with God is free of all coercion, there is nothing dispassionate about the invitation to turn from a self-absorbed life to follow Jesus Christ. The Bible is clear that the stakes are high. That is why, along with the many promises of blessing for those who gladly submit to God's good and perfect will, there are stern warnings of the consequences for those who choose to go after other gods. In a pluralist climate, the perfectly proper notion of tolerance towards

[7] It has also been pointed out that the wager seems to presume the existence of the God of Christian revelation. It may not help, therefore, those who are confused by the variety of images of God to be found in the different religions, see *God, Reason and Theistic Proofs*, p. 166. This objection is dealt with in part in the next section, and more fully in chapter 5.

others' beliefs has unfortunately turned into indifference towards ultimate reality and the semi-conscious expectation that God will be indulgent towards our neglect of his rightful claim on our individual lives.

Paradoxical though it may seem, there are many false absolutes hidden in the oppressive tolerance evident in the extreme subjectivism of contemporary Western culture. The notion of non-discrimination, for example, can become exceedingly discriminatory, for it is based on a set of beliefs and values that have emerged from a social consensus that theoretically tolerates but in practice excludes minority opinion. There are beliefs and actions that do not merit toleration, because they degrade a person's true humanity. Social agreement is a poor guide to the meaning of humanness. The Bible claims to offer a comprehensive model, not only of the true end of human existence in the world, but also the means of achieving it.

In the context of the wager, then, the word addressed to all peoples is the same that God spoke to his ancient people, 'I have set before you life and death, prosperity and destruction. Now choose life' (Deut. 30:19). If the message of Scripture is the final truth about all reality, we can know and enjoy to the full the reason for our existence. If not, there is no adequate alternative; we are condemned to speculation and ultimately a meaningless life.

Amongst the religions and philosophies of the world, the Bible's message is unparalleled

The biblical story of God's relations with humanity is unique in the annals of human history. It is unequalled, not only in the sense of being *different* from all other religions and philosophies, for all are unique in this respect, but by being totally *dissimilar*. The narratives of creation, the entrance of sin into the world, the way of salvation, the person and life of Jesus Christ are all without parallel. This reality was expressed forcefully on one occasion in posters put up to advertise a series of Christian meetings at a university. The wording declared that Moses, the Buddha and Mohammad had all died and remained buried; whilst the grave of Jesus Christ was found empty.[8] The formulation of the statement may not have been the most sensitive, but the statement itself points to certain facts of history that mark a difference in kind between the respective religions. In this, and many other instances, the biblical story cannot be assimilated to any other meta-narrative without completely destroying its integrity.

Naturally, dissimilarity does not necessarily equate with being true. All religions, for a variety of reasons, could be false, making spurious claims and offering specious hopes. By the same logic, they could not all be true. What is remarkable about the Christian faith is its distinctiveness. Many conclude that not only does it not belong to the genus 'religion' but it actually comprises a radical break with this species. There is good evidence to suggest that the central core of the message of Jesus is actually a protest against religion. A careful reading will show that it contradicts most people's natural religious instincts concerning the deity, salvation, prayer and life after death.[9]

Thus, when considering the place of the Christian Scriptures in a pluralist culture, it is necessary to affirm that with regard to ultimate beliefs there are three (not two) main options: the teaching of the various religions, the tenets of secular humanism and the principles of Christian discipleship. Any rational approach to religious conviction, to have credibility, should construct a theory, which does justice to this phenomenon. To put human beings into two categories, either religious or non-religious, is not adequate to experience. The Scripture gives a clear third alternative. This is one reason why, from a Christian perspective, the new search for some kind of spiritual experience as an alternative to the tedious, trivial and nihilistic plight of the post-modern condition can easily be a distraction. Jesus Christ comes as a

---

[8] This latter fact might not seem extraordinary, if one assumes that the dead body was removed either by the Roman or Jewish authorities or by Jesus' disciples. However, such a possibility is historically improbable: the Romans would have had no reason to do this (and, even if they had, it is unlikely that it would have remained a total secret); the Jewish leaders would have produced the body to disprove the notion of resurrection, and the disciples would hardly have suffered martyrdom at a later date on the basis of a known deception.

[9] See J. Andrew Kirk, *Loosing the Chains: Religion as Opium and Liberation* (London: Hodder & Stoughton, 1992), pp. 97–104, 158–201.

wholly singular alternative to the current choice between post-modern futility and esoteric mysticisms.

So, how does one explain this sharp divergence from norma-tive religion? Islam believes that its claim to be the most perfect natural religion is an indication of its truth. The biblical message proclaims the exact opposite. Normal religious sentiments are a sign of alienation from the true and living God. There is only one faith that is audacious enough to stake everything on this appar-ent contradiction. Christian faith, in so far as it consents to its own foundation document, cannot be assimilated to a pluralist paradigm that asserts that all religions are ultimately equivalent. Either pluralism is a statement about reality and Christianity, as a consequence, is false or vice-versa. To be able to fit the Christian view of the world into a general theory of religions, it is necessary first to modify substantially the Bible's teaching. However, such an undertaking simply demonstrates the Christian case against pluralism.[10]

The positive impact of Scripture on individuals and societies has been immense
In millions of cases in all periods of history, in every kind of soci-ety and culture, amongst people of every social background and personality type, the message of the Bible has been the means of bringing substantial healing to disturbed, violated and twisted lives. It has enabled people to forgive their enemies, turning hatred into love. It has transformed meaningless existence into purposeful life and apathy into the sacrificial service of others.

The Bible has been instrumental in breaking superstitious atti-tudes to nature. It has helped to deliver people from the fear of evil forces controlling their destiny. It has motivated people to campaign for the abolition of slavery, child labour and the exploitation of workers by unscrupulous employers. It has inspired those working for prison reform and the eradication of scourges like leprosy, illiteracy, racial discrimination and the caste system. Its fundamental commitment to the equality of all

---

[10] I justify the reasons why Christianity is committed to this perspective in *Loosing the Chains*, ibid. chapter 6: 'Jesus Christ outside religion.'

human beings has ultimately broken down hierarchical approaches to political authority and promoted democracy through universal suffrage. It has been a powerful tool in the struggle for fair trade, debt relief and the alleviation of misery. Believers in the biblical witness have been in the forefront of appropriate and sustainable development projects, such as establishing farming cooperatives and creating low-cost, permanent houses.

However, in spite of the countless examples that can be given of the way in which the biblical message has been instrumental in transforming individual lives and communities for the better, some serious doubts remain about its overall impact on people and nations. It is only right that those who make justified claims for the power of the message to bring hope and healing also face the contrary evidence of the way it has been used to legitimate violence, suffering and oppression. It is only fair to mention some of the more tragic events that have been brought about by people who have used the Scripture as their authority. Only by openly confronting the dark side of Christian history is it possible to offer a satisfactory explanation of why the text of Scripture has been abused to warrant evil deeds.

The use made of certain passages in the Old Testament to sanction the elimination of enemies probably comes top of the list. It has been argued that a state that seeks to uphold the righteousness of God has a duty to rid itself of those elements that openly flout God's laws. By extension, the same 'godly' state has a responsibility to 'cleanse' neighbouring states of evil leaders by conquering their territory. In part, the Crusades against the Muslim 'infidels' were based on a notion of ritual purity. If the land at the East end of the Mediterranean was considered 'holy' but was occupied by a people who practised a false religion, then it was legitimate to purify the land of the offence. The Church developed not only a doctrine of the 'just war' but also promoted the notion of the 'holy' war.[11]

The torture of people who did not accept and practice the official version of Christianity has been justified on the basis of

---

[11] See, further, chapter 6.

the saying, 'if your right eye causes you to sin, tear it out and throw it away; it is better for you to lose one of your members than for your whole body to be thrown into hell' (Matt. 5:29–30; 18:8–9). The logic of torture is that it is better to suffer for a short time in this life than suffer eternally in the life to come. Perhaps, it was argued, by forcing people to conform, they will come to see the error of their ways, repent and accept the truth.

The Bible has been used to endorse the practice of slavery, the inferiority of women and the complete subordination of citizens to the governing authorities. In each case, the justification given is that the world has been eternally ordered in a particular way, so that some are given responsibility to exercise power in the family and the community and the rest are required to submit to their dominion. The Bible, according to this perspective, is concerned with the state of a person's soul and with maintaining the *status quo* of a hierarchically ordered society. Thus neither Jesus nor Paul, it is alleged, challenged the institution of slavery, or even bonded-labour. They were content to admit the full rights of 'Caesar' to govern, whoever Caesar might be and whatever he might do. Paul, at least tacitly, accepted the prevailing patriarchal ordering of family life, including the absolute rights of the husband and father over his wife and children.

Finally, in this very brief survey, we might mention the way the Bible has been used to authorise a doctrine of racial superiority and inferiority. In its most extreme form, the Bible has been used to teach that lighter-skinned people have been specially created to guide and rule over those of darker skin. It has been asserted that they possess a superior intellect and, even, a stronger moral fibre. In a different form, the notion of an elect people has been invested with racial overtones. Thus, white ethnic groups have been given a special commission to bring all the other races to a spiritual and moral maturity of which they are both the precursors and guardians. They have been created to fulfil this particular destiny.

It would not be possible to deny that in the course of its history sections of the Church have sought to substantiate all these views on the basis of the presumed teaching of the Bible. However, the accusation against the Bible itself, rather than against a false mishandling of its meaning, can only stand on the basis of one of two hypotheses: either that it is clear that the Bible does indeed authorise and ratify these practices, which as a result of human moral progress we now see to be unacceptable, or that the Bible is quite ambivalent about the issues. Those who speak against the positive effect of the Bible on human history are likely today to contend that the Bible speaks with so many different voices that it is possible to make it say quite contradictory things. They would argue that the main reason why in contemporary societies the Church adheres to the admirable elements of the text and discards the harmful is because (belatedly) it has accepted the moral values of an enlightened society. In other words, the Bible is judged acceptable in so far as it conforms to the highest moral values of an evolving, critical and self-conscious community.

The debate centres round historical cause and effect. Christians who defend the transforming power of the biblical message argue that the main cause of a certain moral awakening in recent centuries has been a renewed understanding of the underlying dynamic of the New Testament gospel. They can point precisely to those matters that have been in dispute, namely slavery, the use of violence to promote national interests, religious conformity, patriarchy and the dignity of all, especially the vulnerable, and show how the gospel implicitly and explicitly challenges all oppressive readings. The issue is not what may have happened at certain points in history. It is a well-known syndrome that political powers frequently endeavour to use religion to sanction their policies, and religious leaders, in order to maintain their own status, can be found who will endorse whatever interpretation is considered convenient. The question, however, is whether they are justified in doing so.

Obviously, there are areas of dispute among Christians as to the most faithful way of handling the interpretation of the Bible. Nevertheless, it is now generally agreed that properly established criteria exist, which prohibit certain readings of the text. It cannot be made to say whatever the reader wishes to find. Nor can it be made to contradict itself. If an interpretation seems, on the surface, to endorse a morally outrageous practice, at the least the Christian community should collectively revisit such an understanding, to make sure that it is not an instance of ideological rationalisation.

Exegetes are conscious today, as perhaps never before, that they need to pursue their work mindful of ethical discussions going on in particular societies. They will seek to elucidate the text in the light of commonly held values. However, in the last resort, they will acknowledge that the text sometimes supports and sometimes opposes current opinion. To make it always conform to the 'politically correct' would be an act of violation. The text has to be interpreted in the light of its own vision of a transformed humanity. It is the claim of Christians that it is precisely this vision that has been the greatest force for beneficial change in human history, and continues to be so.

Rightly handling the word of truth

The discussion of the previous section highlights the importance of correct procedures for understanding both the original intention of the text and its application to contemporary problems. The authority of Scripture is not overturned just because it does not address directly certain current issues.[12] As I have argued elsewhere at some length, the task of applying Scripture is a matter of designing and building the right kind of bridges.[13] The

---

[12] Michael Martin in his polemic against the legitimacy of Christian belief, *Atheism, Morality and Meaning*, p. 164, mentions abortion, the death penalty, war, slavery, contraception and racial and sexual discrimination. However, he fails to understand the nature of the Bible. He wants to treat it as a moral code-book that gives, presumably, clear instruction on every moral topic that we might be interested in. Apart from the fact that such an approach would contradict his own distaste for the divine command theory of ethics, it ignores the necessity of an historical perspective. His criticism makes the Bible into an anachronistic textbook, seeing that a number of contemporary moral questions (such as abortion, contraception, nuclear power or the right to withhold labour) could not have been explicitly addressed at that time.

[13] See J. Andrew Kirk, *God's Word for a Complex World: Discovering How the Bible Speaks Today* (London: Marshall Pickering, 1987), chapter VI. Here I explore three useful tools that should be used in the construction of the bridge: the model, the middle axiom and dynamic equivalents. I give a number of examples to illustrate the processes, finishing with a discussion of the use of wealth as a test case for the relevance of biblical teaching to a major current moral issue.

task, like most activities in life, requires the acquisition of certain skills, the experience of learning from mistakes, collaboration with others and the humility to admit that one's own views may need correcting. Though distortion of the text does take place, it is not inevitable. There is hope in the fact that, usually, the distortions can be detected and corrected.

Crucial to this enterprise is the place of the whole Christian community as a (virtual) workshop for reliable, well-founded interpretations. The proper way of understanding what is God's word in today's circumstances is a matter for all parts of the world church to debate together. Where one church appears to others to be departing from a well-founded, prevailing interpretation, it should be challenged to justify its unusual use of the text. In particular, it must be careful to show that its unexpected conclusions are the result of following well-tested methods of exposition.

As the history of Christianity shows repeatedly, appeal to the authority of Scripture is not straightforward; sharp differences over the meaning of the text have often divided Christians from one another. Therefore, much attention has to be given to sound methods of interpretation. There are four elements that need particular attention. Firstly, the integrity of the text must be respected by listening to its message on its own terms. The first step in intelligent understanding is to use an inductive method of exegesis, which obliges the interpreter to enter empathetically into the world of the author without making hasty value judgements.

Secondly, the interpreter must be aware of his/her intellectual, ethical, cultural and social assumptions and commitments. Interpretation involves a degree of self-awareness, involving an analytical and critical consciousness about one's predispositions before coming to the text. One's own understanding, therefore, has to be justified to oneself, as well as to other commentators.

Thirdly, the interpreter must learn the hermeneutical skills necessary for relating a message originally transmitted 2,000 or more years ago to a world which has changed dramatically in terms of material production, scientific knowledge, moral sensibility and belief systems, and continues to change. Much has been written about and experimented with in terms of the 'two horizons' – ancient text and contemporary context. Concepts like contextualisation, indigenisation, adaptation and enculturation are employed to try to find ways of doing justice to this process. My own preference is to use the method of translation, and especially the procedure of dynamic equivalents, extending it analogically from the field of linguistics to that of communication theory more generally. Such a process is designed to guarantee both faithfulness to the original meaning, and thus guard the integrity of the text against deformation, and appropriateness to a particular situation.

Finally, there is the articulation of the *sensus fidei*, i.e. the confirmation by the whole believing community of the rightness of certain formulations of faith and certain practical expressions of the Gospel. In some ecclesial traditions this is spoken of as the process of *reception*: the development over time of the acceptance by the community in its life, liturgy and mission of a particular way of formulating belief or walking in the way of Christ.

More important even than right techniques and attitudes is the willingness of the Christian community to 'walk in the truth', i.e. to abide by the word of God, thus showing in practical daily living that its claims about the transforming power of the biblical message are demonstrable. Although it is imperative that Christians argue for the probity and reliability of the Bible against unreasonable scepticism and misrepresentation, in the last analysis, living with consistency the good news of Jesus and the kingdom of God, in the power of God's Spirit, is the most cogent demonstration of the reality of what we declare to be true.

CHAPTER 5

Mission as Evangelism:
The Question of Religious Believers

Current circumstances

The flood of missionaries from Western Europe, who used to travel overseas to tell the story of Jesus and found communities bearing his name, has dwindled to a trickle. However, the number of missionaries from the 'Third Church'[1] going to those lands where the majority of 'un-reached peoples' live[2] has increased in recent years to a steady stream. It so happens that these lands are dominated by one or more of the world's major religions – Buddhism, Hinduism and Islam. There is now a significant group of Christians from the global south and from Eastern Europe living and witnessing to their faith in nations where the majority of the inhabitants are adherents of another religion.

This new situation is raising afresh a host of questions about the acceptability of activities designed to persuade such people to convert to Jesus Christ, and thereby abandon their former beliefs. The concern of this chapter is to explore these questions as thoroughly as possible, given the negative reaction that such a project creates among many people – political authorities and religious leaders in the nations concerned, political leaders in the West, apprehensive about the dangers of provoking religious

---

[1] For the use of this title, see chapter 8.

[2] The term 'un-reached peoples' is a description of communities who share a common language, history and culture, amongst whom a fully indigenous church does not yet exist.

extremism, and those Christians anywhere who object in principle to evangelism 'targeted' at religious believers of other faiths.

Opposition to evangelism

One major objection to Christian evangelism is that such an
enterprise has tended to incite other religious believers to
express their convictions in a more militant form than before.
During the nineteenth century missionary expansion of the West,
the major world religions, which had lain somewhat dormant for
centuries, became reinvigorated. By and large, they managed to
resist the evangelising force unleashed against them. The effect
of evangelism was to awaken these religions from their slumbers
and provoke a renaissance, in which they rediscovered the treas-
ures of their respective heritages.

The 'Christian' nations, up to the time of decolonisation, were
able to control, either through direct governance or through
strategic alliances, the political dimensions of this new life.
However, in recent times, more radical and assertive interpretations of these religions have come to the fore and are threatening
to destabilise the current geo-political world order. Some people
believe that direct evangelism in the heartlands of Islam is likely
to generate further religious unrest and hostility towards more
moderate forms of the faith. In other words, it could contribute
to a greater confrontation with those groups who already believe
that Western liberal democracy is a denial of and threat to their
beliefs. Evangelism is easily interpreted as part of a continuing
covert 'crusade' by the Christian world to undermine or neu-
tralise Islamic republics.

The fear of religious hostility overflowing into major acts of
terrorism is now part of the everyday life of many societies
across the globe. It is based on the reality of New York's 'ground
zero', the Madrid railway stations, the London Underground
network and the Bali nightclubs. It is reinforced by information
being gathered by the intelligence agencies of a number of countries. In the light of this state of affairs, then, it would not be surprising if Christian evangelism among adherents of other
religions were considered dangerously provocative.

This line of reasoning resonates among some groups within churches in the West. However, there are other issues also in play. I will mention two.

There is confusion and hesitancy about evangelism

Reactions against evangelism often arise in people's minds because they have confused the nature of evangelism with the means that may be used to carry it out. Thus they equate evangelism with vigorous marketing techniques, such as knocking on people's doors in the hope of selling another product. Such an activity is identified with sects like the Mormons and Jehovah's Witnesses.[3] Or, they think of evangelism as standing in crowded shopping centres on a Saturday morning, conspicuously waving a Bible around and preaching judgement on unrepentant shoppers. Or, they imagine that evangelism is a special gift, granted only to a few specially chosen people, not a task for the majority of Christians.

There are also more personal reasons to be diffident about evangelism. Many Christians feel unprepared to share their faith with others. They do not know how to initiate an appropriate conversation, how to speak simply and directly about the heart of the Gospel or what to say in answer to challenging questions. They are afraid of giving offence, causing embarrassment or being met with apathy, misunderstanding or ridicule. They may not wish to risk valued friendships. Perhaps the deepest cause of misgivings is the fear of being made to appear foolish, and thus of betraying the faith.

The Christian Gospel, allegedly, is irrelevant for people of other faith

A culture permeated by the view that religious belief is a matter of personal opinion and choice creates an atmosphere antagonis-

---

[3] Unlike the major religious traditions of the world, these two religious groups are considered by the liberal elite of the West as dangerously bigoted and insular. It is now fashionable to find all kinds of generous things to say about the contributions to human life made by the first category of religions. The second, however, is usually treated with an intolerance that paradoxically contradicts the liberal attitude extended to the first group.

tic to the idea that there is only one way of salvation. The 'correct' view appears to be that God's grace leading to salvation is available to a believer, whatever expression his or her faith may take. It follows that the relationship between God's salvation and Christ's sacrifice for the sin of the world becomes remote. For some, salvation is still secured by Christ's work of atonement, but personal faith and discipleship in the community of Christ's followers are not necessary. Openness to God and a life of service to others is sufficient to show that the person has received God's gift of grace (anonymously through Christ) – by their fruits they will be known.

Others believe that each religion's path to salvation is enough. What matters is the conviction and desire with which they pursue it. For people who hold these views, Christian evangelism, in the sense of seeking to persuade others to convert to Jesus Christ, is unnecessary and presumptuous. There are Christian leaders in the West, therefore, who declare that evangelism directed to people of other faiths, particularly Jews, is out of bounds.

Meeting objections
In a previous study, I outlined three major reasons why people oppose evangelism among religious believers.[4] Firstly, it has been connected in many people's minds either with forced conversions imposed on people of other faiths by colonial authorities or with material inducements to join the missionaries' religion. Secondly, it implies that the beliefs of non-Christians are inferior, insufficient or perverse. Thirdly, it is associated with the supposed desire of some missionaries to promote a Western ideological agenda against the legitimate claims of non-Western nations for economic justice and political self-determination. To these might be added the suspicion that evangelism is a cover for the introduction of alien cultural values through educational or social programmes. There is also the observation that evangelism is disruptive of communities,

---

[4] See *What is Mission?*, pp. 57–60.

bringing division into the heart of families, clans and tribes. Some people have even gone as far as to say that evangelism implicitly amounts to religious hatred, racial harassment or cultural genocide.

Obviously, it is important to respond to the seriously bad press that evangelism receives in the contemporary world. In particular, it is essential to distinguish between those objections which are morally valid, and those which spring from fundamental disagreements about the nature of faith and truth.

In context

All Christians can agree that evangelism should not be a pretext for some other agenda. The message of the Gospel is not to be identified too closely with any particular political ideology, social programme or culture. It contains its own criteria for judging the worth of political ideas and is eminently capable of being inserted into any culture. Although it is not always easy to distinguish between the essential beliefs of faith and particular social projects, Christians have always maintained an intrinsic distinction between the future, full realisation of God's intention for creation and present, partial realisations.[5] In other words, all claims to a definitive understanding of what the Gospel requires now have to be questioned in the light of our ignorance of the exact nature of the end of history.

The task of discernment never ends, for contexts change and the Gospel is intended to have a transforming effect on every kind of society in which it is planted. There is, therefore, always the possibility of error and the need, consequently, to admit mistakes and change direction. Such caution, however, does not mean that Christians should never take risks about pointing to concrete social implementations of the Gospel message of the

---

[5] One of the finest discussions of the relation between the fullness of the coming kingdom of God and fragmentary and ambiguous current manfestations remains the book by Jose Miguez Bonino, *Doing Theology in a Revolutionary Situation* (Philadelphia: Fortress Press, 1975), especially chapter 7: 'Kingdom of God, Utopia and Historical Engagement.'

kingdom, only that they should be wary of making over-ambitious claims for particular manifestations of its presence.[6]

Sticks and carrots
Likewise, all Christians can agree that faith cannot be coerced. It is, therefore, inherently wrong to attempt to induce acceptance of the Gospel by means of force or material incentives. If Christians are engaged in works of compassion, such as the relief of suffering, development projects, the promotion of literacy and learning, the protection of vulnerable groups in society (for example, orphaned, abandoned or abused children) or the resolution of conflict, it is essential that they do not impose any conditions on the inclusiveness of their activities. Of course, it would be natural for them to witness to the Christian motivation behind their action and invite people to consider the claims of the Gospel. That, however, is entirely different from saying that people can only benefit from their work if they are willing to undergo instruction in the Christian faith.

Whereas it used to be true that evangelism among adherents of other religions was carried out by citizens of the colonial powers, the situation today is entirely different. As we discuss in chapter 8, much cross-cultural mission today is carried out by people from nations having little influence on global affairs. One, by no means untypical, example of this shows that evangelism can no longer be associated with political, economic or cultural power. Three churches in Bolivia, on all accounts one of the poorest nations on the planet, sent three couples to India to work with the Church there in sharing the message of Christ.[7] All costs were

[6] The debate about the form of social relationships which most approximate to God's ideal for human flourishing was initiated in recent times by liberation theology. The original concern about oppressive or liberative economic structures has been widened to considerations of democracy, civil society, good governance, the environment and the empowerment of minority or excluded communities. Christians believe that the Gospel speaks intrinsically to all these issues. The exact nature of its 'prophetic' word is a matter of 'negotiation' between Christians as they reflect on the Gospel's 'cutting edge'.

[7] This initiative was given as an example of the emerging cross-cultural mission endeavour being undertaken by the churches of the global South at the Latin American Congress on Evangelism in Quito (CLADE IV: 2002).

paid out of local resources. It would be hard to interpret this undertaking as having imperialist overtones of any kind. On the contrary, one could argue that of the two countries, India is technologically and industrially more sophisticated and by no means educationally inferior. The colonialist argument against evangelism is no longer relevant; it has been overtaken by a new Christian global reality.

A superior intelligence?

The other two main arguments against evangelism, both related to the status of the faith of other believers, are of a different kind. It is alleged that evangelism implies necessarily that the religious convictions of non-Christians are inferior to those of Christians. Through evangelism, Christians are seeking to bring people to the full truth about God, the nature of their condition as sinners and the way of salvation. The inference must be that adherents of other religious traditions are ignorant of the truth and, therefore, need to be informed or enlightened.

This view may take one of two forms. Christians may believe that other religions do indeed contain truth about the reality of God and the world, but that this truth needs to be supplemented by the further revelation of God in Jesus Christ. The message of the Gospel, in other words, completes the partial truth already held by the religion in question. Sometimes this view is phrased in terms of fulfilment. Human spiritual aspirations find a fragmentary attainment in the various religions. However, they can only be perfectly completed and consummated in Christ.

Some Christians believe that it is enough that the aspirations (for example, for a mediator between God and humans or for the grace of forgiveness) be held with a deeply sincere desire for salvation in Christ to be secured. Others hold that conscious, personal belief in the name of Jesus is necessary. Salvation is dependent on people actually hearing the Gospel and accepting it for themselves.

On the other hand, Christians may believe that, although other religions have some true knowledge about reality, taken as a whole they mislead their followers as to the true nature of the human condition and the one valid means of salvation. In other words, for religious believers to come to an authentic knowledge of God and his way of salvation they will need to discard some of their central beliefs. So, the Gospel invitation is not to take one more step on the way, in order to attain a fuller panorama of the immense depths of God's truth, but to stop where they are and head in a completely different direction.

In the thought of the first group of Christians, response to the Gospel entails a further step on the same path of faith. For the second group, it means a comprehensive change of mind and heart, abandoning one route to find another.

In either case, whether the faith of the non-Christian is considered incomplete or in error, evangelism seems to presuppose a superior grasp of ultimate truth. How should one respond to this apparently damaging accusation? The language of superiority and inferiority is heavily charged with emotional overtones, leading the discussion in the wrong direction. It suggests that a negative judgement is being applied against the whole culture and way of life of the religious believer. By contrast, the social achievement of the Christian evangelist's culture is deemed to be more advanced and of a higher quality. Here, Christian evangelism is up against a tricky problem. In general terms, it is much more difficult to separate out non-Christian religious beliefs from their embodiment in social and cultural institutions and practices than is the case with Christian faith. So, people from other faiths naturally consider the Gospel as a total package: the message is identified with its historical and social embodiment. A mainly spiritual interpretation would be impossible, and therefore meaningless.

Christians are obliged, therefore, to demonstrate that the identification of the Christian faith with a particular territory or set of static social obligations is a serious misrepresentation of the Gospel.[8] They need to establish the case for making a distinction between the Christian community and the wider human

---

[8] See Andrew Walls, *The Cross-Cultural Process in Christian History* (Edinburgh: T. & T. Clark, 2002); Wilbert Shenk, 'New Wineskins for New Wine: Toward a Post-Christendom Ecclesiology' in *The International Bulletin for Missionary Research*, Vol. 29, No. 2, April 2005, pp. 73–79.

community. Unless the Gospel, communicated cross-culturally, is disentangled from the extraneous cultural characteristics of those who carry the message, it is perfectly legitimate for a person in another culture to hear it as a set of alien ideas and values.

In this respect, an enormous change has taken place in the Western world. Whereas, during the missionary movement of the last two centuries, Christianity and Western 'civilisation' seemed to be inescapably mixed up, now one of the greatest difficulties for evangelism in the West is that its social and intellectual life has become increasingly separate from its original Christian moorings.[9] Given that the heartlands of Christian faith are now in non-Western nations, it is at least feasible to argue that the Gospel is not to be linked intrinsically to a particular social history. If this point can be demonstrated, the language of superior and inferior, with reference to an alleged scale of human progress, is not relevant.

Nevertheless, even if a justifiable distinction can be made between the message of Jesus Christ and any one particular culture, surely the call to believe the Gospel assumes that something is being offered that is lacking in the religious believer's own understanding of reality. If this is the case, then it is logical to conclude that the non-Christian's faith is, at best, inadequate, at worst plain wrong. I think there is no way of escaping this consequence. To be perfectly honest, Christians have either to admit that they know something, hidden so far from non-Christians, or deny the essential core of their own faith. This is the point at which the accusation of arrogance and condescension towards the beliefs of others kicks in. In a climate of relativism towards all beliefs, it seems the height of presumption to claim that one possesses knowledge of the truth that others do not also possess.

In many discussions of these issues that is where the argument is left, at a level highly-charged with feeling, passion and a sense of honour at stake. Many would say that it is impossible to continue a conversation with people who make such pretentious claims about their own beliefs. The latter are then dismissed as

---

[9] We explored evidence for this state of affairs in chapter 3.

doctrinaire, authoritarian, prejudiced and intolerant, in a word, fundamentalists, or worse.[10]

However, to end the discussion by using abusive language of another's opinion does nothing to advance understanding. It may hide the irrational reaction of people who are not prepared even to consider that the reasoning behind the necessity of evangelism might be cogent. As a result, they miss the wider context in which the debate has to be set, if justice is to be done to the different views involved. It is tantamount to dismissing the case before the evidence has been heard. So, what are the features of this wider context?

MAKING TRUTH-CLAIMS

It is not possible to live without asserting that some things are true and others false. An attempt to deny this statement would itself be a claim about what is true. It is not surprising, therefore, to discover that all religions, in different ways and about different matters, claim to know the truth. The corollary is that equally they dismiss the truth-claims of other religions, including of course Christianity. In pressing the truth of its own beliefs against challenges from outside, each religion in effect undertakes a mission.

To realise, then, that in theory and practice the major world religions are missionary-minded is not particularly astonishing. Each one believes that it has access to an understanding of life that is missing in other faiths, and has a duty to share it with them. The intensity of this 'evangelistic' conviction may vary from religion to religion: it is extraordinarily strong among Muslims, quite weak among Jewish believers. In this way, Christian evangelism is not different in kind from that of other religions. It may vary in the methods used and the motivation that impels it, but not in the desire to persuade others to share its understanding of ultimate truth.

Within the Christian community, even those who are thorough-going pluralists, i.e. those who believe that all religions set

---

[10] I return, in chapter 9, to the prejudiced way in which certain terminology can be used in place of the normal conventions of rational discourse, see pp. 195–7.

forth equally valid paths to salvation,[11] are 'evangelists' for their decidedly non-pluralistic, absolute view of what is ultimate. This being so, no one should be scandalised by the notion of Christian evangelism. At the most they may legitimately object to some methods used and some versions of the message communicated.

ACQUIRING KNOWLEDGE NECESSARY TO SALVATION

In relation to this issue, it is easy to be quite mistaken about Christian claims. When people talk about truth they often use language like searching for, acquiring, achieving and arriving at. The emphasis is on the human effort exerted in beginning, persevering in and concluding a journey of personal discovery. This way of looking at truth owes much to the scientific enterprise, where people are engaged in research in order to arrive at the resolution of a problem or the answer to a question. The discovery of the truth of the situation depends on the skills and application of the individual or team engaged in the investigation. Such a view of the path to truth, if transferred from the natural world to the realm of spiritual or moral matters, suggests that religious claims also depend on the ability and exertion of the one who claims to know. Were this the case, it would be legitimate to conclude that the people concerned were implicitly highlighting the excellence and merits of their own intelligence.

However the analogy drawn from science is not exact in the case of Christian claims. There is a parallel, but also a difference. Like scientific discovery, the Christian view of truth accentuates its given nature. If one understands truth to be that which corresponds to reality, human explorers can only uncover what already exists. Science does not proceed by inventing its own world but by working with the world already to hand.

In a similar fashion, Christians accept that a full explanation of the universe, which by definition has to go beyond the discovery of how the material world functions, depends on there being a disclosure whose source is neither human intuition nor cognition. In the tradition, this is referred to as revelation. What we can know ultimately about the meaning and purpose of life, the

[11] See *What is Mission?*, pp. 127–132.

beginning of the universe and the end of history, the nature of right and wrong, the reason for evil and suffering and the essential qualities of human existence are made known by the one who has made all things. In the case of science, it is right to applaud and reward scientists for the work they put in to making discoveries about the natural world. However, such an attitude to knowledge of the non-material world would not be appropriate.

Christians speak of revelation not only as a given but also a gift. In the event that God decided not to reveal the full truth about reality, human beings would not be able to discover it for themselves. Here, human relationships offer a close analogy. Much of what we can know about another human being, beyond their genealogy, genetic make-up and outward appearance, comes from the person concerned. By studying their gestures and behaviour we may be able to surmise something of their nature. However, if we rely wholly on our own observation, it is certain we will not know them properly. We depend on their willingness to disclose their own thoughts, attitudes and feelings.

It is true that in the case of people, being complex and often contradictory beings, what one hears does not always match with the whole reality of that person. We human beings are prone to devise strategies to withhold vital information or to give a particular interpretation of our beliefs and actions. In a conversation we can never be wholly sure whether we have touched the authentic person or an image the person wishes to project. We are dependent largely on what they choose to reveal. The case of God's self-revelation is both similar and different. It is similar in that what we can know about God depends on God's willingness to communicate it. It is different in that God will only make known that which is absolutely true. He does not project what might be a misleading impression of his nature and will. He can only disclose his authentic self.

This rather involved discussion is intended to counteract any impression that, when Christians speak about the Gospel, they are claiming to have gained by their own efforts a greater insight into truth than could be achieved by others. Were that to be the case, the accusation of conceit and self-righteousness would surely apply.

Two further points need to be made. Firstly, Christians not only speak about revelation as a gift, but the nature of its giving as grace. Grace is understood in terms of something that comes free of charge. The gift is not a reward for spiritual insight, intellectual effort, a righteous life or good deeds. It is not the result of a transaction, in which payment is made. It comes without cost. It is usually experienced as a surprise.

Secondly, revelation is open and available to every human being. The glory of the Christian Gospel is that it belongs to every human community. Thus, those who tell the good news of Jesus Christ do not own the story. They are not mediators between God and human beings. Rather, they are witnesses to what they have freely received. Like thirsty travellers on a hot and dusty road they tell other travellers where they can find water. The point is that every human being has equal access to God's truth. Neither one's family background, natural abilities, innate inclinations, social and economic environment nor educational achievements provide any advantage. The only requirement for accepting God's free gift is the ability to drink. We do not think of that as something we achieve. A witness, therefore, can take someone to the source of water. It is up to the person concerned whether she wishes to drink, or not. This line of reasoning should meet the accusation that, implicit in evangelism, is the notion that evangelists are claiming for themselves knowledge and understanding that depend on their own superior wisdom or enlightenment.

RECOGNISING AUTHENTIC REVELATION

There remains one further problem. Accepting that revelation is entirely an unmerited gift of God's graciousness, is there not still a real difficulty in having access to it? Within the context of a multiplicity of apparently contradictory claims about the reality of the non-visible world, how can we know that one set of claims is more valid than another? It is often pointed out in relation to the Christian claim that Christians themselves disagree quite seriously about the content of revelation. Why, then, should we trust one person's interpretation more than another's?

There are three possible answers to this dilemma. The first is to point out that Christians disagree much less about the core affirmations of the Gospel than might be supposed by a cursory glance at church history. Many of the divisions between different Christian groupings can be explained historically by reference to particular political circumstances. In recent years, there has been a notable increase in the level of agreement across all churches about the substance of the apostolic Gospel.[12]

The second response is to invite people to consider the evidence for themselves. Christians base their claims mainly on the witness of the first Christians to Jesus of Nazareth. This has been recorded for all time in the Gospels and other writings of the Christian Scriptures. However, knowledge of the truth does not depend, they would argue, wholly on the willingness to consider the reliability[13] of these early witnesses. There is also the evidence that the Christian interpretation of reality corresponds precisely to the way human beings experience it. Or, to put it another way, the Christian explanation of reality, as we encounter it, gives the fullest, deepest, most satisfying and most coherent answers to the permanent questions about existence that humans persistently pose. It claims to be a comprehensive view of the world that can be lived out consistently in practice.

So, thirdly, the best reply of all is to invite people to taste for themselves the reality of what is being proclaimed. The proof that water quenches thirst is given by drinking it. If anyone suspects that the source of the water is contaminated, the best response is to show that those who have already drunk from it are more, rather than less, healthy as a result.

---

[12] Evidence for this can be found in a recent document of the Faith and Order Commission of the World Council of Churches, which records the agreements, as well as the still outstanding disputes, arrived at by representatives of all the major Christian traditions – Orthodox, Catholic, Protestant and Pentecostal: see *The Nature and Purpose of the Church: A Stage on the Way to a Common Statement* (Faith and Order Paper No. 181) (Geneva: WCC, 1998).

[13] The question of the credibility of the New Testament is examined in chapter 4.

The nature of evangelism

One way of answering some of the objections to evangelism is to clarify its nature. Quite often, as already mentioned, the problem has to do with misunderstanding its main characteristics. Therefore, although not all doubts will be met, it may help to give a brief summary of the core elements.[14]

Essentially it is sharing, with all who care to listen, a message about Jesus Christ. The message is the good news that God cares for the whole human race and longs to heal and transform, through Jesus Christ, every aspect of our disordered human existence. It follows, and only makes sense in the light of, the bad news that we human beings, without exception, have strayed from God's perfect purpose for our lives. We are lost in an ugly and threatening world of our own creation. We are unable to find our own way back to the One in whom alone we can find our true selves. The task of evangelism, then, is to tell people the story of what God has done to make their homecoming possible and to persuade them to be reconciled to God, letting him fully into their lives.

Through Jesus Christ, God has taken upon himself the full range of human hostility, anger, fear and destruction. As God has transferred all wrong to himself and borne its full consequences, humans are potentially free of all that distorts life and turns it into one of misery, grief and suffering. To benefit from God's offer of freedom from sin, a person naturally has to believe that the message about Jesus is true, humbly acknowledge their need of forgiveness and cleansing, and allow God to transform their lives into the beautiful existence he intends for them.

So, evangelism is the process of communicating the most crucial piece of knowledge possible about real life in such a way that the recipient has the maximum opportunity to understand and act on it. This way of defining evangelism does not connect it immediately either to the Christian faith, as a body of doctrine or to the church. This is particularly important in the context of religious believers. Christians should be careful not to give the

[14] For a much fuller discussion of the meaning, I would refer readers to the chapter 'Announcing Good News' in *What is Mission?*, pp. 56ff., and the literature cited there.

impression that they are promoting particular articles of faith or an institution. Through evangelism people are not being invited to convert either to Christianity or to the church but to Jesus Christ as God's full and final resolution of the problem of evil.

It would, of course, be misleading and dishonest not to mention that new life in Christ has to be conducted within a community of other followers of Jesus. The reason for belonging to a community is simple. Reconciliation does not envisage only a personal relationship with God but also the mending of relations with other human beings. The good news of Jesus Christ is not a matter only of restoring a broken friendship with God but also of healing all manner of deformed human relationships. As individuals cannot exist outside of communities, so the new believer in Jesus Christ cannot flourish outside the new society which is being created by God's Spirit.

Motives for evangelism

In the context of religious believers, it is particularly important to ensure that evangelistic motives are as pure as possible. The Christian, in telling the story of Jesus, is responsible for making certain that his or her reasons are free of unworthy motives. In my opinion, three valid ones stand out.

A sense of indebtedness

If a person has received freely and unconditionally from God a gift of such magnitude as salvation through Jesus Christ, it would be truly amazing if they kept it to themselves. It is a wholly natural human desire to want to pass on a piece of good news (such as the safe arrival of a long-awaited baby) to everyone one meets. As in this example, the good news is that the gift of real life is on offer free of charge. Not to evangelise, therefore, signifies an incomprehensible refusal to share with others a personal blessing and joy.

A way back from ineffective spiritual searching
Part of humanity's alienated condition is manifest in the pursuit of mistaken paths to salvation. They arise from a wrong diagnosis of the basic human predicament. This may be understood either as ignorance of true moral virtue, being out of harmony with the creative energies of the universe or a failure to understand the real nature of suffering. Coming to terms with spiritual reality is, as a consequence, interpreted as embarking on a path of enlightenment which eventually will reunite our being with fundamental cosmic forces. Spiritual searching of this kind may pursue either a personal or impersonal goal.

At the level of popular religious beliefs, the basic consideration is to maintain a good relationship with the power/s that determines one's destiny in life. The overriding concern is to ensure well-being and avoid bad fortune. This can be achieved through rituals of various kinds, which alleviate insecurity in the face of the unknown and guarantee that the future is benevolent and not capricious. A major part of the ritual is to accumulate merit in order to counteract unintentional offences against the moral order or appease the supposed anger of unseen spirits or ancestors, and thus avoid suffering and misadventures.

Ways of responding to the ever present threats of pain, distress and misery are numerous. They form part of most religions. The good news of Jesus Christ is of a wholly different variety. He reveals a divine order which does not have to be appeased by human actions, in order that it may align itself with human aspirations. He reveals a God who, through the sacrifice of himself once for all, eternally wills the very best for those who love and trust him. So, evangelism may be seen as a way of breaking dread of the 'gods' whose favour religion has been invented to secure. It offers a power that ends once for all the twin evils of fear and fatalism.

The liberating project of Jesus
Decisively, evangelism is not just a matter of words. It is not a case of presenting a more convincing rational demonstration

of the truth than any other system of belief and, therefore, of winning arguments. The Christian faith can, of course, more than hold its own intellectually in the concourse of religions, philosophies and other world-views. There is a place for rational demonstration.[15] However, the point of the good news is that lives are transformed in a way that is not possible outside of faith in Jesus Christ.

> Liberation is release from every attitude and conduct which is contradicted by the life of Jesus. It is to be free from all that damages and restrains the possibility of human beings becoming fully human *in the image of Jesus*.[16]

Conclusions
Given the features of the contemporary world already mentioned, the issue of Christians evangelising religious believers remains problematic. In concluding the discussion, I will tackle one or two still outstanding questions.

Those who never hear the Gospel?
Some people wonder why, if it is vital to respond in person to the story of Jesus, so many people have lived and died without having had the chance of hearing about him. For centuries the Church apparently lost its missionary vision and, apart from sporadic attempts, did not reach out far beyond the borders of already 'Christianised' nations. Why, then, did God not ensure that his people were more adventurous in penetrating unknown regions for the sake of making known the good news? Or, why did God not reveal himself in a more conspicuous way to those who lived in places remote from the centres of Christian faith?

These are good and important questions. However, because they are hypothetical, they are not easy to answer. Any attempt

---

[15] Such as given, for example, in Paul Copan and Paul K. Moser (eds.), *The Rationality of Theism* (London and New York: Routledge, 2003), passim.
[16] *Loosing the Chains*, p. 196.

to do so involves speculation, which may be unwise and unprofitable. There are some aspects of the question that we can know; others remain mere conjectures. However, God has not left himself without witnesses. In the case of millions of people these may not be other people, but the natural world (on which they depend for life) and their consciences. They are able to know enough of the invisible reality behind the visible world of the senses by observation and introspection. At the least, it is possible to come to believe in a personal deity who has brought the universe into being and sustains it constantly. It is also possible to accept that the universe is regulated by a moral order, which sets an external standard of right and wrong, and that justice demands that those who break the law deserve punishment. Human beings are also aware of the reality of mercy and forgiveness. In addition, there have been many remarkable stories of God revealing himself in dreams and visions.

We do not know to what degree these partial revelations have been sufficient to draw people to recognise their need of God's forbearance and forgiveness and to throw themselves upon his mercy. We do know, however, that God is the very meaning and measure of justice and compassion. He can only act with complete fairness. Thus, if we were in receipt of all the facts, we would come to the conclusion that God has acted with perfect justice in his judgement of every individual human being. Any other conjecture is pure hypothesis, beyond either confirmation or refutation.

Many paths to salvation?
One response given to the question about the destiny of those who do not hear the Gospel is that people of faith can be saved by their commitment to the light they have received. Although they do not believe in the Christ of God, they believe earnestly in the teaching they have received. However, it is unlikely that such believing could be counted as the equivalent of accepting the Gospel of Christ. When one examines the different notions of salvation in the religions, it becomes clear that in all cases they are widely divergent from the Christian view. This is not a

conclusion that Christians draw from biased and prejudiced
convictions. It is what other religions say about themselves.
Indeed, many are proud of the fact that they do not share the
same outlook on the nature of the human predicament as
Christians. They accuse the latter of having far too morbid a
view of human nature. They tend to argue that Christians promote an unwholesome sense of guilt, in order that their view of
salvation then becomes the answer to the problem as they define
it. This is a particularly telling criticism, where Christians
emphasise the sacramental nature of forgiveness, for the means
of salvation can then become a matter of institutional manipulation. Thus, many non-Christians do not wish to have anything to
do with the Christian understanding of salvation.

If all ways of salvation are equally valid, as even some
Christians claim, it is a curious fact that all the world religions
categorically deny the Christian affirmation that God is to be
found most truly in the death of his son. For some, the notion is
completely absurd; for others it is blasphemous. Speaking in
general terms, the religions conceive of the way to God as an
'ascent'.[17] It is a path that leads upwards, away from impurities
and physical desires. God, or ultimate reality, is to be reached
through a disciplined, even ascetic, life. The surest way of
achieving the goal is by following particular teachings, spiritual
exercises or codes of practice. The ascent is gradual, with pauses
and diversions on the way.

For Christian faith, however, the very reverse is true: fellowship with God is dependent on 'descent'. Salvation is found in
the depths of the humiliation of the Son of God, who allowed
himself to be killed by political opportunists. He was executed
outside the walls of the holy city, on the municipal rubbish tip of
Jerusalem. For the religious sensibility this was (and is) the most
impure place on earth:

---

[17] This observation is not contradicted by the fact that some faiths – Judaism and
Islam – are centred on God's personal revelation. 'Ascent' is still the human
response to God. The point at issue here is that of the equivalence of beliefs.
Manifestly, unless its very heart is torn out, Christian faith, rooted in God
becoming human, is vastly different from all others.

> It was absolutely logical that Jesus would be judicially
> murdered in the place where the remains of the (temple)
> sacrifices were thrown . . . Religion threw him away, just as
> the carcasses of the animals were discarded and burned.[18]

The contrast between two views of salvation could hardly be
greater. This being so, it is impossible to talk meaningfully of
many paths to salvation. It could only make sense if the nature
of salvation was similar in all cases.

Many means of evangelising?

It is worth stressing again that the methods which Christians use
to bring the Gospel to people must be appropriate to the ends in
view. It is a principle of Christian ethical practice that the ends
being sought determine the means to achieve them. It is also
worth pointing out that many religious people expect Christians
to share their faith. They also will demand the same right to
share their own. That is why dialogue, as we have argued in
chapter two, is a fitting means to use. Legitimate concern about
Christian evangelism has to do with the fear that Christians may
try to exert a wrong kind of pressure, particularly on young
people. There is a danger that in some societies they may be
tempted to use their privileged place in culture to take advantage of weaker, minority communities.

It should go without saying that genuine evangelism always
honours the full integrity and worth of other people. This has to
include respect for the other's beliefs and culture. The object of
evangelism, therefore, is not to denigrate the teachings and practice of another person's religion. It is to tell the story of what
great things God has done for that person in the life and work of
Jesus (Mark. 5:19–20). Moreover, communication of the message
has to be from alongside a person, not from the other side of the
street. Sharing can only happen where there is real friendship
and trust. Integrity demands that evangelism does not spring
from ulterior motives, only out of genuine concern that a fellow

---

[26] Ibid. p. 120.

human being may share the joy of knowing the significance of Jesus.

If we accept the famous definition that evangelism is 'one beggar telling another beggar where to find the bread of life', religious belief is irrelevant to evangelism; in terms of our need of new life in Christ everyone is a beggar. So, in a way, any one (including professing Christians, atheists and agnostics) who has not yet responded to Jesus' call to 'come and see' (John 1:39) belongs to another faith. Irrespective of religious convictions and commitments, everyone possesses an entitlement to hear the good news that Christ restores our lost humanity.

CHAPTER 6

The Role of Religion in Conflict

Introduction

It would be hard to find a more sensitive issue in the geo-political arena than the linkage between religious faith and acts of violence. Due to high profile cases of brutality, committed apparently in the name of extreme religious belief, there is a new dimension to concerns about security across the world. The attacks on Manhattan and Washington in 2001, in which young militant activists were prepared not only to sacrifice their own lives but indiscriminately kill hundreds of people of all ages, both genders, diverse religions and many ethnic groups, have raised the stakes.

There are a number of facets of this extraordinary saga that have changed perceptions of what terrorists[1] may attempt. In the first place, both the motivation for the attack and the conviction that sustained its perpetration come from particular religious beliefs. Whereas armed conflict in the second half of the twenti-eth century was largely inspired and driven by ideological the-

---

[1] The usual definition of terrorism is 'a form of political violence, directed at gov-ernment but often involving ordinary citizens, whose aim is to create a climate of fear in which the aims of the terrorists will be granted by the government in question', David Miller (ed.), *The Blackwell Encyclopaedia of Political Thought* (Oxford: Blackwell, 1991), p. 514. Part of the chaos sown by undiscriminating acts of destruction is the sense of public confusion about the realistic objectives of the terrorists in committing their acts of intimidation.

ory, either the dream of a new socialist order or of national or ethnic self-determination and independence, now the motive is religious. Secondly, part of the religious foundation is the belief that suicide, in the name of a serious enough cause, merits the 'spiritual' benefits of martyrdom. Clearly, where there is a threat of violence in which the perpetrator is not afraid to be one of the victims, danger has increased from anything known before. Thirdly, there is a total indifference and callousness towards innocent people. No exceptions are made, as has been usual in other conflicts, with regard to women and children.[2] Whoever happens to be in the wrong place at the wrong time, in an office in a New York skyscraper or Tel Aviv restaurant, is destined for slaughter. There is no calculation about the (unfortunate) collateral damage done to bystanders, as may be the case, for example, in urban warfare.

The unprecedented savagery committed by religious groups in the name of an extreme and deviant interpretation of Islam, which include factions operating in Palestine, Saudi Arabia, Afghanistan and Iraq is one example of a trend that includes other parts of the world and other religions. The destruction of life in Northern Ireland and, by extension, on the British mainland and the ruthless attempts at ethnic cleansing in Bosnia and Kosovo might be said to have a Christian religious underpinning.[3] Likewise, the ruthless suppression of dissent during the 1970s and early 80s in many Latin American nations under military dictatorships was carried out in the name of 'Christian civilisation' against the ungodly and immoral forces of Communism. Some of the atrocities committed in Sri Lanka in the prolonged civil war between the government and the Tamil Tigers have been legitimised with reference to Buddhism or Hinduism, often in the form of a struggle to hold on to 'sacred territory'. The acts of barbarity committed in North Eastern Uganda by the self-

---

[2] Tragically these exceptions are increasingly less commonplace. For example, systematic rape is now considered by some as a legitimate weapon of war in places like the Sudan and the Democratic Republic of the Congo. The taking of children as hostages has happened in conflicts in Colombia and North Ossetian.

[3] See, for example, Gerald Shenk, *God with Us? The Roles of Religion in the Former Yugoslavia* (Uppsala: Life and Peace Institute, 1993).

styled 'Lord's Deliverance Army' are said to spring from bizarre religious beliefs.

Before we continue, it is necessary to make one important clarification. Although interest in this topic has centred on the dark side of religion, i.e. the use that has been made of religion to initiate and perpetrate conflict, the title of the chapter is intended to be neutral. It allows for a negative interpretation, but also for a positive one. In the latter case, religion has an excellent track record, as we shall go on to see, in the resolution and transformation of conflict. Therefore, part of this discussion will be descriptive, for both the negative and the positive elements are part of the reality of the contemporary world. We begin by attempting to outline what is meant by the two major words of the title, namely religion and conflict.

Understanding religion

Descriptions of religion are fraught with difficulties. The main problem is finding a designation inclusive enough to embrace widely diverse sets of beliefs, and yet not so inclusive that absolutely every kind of belief somehow becomes religious. The best approach is to try to describe religions according to their own self-understanding. What counts as a religion is that it possesses at least some of a number of well-recognised elements that sets it apart from the beliefs of a secular world-view.[4]

To have as comprehensive an understanding as possible, we might add one or two more elements to the basic list mentioned in chapter 2.[5] Along with the message, experience, community and historical tradition, religions usually possess a number of *institutions*, such as buildings, societies, training establishments and schools, traditions of *worship*, like prayer and meditation, often including symbolic rituals, a special *language* or the use of common words, but with a particular designation, like 'peace', 'reconciliation' and 'justice', *ethical norms* and codes of behaviour

---

[4] I have tried to clarify the distinction between the two in chapter 2.
[5] See p. 19.

that reflect the basic message of the religion and, finally, *charitable works*.

One has to bear in mind that, although these elements are present in the major religions, they have different manifestations and are open to widely divergent interpretations in some cases. This is partly what makes a discussion of the role of religion in conflict such a tricky and delicate matter. The proneness of some politicians and certain elements of the mass media to make sweeping generalisations is not helpful, for it obscures deeper perceptions about the nature of the religion in question. That is why part of the effort to overcome conflict is an attentive listening to respected authorities as they explain the meaning of their faith. Once the self-definition has been heard and understood, it is legitimate for those who stand outside the religion to hold it to its own finest interpretation, or to criticise it in the name of some other principle or belief. In this study, though taking examples from various religions, I will deal mostly with the Christian faith.

Defining conflict

Recognising how easily definitions can be disputed, only a preliminary understanding will be offered at this juncture. The notion may be refined and expanded as a result of subsequent discussion. Conflict can be identified as:

> a state of antagonism that is the result of disagreements that
> arise between two or more people, or groups of people, that
> either have produced or threaten to produce loss of life,
> freedoms, land, property, or livelihood, or cause mental
> suffering or physical abuse.[6]

In the context of this book, overcoming conflict, achieving reconciliation and building peace are seen as integral parts of the Church's mission, even though they do not always receive a high profile in books written on mission and missiology.

---

[6] This is my own definition.

The role of religion in conflict: a cause or contributing factor
A direct cause
It is rare that religion is the main or only cause of a particular conflict. When it is, the religion in question is seen as both reason for the conflict and also the motivating force for sustaining the aggression. The classical example from history is that of the Crusades. The purpose of sending armies to the 'Holy Land' was to remove the Muslims, regarded as infidels, from 'sanctified' territory. The Christian monarchs of Europe considered that the presence of militant unbelievers in the sacred sites of Christian faith was unacceptable. They had to be removed, so that the sites could be returned to the tender protection of Christians dedicated to preserving the memory of the original events of salvation that happened at these precise places. The means used to motivate the raising and sending of armies was self-sacrifice, leading quite possibly to martyrdom, to the greater glory of God. Religion as a direct cause derives from the notion of a holy war: it is God's will that all that pollutes a land should be exterminated:

> In the process, the precept that killing even in a just war occasioned guilt . . . came increasingly under pressure. One church leader after another, who had persistently paved the way for the First Crusade (1096), differentiated less and less between pagans on the one hand and heretics or apostates on the other. Anybody belonging to any of these categories could be killed with impunity . . . The killing of a heathen or an apostate, it was now suggested, was exceptionally pleasing to God.[7]

Another example would be that of the Zealot movement at the time of Jesus. The various groups of Zealots also believed in the sacredness of the land, which at that time was being desecrated

[7] *Transforming Mission*, p. 225. Aquinas, writing his *Summa Theologica* at the time of the seventh and eighth crusades, gave as the reason for waging war against infidels, not that of forced conversion, but for the purpose of stopping them obstructing the faith of Christ, see Norman Thomas (ed.), *Classic Texts in Mission and World Christianity* (Maryknoll: Orbis Books, 1995), p. 25.

by the pagan Roman occupation. For some years, culminating in the heroic defense of the citadel of Massada, bands of armed men carried out a guerrilla war against the Roman forces. A much more recent case would be that of the destruction of a Mosque by Hindu militants in Ayodhia, on the grounds that once it marked the spot of a holy Hindu site. In this latter example, although such communal violence also contains political elements, the major motivation is that of religious factionalism.

An indirect cause

The place of religion as one contributory cause of conflict among others is much more frequent. It may be used as a motivation, where the end to be gained is more mundane or 'secular'. Perhaps Palestinian suicide bombers would be a case in point. The willingness to blow themselves up alongside their largely innocent victims is the result of certain religious beliefs held with great tenacity. Nevertheless, the wider purpose appears to be to cause political damage, such as that of undermining attempts to negotiate sustainable geo-political solutions to long-term disputes by peaceful means. At the time of the Vietnam war between the Vietcong and the US military, a number of Buddhist monks burnt themselves to death as a protest against the foreign occupation of their country. Again, the motivation appears to be religious, but the end is political, namely self-determination without external interference.

The reverse of this process can also be observed. The ends may be religious, but the motivation is of a more secular nature. In the case of Sudan's long-running civil war, the objective of the Sudanese government, in attempting to crush the resistance of the rebels in the South, may have been that of the Islamisation of the whole nation. However, the more immediate motivation could have been the desire to maintain the unity and integrity of the state and, therefore, access to vital natural resources in the southern part of the terrritory.

A contributory factor

This is undoubtedly the most frequent way in which religion becomes involved as a cause of conflict. In these cases, religion may be used not so much as a reason, more as an excuse, for the disproportionate employment of force in certain circumstances. One of the most infamous examples of the manipulation of religion in the interests of maintaining a social and economic status quo happened in Latin America in the 1970s. Then there was an upsurge of popular feeling against the dominance of Latin American political life by the oligarchical elite, who sought to maintain societies favourable to their own economic interests. Part of the method of combatting popular unrest was to label it an international, communist plot against the integrity of a 'Catholic' continent. Then, it was a short step to using the ends to justify all possible means: Christian and Western values must be upheld against godless Communism, employing whatever level of violence was deemed adequate to get the job done.

Another example in this category is that of the pro-Zionist defence of Israel's excessive violence against Palestinians. Religion is a factor, in that appeal can be made to some passages from the Hebrew Bible to defend the right of Israelis to settle anywhere in the land believed to have been promised to the descendents of Abraham through Isaac. However, the expansion of Jewish settlements into land claimed through centuries of continuous occupation by the Palestinians as part of their homeland is extremely provocative and aggravating. It is one of the major causes of the conflict between the two peoples. Religion is used here as a tool (or weapon) to override international treaties and United Nations resolutions.[8]

Reasons why religion may be a motive for conflict
A territorial understanding of religion
In different parts of the world, a particular piece of land may be seen as dedicated, or belonging, to a particular religion. All those living within the bounds of that territory who are not adherents of that religion are experienced as a threat. Correspondence between being a citizen and being a member of the privileged

---

[8] The most relevant resolutions are those of the Security Council: Nos. 242 (1967), 338 (1973), 446 (1979), 465 (1980), 476 (1980).

religious community is then made a question of patriotic loyalty. As a result, minority groups may well be denied the full panoply of civil liberties and human rights. The constitution itself discriminates against certain citizens, because of their religious affiliation.

In Argentina, in the late 1960s, an attempt was made by the then military government to fortify the nation's resolve to withstand the alien forces of secularism and communism. It took the form of a proposal solemnly to dedicate the whole nation to the heart of the Blessed Virgin Mary in the national Catholic shrine of Lujan, outside Buenos Aires. After considerable objections from many sectors of the nation, on the grounds that such an action would be discriminatory, divisive and counter-productive, the idea was dropped.

In the 1990s, in the Balkans, part of the motivation for the war between Croatia and Serbia was the religious division between Catholics and Orthodox. Defending the territorial integrity of the nation, identified with one or other of the churches, became a matter of religious conscience. The external threat against the life and livelihood of the people was interpreted as a threat against their religious identity.

Clearly, the intention of identifying so closely a particular geographical space with one expression of religious commitment is anti-pluralist. Those who do not belong to the religion do not properly belong to the nation either. They are inferior citizens, treated always as potential subversives. To link territory (or, in some formulations of the matter, the very soil itself) to a particular religious expression is a sure recipe for ongoing strife. The right to religious freedom, even if enshrined in a constitution or charter of rights, is a dead letter, unless the full rights and responsibilities of citizenship are also guaranteed in practice for all minority communities.

A spatial notion of holiness

A particular location, regarded as being of supreme significance to a particular religion, may be wittingly, or unwittingly, seen as having been 'desecrated' or 'defiled' by a deliberate or unintended dishonour. A classical example of religious insensitivity which became a major cause for the renewal of the Palestinian 'intifada' was Ariel Sharon's infamous visit to the Al Askar mosque in Jerusalem in September 2000. It was interpreted by most devout Muslims as a provocative, scandalous invasion of a 'sacred' space by someone bent on causing trouble and harm.

Israelis might argue that the event has a pefectly proper explanation, in that the mosque is built on the site of the temple mount, a place of immense religious significance to orthodox Jews. Access to this space ought, therefore, to be granted to Jews as well as Muslims. In a different kind of world, such an aspiration might find its fulfilment. However, in the real world, given that the mosque has been there for many centuries, long before the Jews returned to their original home, and given that such an action predictably would inflame passions, to make a unilateral decision of this nature was bound to cause deep offence. No doubt the motive was more political than religious, designed to show, by a display of overwhelming military force, that might and control was with the Israeli nation not with the Palestinians.[9]

Ethnic identity

There are many cases, where one community (generally a minority) feels a strong sense of grievance and resentment either because of the privileges and power of another group, the suppression of their culture or the denial of their religious freedoms. Contemporary examples of this might be the Catholic community in Northern Ireland or the Christians in Northern Nigeria. This can certainly lead to violence, as the excluded group wishes the authorities to pay them a proper respect on the basis of who they are. In a sense, this is the reverse side of the identification of one religion with a specific region. Those who do not belong to the religion are claiming a due recognition that they belong equally to the region.

In each of these cases, religion is being used as an *instrument* to further sectarian interests. They are classical cases of ideo-

---

[9] On the significance of Jerusalem as a centre for religious devotion, see Colin Chapman, *Whose Holy City?* (Oxford: Lion Publishing, 2004).

logical manipulation of deep cultural sensitivities, which gain their strength from profound human feelings of identity, belonging, solidarity and ownership. In a word, conflict can arise because people experience, or are induced to feel, a threat to their security, one of the deepest strands of their psychological make-up.

The role of religion in conflict: is it always unwarranted?

Up to now, we have only highlighted those aspects of religion which have been widely used as a justification or excuse for conflict. It is right to ask, however, whether the involvement of religion in conflict is always a perversion of religion. The answer depends, in part, on the religious tradition's teaching about the use of lethal force. The majority of Christians (and Muslims) believe, on principled ethical grounds, that the use of force may be justified in certain circumstances. In those cases, therefore, a religion would be acting according to its precepts in defending such a use. For Christians, following the principles of the theory of a just war,[10] the conditions have to include the following elements: just cause, last resort, self-defence and the lesser of two evils. This means that war might be justified, if all peaceful means for resolving disputes have been exhausted, the military action is not a pre-emptive strike and the result of not going to war would be greater oppression, increased violence and more misery.

It is interesting to note that, on these grounds, some liberation theologians in Latin America defended the violence of the guerrilla groups as a legitimate resistance to tyranny. They spoke eloquently about such action as the 'second' violence: i.e., the response to an intolerable situation of state-sponsored brutality and suppression of human rights, carried out in contravention to

---

[10] An account of the background, development and reasons behind the theory can be found in most standard text-books on Christian Ethics. I have discussed it in some detail in the context of the Christian call to be peacemakers in *What is Mission?*, pp. 148–152. I discuss some of the difficulties in the theory in chapter 7.

the state's own constitution and to internationally agreed conventions on human rights.[11]

External force might be justified, on the grounds of the lesser of two evils, to separate two, or more, warring parties. This would certainly be an argument for the use of an outside military force in Rwanda in the 1990s and the use of troops under the flag of the United Nations in peacekeeping roles (for example, to enforce or maintain a cessation of hostilities between communities or ethnic groups in dispute, such as in Sierra Leone in the 1990s). It was also one of the arguments used for the intervention of NATO forces in Kosovo in 1997.

Using the same criteria, it would be correct to say that the US-led invasion of Iraq in 2003 cannot be justified by the principles of the just war. It was not fought in self-defence, as there was no evidence of any credible threat by the regime towards external third parties. It was certainly not the last resort, as the United Nations had not exhausted all means to make Saddam Hussein comply with its resolutions. As predicted at the time, and subsequently borne out in real situations, it was not the lesser of two evils. Although trumpeted by the US, British and other governments as a war of liberation, in fact it became the cause of increased violence, the breakdown of law and order, the escalation of the threat of international terrorism and the worsening of the social circumstances of the population. Finally, it was not authorised by a competent authority, as the UN Security Council refused, at that juncture, to issue the invading powers with a mandate under the UN Charter. It was right, therefore, for church leaders to speak out in opposition to the war, on the basis of unambiguous principles long since included within the historical tradition of the Christian faith.

Over against the religious defence of war even in very special circumstances, and it cannot be over-stressed that the just war criteria are intended not to legitimate war in one's own interests but to make it as difficult as possible, a minority of Christians (and Buddhists) are committed to wholly non-violent means of

[11] See J. Andrew Kirk, *Liberation Theology: An Evangelical View from the Third World* (London: Marshall, Morgan & Scott, 1979), p. 31; Dom Helder Camara, *The Spiral of Violence* (London: Sheed & Ward, 1971), pp. 30–34.

resolving conflicts and bringing about change. They are, therefore, resolutely opposed to any justification of lethal force on religious grounds, understanding that their faith forbids them to
participate as combatants in the use of military force of any
kind.[12]

Finally, it is necessary, in the light of current misconceptions,
to stress that there is no religion, true to its own self-understanding, that proposes a theory of holy war. A holy war is
understood as the use of military might to further the interests of
God as interpreted by the religion in question. As we have
already seen, the notion of holy war, even when the language has
not necessarily been used, has been employed in the history of
both the Christian church and the Islamic *dhumma*. The concepts
of 'crusade' and *jihad* have been diverted from the realm of spiritual warfare, i.e. the struggle against all forces that hinder closer
communion with God, to that of real warfare. Thus, war, torture,
execution and bannishment have all been justified, not only on
the basis of self-defence, the lesser evil and a last resort (or even
first resort), but also to exterminate (supposed) evil from the religious community or the body politic.

However, it is now widely recognised that the purposes of religion cannot be accomplished by using coercive, physical means.
It is, perhaps, an encouraging sign that, in the best ethical traditions of the major religions, means and ends are firmly separated,
so that it cannot be taken for granted that the latter (the furtherance of faith) justify the former (the use of force). In a much wider
context, means-ends moral theory is also a principled counter-
weight to the kind of overly pragmatic, utilitarian and consequentialist ethics of today's secular world that found it possible to
justify a pre-emptive invasion of a non-belligerent nation.

The rose of religion in conflict: a means of resolution

In this section I shall be dealing exclusively with the Christian
contribution to both theoretical and practical means of resolving

---

[12] I attempt to tackle more extensively the moral and theological issues raised by
the Christian peace tradition, and seek to determine how far the prohibition on
violence can go in chapter 7.

conflict. This is not intended to suggest that other religions do not make valuable contributions towards the overcoming of a conflict. Rather, it is an acknowledgement that I am more aware of Christian resources than those of other faith traditions.

The anthropological causes of conflict

    The causes of conflict are multiple: it may, for example, be due to the unrelenting pressure of fear (real or imagined), which one community has about the intentions of another. Likewise, it may arise from the seemingly universal human desire to exact retribution or wreak vengeance . . . or the experience of military humiliation, cultural degradation . . . or the primitive urge to dominate others or expand one's influence or power.[13]

In the letter of James, in the New Testament, the author reflects on the consequences of flawed human nature.[14] He poses first the rhetorical question, 'What causes fights and quarrels among you?' Then, he answers it by referring to a number of realities, which have produced the tensions and antagonisms within the community: 'conflicting desires', 'covetousness', 'envy', and 'pride'. All of these, he affirms, spring from the natural human inclination to substitute idols and ideologies for the living God. Paradoxically, religion itself can be a manifestation of this substitution, whereby people fanatically follow ideas, dogmas and structures in place of the one true God.

    Rene Girard, although he does not cite the passage in James, gives a running commentary on desire as the fundamental cause of conflict. He calls it 'mimetic' desire, meaning the desire that wishes to possess what belongs to another, or to imitate another of whom one is envious. It is the desire prohibited in the tenth commandment ('you shall not covet . . .'), which motivates the acts forbidden in the preceding four commandments: 'You shall not murder. You shall not commit adultery. You shall not steal. You shall not bear false witness.' (Exod. 20:13–17). Mimetic desire is motivated by rivalry, fuelled by the perception that the

---

[13] *What is Mission?*, p. 144.
[14] James 4. 1–6.

person (or group) that refuses to allow my desire to be satisfied is my enemy.[15] Girard's analysis is fascinating, based as it is on anthropological research. However, as he acknowledges that not all desire is evil-inclined, there must be a deeper cause of conflict. He hints at this himself, when he says:

> The conflicts resulting from this double idolatry of self and other are the principal source of human violence. When we are devoted to adoring our neighbour, this adoration can easily turn to hatred because we seek desperately to adore ourselves, and we fall.[16]

This statement suggests that idolatry, i.e. worshipping the wrong object, is the basic problem. The prohibitions of the second part of the Decalogue would be unnecessary, if there was a guarantee that all would keep the first commandment: 'You shall have no other gods before me.' (Exod. 20:3).

Just because the deepest roots of conflict are to be found in false objectives, the Christian tradition, even when it may justify war in carefully defined and limited circumstances, nevertheless declares it to be evil. It arises always as the result of the breakdown of proper human relations, which in turn have their ultimate origin in the refusal to heed God. War, then, cannot deal with the basic cause of violence, only the symptoms. And, of course, God does not need to be defended by the puny efforts of human, physical force! This is precisely what Jesus meant, when he declared before Pontus Pilate, 'my kingdom is not of (does not originate from) this world. If it did, my servants would fight, so that I might not be handed over to the Jews. No, my kingdom is not from here.'[17] The rule of God cannot be achieved by resorting to human weapons.

---

[15] *I See Satan Fall Like Lightning* (Maryknoll: Orbis Books, 2001), chapter 1.
[16] Ibid. p. 11.
[17] John 18. 36.

The vision of a new creation
In a number of Old Testament passages, particularly in Isaiah, we find promises of the universal reign of God's *shalom*.[18] These texts have been the inspiration for many a secular utopia:

> Nation will not take up sword against nation, nor will they train for war any more;

> Every warrior's boot used in battle . . . will be destined for burning;

> My people will live in peaceful dwelling-places, in secure homes, in undisturbed places of rest;

> No longer will they build houses and others live in them, or plant and others eat.[19]

It is because of both the nature of *shalom* and the means by which it is brought into being that the Christian tradition asserts that real peace cannot be brought about by war. *Shalom* is the result of reconciliation and genuinely new beginnings. These are only possible on the basis of uncovering the truth of a situation, recognising and admitting wrong-doing and exercising forgiveness. Although it is true that there cannot be *shalom* where there is an absence of justice, it is every bit as true that *shalom* is impossible until truth is known and faced and authentic reconciliation between two parties in conflict happens. It is not without

---

[18] Unlike the English word 'peace', uniformly used as a translation, the Hebrew word conveys a positive rather than negative meaning. Whereas 'peace' conveys a sense of the absence of conflict and strife, being interchangeable with synonyms like tranquility, calm, stillness, serenity, rest, non-aggression, cease-fire, *shalom* expresses a sense of constructive well-being, a community in which everyone is able to develop fully their human potential. It depicts a situation of security, prosperity, care and respect. It presupposes, of course, an end of violence as a means of bringing change and the reconciliation of parties formerly in conflict.
[19] Isaiah 2.4, 9.5, 32.18, 65.22.

significance that commissions exploring truth and reconciliation in post-dictatorship situations (like South Africa, Chile and Argentina) have been inspired by an explicitly Christian under-standing of redemption.[20]

The insistence on justice

It is important to establish a position where parties in conflict can be held to account at the highest possible level, the level of con-science and moral rationality. Then it may be possible to present cogently all the arguments that delegitimise the use of force to settle disputes. For example, if the means used in the pursuit of violence involve the killing of innocent people, then they are not justified. It would constitute a grave injustice to take away the life of those who are not responsible for either the cause or the pursuit of the conflict. In this context justice cannot be achieved by violent means, if it is inevitable that a grave injustice will be committed on human beings not involved in the conflict. The means used simply invalidate the ends in view.

The burden of justification for violence must fall on those who wish to use it. The only set of criteria that has been developed in moral and political thinking is that of the 'just war'. However, the criteria, such as *a just cause*, are seldom met. In fact, they are designed to limit war and end violence, not justify it. If applied perceptively and strictly, they have the capacity to stop low-level conflict from escalating into something much more serious and all-encompassing.

In rare cases, though it may happen,[21] to reject any recourse to the use of force may actually promote the sum total of violence.[22] In such situations, the sin of omission outweighs the sin of com-mission. The Christian ideal is the rule of the law of love.

[20] See Walter Wink, *Healing a Nation's Wounds: Reconciliation on the Road to Democracy* (Uppsala: Life and Peace Institute, 1996).

[21] The declaration of war against the German Third Reich is still the most power-ful example.

[22] Such a view is disputed by total pacifists. In the case of the Second World War, they would argue, for example, that the armed struggle against Hitler hastened, and perhaps made inevitable, the systematic extermination of the Jews and other racial minorities.

However, where the Gospel does not rule over the hearts, minds and lives of men and women, the coercive law of restraint and judgement may have to be implemented.

Using practical, pastoral experience

It should go without saying that the Christian community is called, as part of its witness to the reality of the kingdom of God, to be both a model of and an agent for the resolution of conflict in all its manifestations. The work of Christians in society to bring healing and reconciliation is dependent for its credibility on the Christian community itself being able to achieve reconciliation in its own inner life. The following practises are key elements in defusing situations of tension and in seeking lasting solutions to suspicion, fear, insecurity, the desire for revenge, or any other reason for the outbreak of violence.

To end discrimination against genuine diversity

According to the Christian view of reality, diversity is an enriching experience, when it is part of the normative variety of creation expressed in different races, cultures, genders and ages. The logic of the Gospel drives towards a pluralist society, that is one in which variety is accepted and celebrated.

However, diversity is not completely open-ended. No society can allow people to claim that they should be permitted to exercise their differences, irrespective of what these may be. Every human community draws a line at certain points and imposes a policy of discrimination. Thus, the argument that I should be allowed to follow my natural instincts, because this is the way I am, is certainly not acceptable in every case. Tolerance has its limits. For example, the attraction of adults for young people, which leads to sexual relationships, is inadmissable. It is rightly called abuse, because the adult imposes a superior power derived from social standing and psychological advantage on a vulnerable human being. Violent behaviour by people, even if they suffer with severe emotional disabilities, is also unacceptable. In neither case can it be argued that the person concerned is simply expressing the outcome of the way he or she was born.

So, every society and culture draws boundaries. For either good reasons or quite arbitrary considerations, standards of normality and abnormality are agreed and enforced. Sometimes, there are deep divisions in society about where the boundaries should lie. The most controversial and difficult concern adults sexually attracted to their own gender. Liberal societies have come to accept that, for a small percentage of any population, there is an inherent disposition towards the same sex. As long as the relationship is entirely mutual, there being no exploitation of a younger person by an older, it should be accepted. The majority of Christians, however, do not accept that this kind of partnership is normal for some. In the light of how they perceive God's intention for human well-being, they are convinced that men and women come to realise the fulness of their humanity only in a relationship with someone who is other than themselves. So, they disagree with the liberal consensus about normality and draw the boundaries, in this case, at a different point.[23]

There is, however, no excuse for differentiating between people on the basis of ethnic or cultural backgrounds, gender, age or disability. Moreover, non-discrimination has to become pro-active in the case of the weaker and more vulnerable members of society, especially those with permanent incapacities, the chronically sick, poor families and refugees fleeing from persecution. Such a task is enormously challenging, given the difficulties, which most people find, in handling the different and the unfamiliar.

To practise forgiveness in place of condemnation, vengeance and retaliation
When offended or affronted, the natural human inclination is to seek to repay evil for evil. The first reaction is to defend one's human integrity against the the other's wilful disregard of my

---

[23] I will explore in much more depth this vexed question of human sexuality in chapter 9. Although such a topic might seem incongruous in a book about mission, I include it because I believe it illustrates in a most forceful way the missiological issue of the relationship between the Gospel and culture.

humanity by inflicting some kind of hurt upon him or her. Our natural tendency is to mete out our own form of punishment on the person or group who is guilty (in our judgement) of the crime of disrespect or dishonour.

Within the bounds of a process of judgement under the rule of law, punishment is an indispensable part of society's conviction that right and wrong have to be distinguished. The ancient stipulation of 'an eye for an eye, and a tooth for a tooth' was intended to limit the amount of punishment so that it was appropriate to the crime committed. When left to the offended party, just punishment can easily give way to unjust vengeance. Thus, it would be wrong to make perpetrators of offences pay double for what they had done, merely to express society's anger and deter others. Punishment is based on the principle of justice. The inviolability of human personhood has to be defended against physical or psychological assault.

However, the matter of crime and punishment does not end with a due and fair judicial process. A situation is only transformed when the victim is ready to forgive and the victimiser is ready to say sorry from the heart. There is, however, a genuine and complex question concerning the refusal of the aggressor to ask for forgiveness. Can the aggrieved party, nevertheless, still forgive? To what extent is forgiveness only meaningful as a response to genuine contrition? To what extent is it a movement of grace that intends to initiate a changed attitude on the part of the perpetrator of the crime? Perhaps it is both, being a necessary step on the way to a changed relationship. It is not yet full reconciliation.

To practise reconciliation

This takes the process of ending conflict one step further forward. Indeed, some would see this as the genuine goal of all attempts to resolve confrontations. It is the conclusion of a process whereby alienated and estranged people are brought together, so that they can accept each other as full human persons, with the same rights and responsibilities. It can only happen if a number of barriers are removed, such as misrepresentation, prejudice, scapegoating, stereotyping and demonising the other.

'Strangers' who, by definition, live far from me (culturally, geographically, religiously, politically or economically) have to be converted into my neighbours (welcome in my neighbourhood, near to me). Strangers are estranged from me by being distant and being strange (not like me). The neighbour is one who lives next door (who is *nigh*), who shares, so to speak, the same space as I do. It is easier to regard the first as an enemy, because they are absent. For reconciliation to happen they have to be transformed into a neighbour, one for whom I feel the responsibility to care.

Reconciliation is not an easy matter. In terms of the Christian story, the solution to conflict is what it has cost God to repair the damage caused by human alienation and enmity (2 Cor. 5:18–21). Jesus Christ during his public life penetrated to the very heart of problems. He knew intimately the deep causes of alienation – fear, insecurity and hatred. He experienced in his own being the anger and enmity of opponents and the fear and disloyalty of friends. He bore them all in his own body in the crucifixion, the supreme place and moment of alienation. The death of Jesus was the moment of absolute abnormality, of total estrangement – 'my God, my God, why have you forsaken me?' (Mark 15:34). The curse of abnormality was born to its uttermost, but was then followed by three great cries of triumph: 'it is finished'; 'Father, into your hands, I commend my spirit'; 'he is not here, but has risen' (John 19:30; Luke 23:46, 24:5). In the resurrection of Jesus Christ from death, the reality and consequences of alienation have been resolved.

So, restoration to a situation of full reconciliation and healing is a costly process. As a *first step* human beings need to admit to the abnormality of their lives, demonstrated in acts of violence towards others. As a *second step*, they have to own up to their own guilt. A *third step* is repentance. This is more than the emotions of sorrow, regret or remorse; it is an act of the will, turning away deliberately from a past life, in order to embrace a new one. The *fourth step* is restitution. This may take the form of punishment. In public, it is administered judicially under a proper rule of law; privately, it may happen in acts of penance, such as an unconditional apology for wrongs done. It has to include reparations for damage done to and a costly embrace of the person wronged. The object is to ensure that justice is seen to be done and injustices rectified. The *fifth step* is unconditional forgiveness. This is not the same as forgetting, for memory is one way of guarding against repetition of wrongs committed; nor is it the overlooking or minimizing of wrong-doing. The purpose and consequence of forgiveness is to release (the same word – *aphiemi* - is used for both in the New Testament) the wrong-doer from his or her guilt and the wronged from bitterness, hatred and the spiral of violence.

To exercise power to further human dignity

A good number of conflicts are caused by disadvantageous social and economic conditions. Peasants are permanently excluded by absentee landlords from land, which is their only means of livelihood, even though it is quite probable that the former's ancestors had tilled it for many generations. Factory workers are exploited by ruthless owners, in situations of scarce employment, being made to work long hours for miserable pay. Minority groups are penalised by having to bear the burden of extra taxation and discrimination in the job market.

Resolving conflict entails the advocation and enforcement of just economic, social, political and legal structures. This may be done in two ways: by monitoring and publishing unjust practices, wherever they occur and by whoever perpetrated, and by empowering the vulnerable and excluded, so that they are able to participate fully in society. There is no question that both of these strategies are risky, in the sense that those who enjoy economic power and political privileges are not generally willing to see them curtailed. Equality of opportunity, meaning extra support given to the disadvantaged to enable them to have a genuine stake in society, may sound good as an abstract principle. However, if the implications are that the present assets of the advantaged may be partly stripped away, either through land reform, taxation or the obligation to pay a minimum wage, the idea may well be vehemently opposed. In so far as this is the case, conflict is bound to continue.

Conclusion

With regard to incidents of conflict, religion has received a bad press recently. This is partly the fault of people who misuse religion in order to justify various forms of violence. However, it is also the fault of the press, which tends to emphasise exclusively those events where religion could be said to be a contributory factor. For some media commentators the link between religion and violence is another reason to dismiss religion as a divisive, anachronistic relic from a bygone age, not capable of being trusted as a serious force for progressive attitudes and policies.

The problem with this stance is that it is hopelessly selective. Even when parts of the media do pay attention to the considerable role that religious leaders have played in averting some conflicts and resolving others, the actual contribution of the message of faith itself is often omitted or sidelined. The greater reality is that much of the work done in the name of a faith perspective is not acknowledged at all. Perhaps, this is as it should be. Christians in particular are not motivated by the praise they may receive from the secular world. They like to receive the praise of their divine Lord, 'blessed are (you) the peacemakers', (Matt. 5;9) only because to fulfil the will of the one who sends them is completely satisfying and worthwhile.

So, the role of Christians as mediators and healers in situations of conflict is at the heart of the missionary call of the Church, for it represents a concrete example of the mandate to be ministers of reconciliation (2 Cor. 5:18). This task lies at the heart of the Gospel, for in all Christian involvement in transforming conflict an invitation to escape from the deepest of all alienations by being reconciled to God through Christ is implicitly enshrined. The root cause of all conflict is a life out of kilter with the loving purposes of God. So, the only hope for a lasting peace between individuals and peoples is to be at peace with God through Jesus Christ.

CHAPTER 7

Overcoming Violence with Violence: Is It Ever Justified?

The wholeness of truth

Through the help of wise teachers I learnt as a young Christian that human life cannot be fully human unless truth and absolutes, corresponding to an objectively real world and not relative to circumstances, actually exist. I also began to appreciate that truth is not an abstract, rational theory, but integrates all dimensions of the human world – intellectual, spiritual, emotional, aesthetic and ethical. I also learnt that truth and absolutes have to do with all aspects of the mundane world, social, political and economic. Truth, by its very nature, covers the whole of life. If it is limited to personal belief, it simply ceases to be truth.

The consequence of this reality is that the individual's inner life is deeply affected by his or her external social situation. Who people are and how they behave is the result, to a considerable degree, of the context in which they live. So, in thinking about the relationship between individual and social change, the main issue is not which comes first but how do changed people change society and in what ways does the latter affect our ways of believing and behaving.

A realisation of the completeness of truth bears upon the nature of Christian conversion and spirituality. Conversion is a continuous process in which the whole human person is gradually transformed into the likeness of Jesus Christ: to think and act in every small detail of life like Christ. Spirituality is much more than a life of prayer, meditation and reflection. It embraces the way Christians respond to every situation in which they find themselves. It has to do with the breadth of our vision of God's concerns for the whole of creation. It impels us to discover and become a part of God's missionary activity. Not least, among the issues with which many Christians have to deal, is the reality of social deprivation, dislocation and injustice. Along with this, comes the question about the legitimacy of violence, in certain circumstances, to bring about a political change that will benefit those excluded from a dignified life by the present system. To what extent, if at all, could it be part of the church's mission to endorse the use of lethal force to bring about such a change?

The violent you always have with you

Another important aspect of my Christian development was encountering the 'peace-church' tradition. This happened in Buenos Aires in 1971 through meeting John Howard Yoder, on a year's sabbatical at the time.[1] That year was a particularly crucial time for the people of God in Latin America as they were confronted with the question of revolutionary politics and violence as a means of achieving radical social change.[2]

Positions among Christians became easily polarised. On the one side, conservatives and traditionalists held to the semi-sacred nature of the existing political equilibrium, meaning the effective control of political life by the oligarchies, whichever political party happened to be in power. Where possible, the sta-

---

[1] Yoder is the author of numerous books outlining the biblical, theological and ethical stance of the peace-church tradition. The most influential has been *The Politics of Jesus* (Grand Rapids: Eerdmans, 1972); see also, *The Original Revolution: Essays on Christian Pacifism* (Scottdale: Herald Press, 1972); *Nevertheless:The Varieties of Religious Pacifism* (Scottdale: Herald Press, 1971); *The Priestly Kingdom: Social Ethics as Gospel* (Notre Dame: University of Notre Dame Press, 1984).

[2] It will be remembered, among other significant events, that in September 1971 Salvador Allende, the socialist president of Chile, was killed in a coup that ushered in the military government of Pinochet.

tus quo was supported by the rhetoric of democracy and propaganda aimed against anarchistic tendencies. However, where necessary, the status quo was maintained by wholly undemocratic, fascist-leaning military regimes. The use of violence for these people was quite unproblematic. The state, identified with the most powerful ruling elites, had monopoly rights on the deployment of force. In terms of classic just-war theory, the emphasis was on *legitimate authority*.

On the other side, radical forces, represented within the Christian churches by a group calling itself 'Christians for Socialism'[3] used the just-war theory for their own ends. They developed the notion of the *just rebellion:* the justifiable duty of citizens to rise up against intolerable oppression and brutality. The emphasis was on *the lesser of two evils* (a kind of consequential ethic) and *legitimate self-defence*. It was common to hear people sympathising with this line of argument speak about the 'first' and 'second' violence. The first was perpetrated by the state in callous disregard for elementary human rights. The second was employed as a response to an unprovoked violence already unleashed. However, at the same time, some in the revolutionary parties would speak, using imagery employed by Karl Marx and Franz Fanon,[4] of violence as a 'midwife' for the birth of a new order of justice and progressive policies.

Certainly Latin America, and particularly Argentina, was living through violent times. Guerrilla movements resorted to kidnapping and summary executions. They bombed civilian targets like supermarkets and offices (though only when closed) and raided military establishments. The military detained people

---

[3] The actual title is significant. They did not call themselves either Christian socialists or socialist Christians, where in each case the use of the adjective modifies the noun. Christians for socialism denotes the priority of socialism, with this group identifying themselves as Christians on behalf of socialism. Further, see, Peter Hebblethwaite, *The Christian-Marxist Dialogue and Beyond* (London: Darton, Longman & Todd, 1977), chapter 4.

[4] See David McLellan, *The Thought of Karl Marx* (Basingstoke: Macmillan, 1995), pp. 227–228; Franz Fanon, *The Wretched of the Earth* (Harmondsworth: Penguin Books, 1970).

without trial, practised torture and began to abduct people from their homes, never to be heard of again. Those sympathetic to the actions of either side had no qualms about the use of violence as a justified means to further their ends. Whatever else may have been a matter of dispute between the groups in conflict, a challenge to the principle of violence was not one of them. In a supposedly Christian continent, both sides appealed to the long church tradition of justified violence to achieve certain ends. The only disagreement was about the ends in view and their respective interpretations of the geo-political situation on the continent.

Violence is not an option

In the midst of the tensions, confusions and confrontations among Christians, Yoder presented a significantly different message. At the risk of simplifying his message, it seemed to consist of two fundamental and quite simple affirmations. First, the use of violence by Christians for political, social or personal ends is a denial of the Gospel. If Christians, by definition, are bound to follow in the way of Jesus Christ, then the use of the sword is the use of an alien weapon.[5] The only legitimate power that they can exercise, in circumstances of terror and violence, is to suffer it without violent retaliation.

Although the refusal to retaliate, when being subjected to violence, suggests a position of great weakness and ineffectiveness, it actually displays a type of power that others find difficult to cope with. Not to strike back is unexpected, creating for the violent agent a state of uncertainty. He is not used to dealing with such an unusual reaction and may, as a consequence, become confused. More importantly, non-retaliation is powerful because it is the only effective strategy that has the possibility of ending a cycle of self-righteous anger, bitterness and revenge. It introduces a genuinely brand new factor into the situation. Thus, the death of Jesus, interpreted as the willingness to suffer the vio-

---

[5] An excellent short presentation of the reasons why pacifism is the only option for a disciple of Jesus is given in Alan Kreider, 'Following Jesus Implies Unconditional Pacifism' in J. Andrew Kirk (ed.), *Handling Problems of Peace and War: An Evangelical Debate* (Basingstoke: Marshall Pickering, 1988), chapter 2.

lence of those whose policies depended on violence, was able to break the vicious circle of the use of force as a means of gaining religiously sanctioned political ends. Moreover, the subsequent history of Jesus' people shows how futile was the violence perpetrated on the man from Nazareth and the long list of persecutions endured by his followers.

This second argument for non-violent resistance to evil is more pragmatic, but nevertheless effective. Violence is always counterproductive. Experience teaches that the use of force never solves the problem it is designed to address. This is true for two reasons. On the one hand, its logic is to engender a never-ending spiral of force and counter-force, in which too easily the original reasons for the use of violence get twisted or forgotten. Violence creates its own dynamic situation, in which the boundaries of the original dispute are often expanded by new causes for bitterness and hatred. On the other hand, violence cannot achieve a genuinely new situation. Only when forces in dispute openly acknowledge the humanity and, therefore, inherent dignity of the other, can a real conversation between two groups of human beings have any chance of success. Violence, to succeed, has to be conducted in an environment in which the enemy is dehumanised by being reduced to a level of humanity inferior to one's own.

This is, in bare outline, the substance of the position of Yoder and other Christian 'pacifists'.[6] However, to do justice to this point of view, it is necessary to expand further those elements in the 'peace-Church' tradition, which carry the most weight. After I have attempted to set them out as lucidly and fairly as I can, I will raise some questions. These, I believe, show that this tradition, though persuasive, is not ultimately entirely satisfactory.

---

[6] Writing at roughly the same time as Yoder, Jacques Ellul, a French lay theologian (from the Reformed tradition) came to remarkably similar conclusions: see *Violence: reflections from a Christian Perspective* (London: SCM Press, 1970). From a self-consciously secular stance, Hannah Arendt's book *On Violence* (London: Penguin Press, 1970) portrayed the tragedy and futility of violence as a response to violence.

The relationship between means and ends
The peace tradition appears to take the relationship between means and ends more seriously than just-war theory. Ostensibly, the latter is about measuring the validity of means and ensuring that they are never overridden by the urgency of the ends. Nevertheless, however carefully they are applied (and often they are not), they remain means. They tend, therefore, to be judged by their utilitarian value.

By definition, violence or the threat of violence is always tainted by evil.[7] So, it can only be justified, if at all, by the possibility that achieving a greater good will outweigh its destructive consequences. It is impossible to consider that it could ever be an end in itself or, in some amazing way, part of the final redemption of creation. In contrast, non-violence, although a means for producing change, *is* also a manifestation of the coming kingdom of God, the realisation of the final *shalom* on earth as it is in heaven. Its use, therefore, does not require a suspension of the kingdom to some future date. In itself it is already a visible, tangible proclamation of the Gospel of mercy, grace, forgiveness and reconciliation.

The burden of proof
It would seem that the burden of proof in this dispute falls on those who wish to justify the use of force by appealing to Christian belief. This assumption is based partly on history. The stance of Christians in the early centuries towards military service has been a matter of dispute among historians. However, current research indicates that most Christians found military service incompatible with their confession of Jesus.[8] Those who wish to argue that, nevertheless, it was right for Christians at a

---

[7] In the thinking of John Milbank, violence is the primeval sin. He interprets it as the refusal of the gift of creation and grace, see *Being Reconciled: Ontology and Pardon* (London: Routledge, 2003), pp. ix, 26ff.

[8] See Alan Kreider, 'Military service in the Church Orders,' *Journal of Religious Ethics*, 31:3 (2003), pp. 415–442; Alan Kreider, *The Change of Conversion and the Origin of Christendom* (Harrisburg: Trinity Press International, 1999); Alan Kreider (ed.), *The Origins of Christendom in the West* (London: T. & T. Clark, 2001).

later date to change their stance need to demonstrate why it was justified to abandon the position of the earliest believers.

This might be done on the basis of one of two arguments, or perhaps a combination of both. Firstly, it might be pointed out that in subsequent centuries the historic situation had changed to such a degree that Christians were obliged to reinterpret the tradition. Now, so it is argued, as the church became a significant power in society, Christians had to take some responsibility for maintaining order and stability through the use of force. To act as a persecuted minority was no longer an historical option. Secondly, even if a changed context did not oblige a later generation of Christians to alter their stance, they might have come to the conclusion that the earliest Christians were simply mistaken. Thus, it might be claimed that they had misunderstood the implications of following Jesus in the Gentile world. If there was a pacifist strain in early Christianity, it was linked securely to a Palestinian tradition that rejected the pressure on Christians to join in the armed struggle against the Roman occupying forces. Whichever of these two arguments may seem the most cogent to the subsequent non-pacifist tradition, the just-war theory, in its initial elaboration by Augustine, was an excellent example of an early piece of contextual theology!

The inadequacies of the just-war tradition

If it can be shown that the Christian community came to change its original attitude towards participation in war, the theory becomes largely irrelevant. In the best of circumstances, the theory is designed to limit the possibility of war and violence in situations of conflict. However, it is already based on the premise that force is legitimate in certain situations. The criteria have been elaborated to discern when exactly that situation has been reached. They are intended to be applied with rigour and objectivity. They do not, however, address the deeper question of whether a disciple of Jesus, in any circumstances, may be an instrument of war.

Apart from this major shortcoming, the theory is defective on its own terms. The analogy, often used, of a police force controlling wrongdoing in a democratic state is inadmissible when projected onto an extra-territorial situation. In the first case, the police are restricted by law in what they are able to do, and in the means they can employ to do it. They are also account-able to legitimately elected civilian powers. If members of the public wish to object to any police action, there is a proper com-plaints procedure they can follow. In the second case, there is no universally recognised legitimate authority, which has the right to sanction war in the case of the outbreak of hostilities. Even the United Nations Security Council cannot act in the same way, and with the same justification, as a national government defending its own territory. The Security Council is made up of five perma-nent members, who have a perennial right of veto, and ten rotat-ing members from the different continents. It is unusual, even with only fifteen votes to be cast, that the Council will come up with a unanimous decision. A split vote, even if it gives one group a majority, is unsatisfactory. The problem is in the bar-gaining and the surreptitious arm-twisting that goes on by the major powers. It is rare for the vote to be entirely free and fair. Some might say, it is the best arrangement that is possible. However, as the recent cases of Bosnia, Somalia, Kosovo, Rwanda, Iraq and the Sudan demonstrate, it is still inadequate.

Then, it is pertinent to ask when in practice has the just-war theory ever been used to demonstrate the illegitimacy of partic-ular use of force, in such a way that authorities bent on declaring war have been persuaded to change their mind. The case of the invasion of Iraq by the so-called 'coalition of the willing' is pow-erful evidence of the failure of the theory. There could not have been a clearer case, according to just war criteria, of the illegiti-macy of a pre-emptive strike against the regime of Saddam Hussein.[9] In Britain, even before the highly dubious intelligence reports became publicly known, the Churches were completely unanimous in condemning the action as an unfounded war of aggression against a sovereign nation. None of the major criteria – last resort, self-defence, legitimate authority, proportionate

[9] See J. Andrew Kirk, 'Letters to World Leaders' in *New Routes: A Journal of Peace Research and Action*, vol. 7, No. 1, 2003, pp. 3–6.

means or improved end result – were present. Nevertheless, the British Prime Minister and most of the Cabinet, on the basis of false information, against the express wish of the Security Council, the advice of UN inspectors working in Iraq and the overwhelming majority of the population, supported the ill-conceived adventure of President George Bush.

Where, then, is the much vaunted ability of the just-war theory, in such a clear-cut case, to restrain the will of powerful nations? Or, possibly, the problem is that the theory is just that. Powerful nations, aware that they are immune to political and economic pressure from the world community, do not feel the need to justify their actions in the light of the evidence stacked against them. They do not accept that they are under any obligation to submit their plans to an independent panel of judges. So, advocates of just war principles may finish their campaigns against recalcitrant politicians knowing themselves to be right; yet the war goes on nevertheless.

One of the logical corollaries of just-war politics is the universal right of conscientious objection. It must be morally self-evident that a person who is able to show that a particular war is manifestly unjustified has a duty not to fight in that war. Although some advances have been made in some countries on the right to refuse military service in terms of specific engagements, the principle has had a pretty rough ride. Usually, arguments derived from the principle of obedience to the chain of command and considerations of national solidarity are made to override individual conscience. It is hard, especially for young people, who are still forming their moral opinions, to withstand the pressure of the majority. It would be easy for them to succumb to taunts of cowardice and betrayal and, thereby, act against their better moral judgement. By selective use of the criteria, the just-war theory, which actually supports their case, is made to work against their convictions. It is certainly no guarantee of a fair and objective hearing.

Finally, under this section, the criterion of proportionality – that the means used to secure victory must be in proportion to the ends that are being pursued – is fertile ground for an arch-casuist. Who can possibly measure the carnage suffered in

Dresden in 1945, caused by the Allied campaign of incendiary bombing, against the possible saving of lives as a result of shortening the war? Or, who can measure the total devastation of Hiroshima and Nagasaki against the known threat of the Japanese war machine to fight until the bitter end. The problem is that in the midst of war, the stakes get raised ever higher. After many years of bitter fighting, leading to the mass slaughter of millions of soldiers, sailors and airmen and the loss of life of countless civilians, there is an enormous desire to achieve the end by one last massive knock-out blow. William Shakespeare, as always, has put the sentiment succinctly and poignantly:

> Bruis'd underneath the yoke of tyranny, . . .
> In God's name, cheerly on, courageous friends,
> To reap the harvest of perpetual peace
> By this one bloody trial of sharp war.[10]

The excellent intention, with which a war may be prosecuted at the beginning, to take every precaution to safeguard the lives of non-combatants, easily gets compromised as the war becomes more ferocious. Innocent victims become the unavoidable or deliberate consequence of the escalation of hostility and hatred. Why does war, apparently, make acceptable what could never be tolerated in normal circumstances, namely collateral damage to people who just happen to be in the wrong place at the wrong time. It is morally dubious to draw a firm distinction between a group of insurgents who kill innocent bystanders in the attempt to inflict damage on the military forces of the government they are opposing and those same military forces causing similar deaths in their attempt to defeat the insurgents. The point is not who is doing the killing nor even the motivation, but who are the killed. If the price of war is calculated on the basis of what is an acceptable rate of civilian casualties, so much worse for the war. Again, bearing in mind that we are talking about real human beings who, according to all human rights conventions, have a right to life, whether or not the killing is intentional is irrelevant.

---

[10] The Earl of Richmond in *King Richard III*, Act V, Scene II.

Non-combatant casualties can never be inadvertent, seeing that modern weapons make them inevitable.

Peace-making

The peace churches have an impressive record in resolving conflict and being agents of peace. Pacifism has too easily been dismissed by some that do not share its principles as passivism. Of course, one can find instances of quietism, where Christians advocate withdrawal from all political and social engagement. However, such a position is so obviously based on an inadequate understanding of the nature of Christian mission that it no longer needs to be refuted. There is an invincible ignorance that no amount of persuasion can budge!

This, however, is not the way of the peace churches, when they are true to their deepest beliefs. One example, with which I am familiar, out of the many that could be quoted[11] is the effort to bring a lasting peace to the havoc of Somalia. Following, even during, the fiasco of the UN intervention, which had the counter-productive effect of strengthening the power and influence of the war-lords, a grass-roots revolution went on. The successful mobilisation of ordinary people, particularly women, to rehabilitate traditional, non-violent, cultural methods of deciding disputes, based on the authority of recognised leaders (which war-lords were not) took place, with a view to reaching a consensus.[12] These are methods which have been located and refined by a Mennonite scholar and peace-activist, John Paul Lederach, and through countless workshops and other means have been

[11] Another is the contribution made to the weakening of apartheid in South Africa by the willingness of white conscientious objectors to the regime's use of force to go to gaol. See Frederick Hale, 'Conscientious Objection to Military Service in South Africa: the Watershed Case of Richard Steele', *Fides et Historia*, 37:1 (2005), pp. 53–70.

[12] The stories have been told in a number of monographs: Wolfgang Heinrich, *Building the Peace: Experiences of Collaborative Peace-building in Somalia 1993–1995* (Uppsala: Life and Peace Institute, 1997); Thania Paffenholz, *Community-based, bottom-up Peace-building* (Uppsala: Life and Peace Institute, 2003); Amina Mohamoud Warsame, *Queens without Crowns: Somaliland women's changing roles and peace-building* (Uppsala: Life and Peace Institute, 2002).

passed back to the people themselves to practise. It goes without saying that the methods are entirely peaceful, in the sense that they presuppose that all parties are willing to put aside all weapons of coercion.

Critical assessment

In spite of the powerful intellectual and practical testimony of the Christian peace tradition, a number of familiar questions remain. Some time ago, I wrote:

> The pacifist can refuse to participate in war and revolutionary war. But consistently to refuse support to a police force, he must withhold a portion of his income tax and reject all physical protection for himself. Here we reach, perhaps, the limit-point between life in two ages.[13]

On reflection, I think I could have phrased the thought in a more coherent way. The question for pacifists concerns the consequences for their lives, and the lives of others, of the consistency with which they wish to pursue their pacifism. It may be, for example, that they will consciously decide that it would be wrong, whatever the circumstances, to use force (even non-lethal force) to defend themselves against physical aggression. Would they be right, however, to refuse it on behalf of others? It might be that a married couple had covenanted together not to use physical force to resist physical abuse and coercion against their persons. So that, if one of them were attacked, the other would not personally use force to come to their aid nor call in a third party (e.g. the police) to remove the threat. That might be the answer, if a pacifist was asked, what would you do if your wife was being threatened with rape? [14] However, would they be just as ready to refrain from all physical interference, if the threatened victim was their ten year old daughter? How could it make

---

[13] *Theology encounters Revolution* (Leicester: Intervarsity Press, 1980), p. 160.
[14] See J. H. Yoder, *What Would You Do? A Serious Answer to a Standard Question* (Scottdale: Herald Press, 1992).

sense for someone of that age to enter into a similar kind of covenant?

A pacifist might respond that this is a very extreme case. However, tragically, the rape of ten-year-old girls or the sexual abuse of ten-year-old boys is not so terribly rare. In any case, for the purposes of consistent moral decision-making, even highly unusual cases must be allowed as potential examples that might have to be faced. It certainly is not just a hypothetical example. It may be that an instance such as this lies behind John Milbank's rather curious argument that the pacifist is guilty of violence by simply *gazing* at violence as an onlooker: 'Pacifism, as looking at violence, is at least as violent, and probably more absolutely violent, than actual physically violent interventions.'[15]

In this situation, as in others that could be mentioned, there is an intuitive sense that by seeking to carry through a wholly consistent rejection of force to counter force, the sum total of violence may be increased, even promoted. To follow, for a moment, the example under review, if the rapist is not captured and deprived of liberty, then inevitably (for experience shows that rapists tend to be multiple offenders) he will act again. Additional violence will be inflicted on another innocent person, because perhaps violence was refused in the previous case.

Now, it seems to me that a pacifist, caught in this dilemma, cannot actually escape from involvement in the cycle of violence in a case like this (Milbank's point). To refuse its use means that he or she has foregone the opportunity of preventing further violence occurring. The sin of omission, if you like, is neglected by concentrating so heavily on the sin of commission; but it is a sin nevertheless. The pacifist does not escape the verdict of guilty, by trying to maintain a consistent principle.

The issues in such an individual situation appear to be relatively clear-cut. There really are not more than two practical alternatives: either to try to restrain violence with violence, whether personally or through an outside agent, or allow the violent person to walk away and continue further acts of violence on as yet unsuspecting victims. If I were to choose the lat-

[15] *Being Reconciled*, p. 30.

ter course, and later heard that someone else had suffered, how could my conscience remain clean? I would suppose that most people adhering to the peace-church tradition would be inclined to answer that the issue is ultimately that of the use of lethal violence. It is ultimately killing that is forbidden to a Christian.

When the situation involves small groups, communities and right up to nations committing unprovoked and gratuitous violence on others, the situation becomes more complex. However, it is not inconceivable that a situation could arise, even on a grand scale, where, after every conceivable attempt has been made to bring an end to violence by non-violent means without a positive result, counter-violence will have to be employed. This is carried out, with great regret and misgiving, in order to lessen the predicted violence and bear witness to the rule of law as a means of respecting the dignity and rights of all peoples. The impulse to protect the innocent, and particularly the highly vulnerable committed to our care, is an intuition that springs from our existence as beings created in God's image, not from our fallen nature. Is it not inherent in God's nature to shield and defend the weak? And, are we not called to be imitators of God (1 Thess. 1:6; Eph. 5:1)?

It may be that Christians in the peace tradition do not sufficiently acknowledge the tensions of having to take responsibility for actual, present existence. Are they, perhaps, trying to resolve too early the tension between the present reality of the kingdom and its future manifestation? There is no escape from living in two realities simultaneously: the old disorder of Adam and the new order of Christ's resurrection life. To a certain extent they have to be regulated by different aspects of justice: one is achieved through the coercive implementation of the law of proportionate punishment and the other secured through a voluntary acceptance of the law of love, made possible by God's saving grace.[16] In terms of the meaning of being joined to Christ through God's act of justification and regeneration, it is not possible to expect an unregenerate person, who has not experienced God's gift of salvation in Christ, to live out the law of (agape)

---

[16] Paul speaks of 'the kindness and the severity of God' (Rom. 11:22).

love. Only as Christ's new life transforms the old life of fear and corruption can people begin to live on the basis of non-violence and non-retaliation. In the meanwhile, where people continue to live 'in the passions of the flesh, following the desires of flesh and senses' (Eph. 2:3), sanctions against anti-human behaviour have to be enforced, by coercive means if necessary (Rom. 13:4).

Unless Christians, as Paul says, 'leave this world' (1 Cor. 5:10), they have simultaneous, though distinct, responsibilities to the two orders. It does not seem biblically and theologically well-founded to pretend that our commitment is exclusively to an existence at the end of the age, when, and only when, all enemies of peace, justice and righteousness will be subjected to Christ (1 Cor. 15:24–28). The missiological concern in this debate between two strong Christian traditions is to discern the political and social implications of witnessing to both the radically destructive nature of sin and evil and to the life-changing power of Jesus' redemption and resurrection.

Given the tension, which one has to live out in the real world, it is conceivable that a person in the peace tradition would agree that in relatively circumscribed situations, and as long as lethal violence was not envisaged, the physical restraint of a violent individual does become unavoidable. However, where the situation involves large masses of people, the conditions under which force would be used implies a wholly different set of conditions. Thus, a pacifist could argue that the circumstance of limited violence, however brutal and ugly to the person suffering, where there was no chance of the violence escalating to involve others, is qualitatively different from that in which military forces are deployed in great numbers. In the latter case, the context is too unpredictable to say with any degree of confidence that the violence can be contained within 'acceptable' limits.

One wonders, though, whether as a matter of principle there is any distinction. If the major concern in the second example is the reality that non-combatant casualties are uncontrollable, the difference seems to be a matter of the calculation of numbers, i.e. it is quantitative, not qualitative. How does one draw an absolute moral line between the rape of the neighbour's young daughter by an isolated sexual pervert and the systematic rape of children by unrestrained soldiers? If the first calls for physical restraint (in part to save the perpetrator from the lynch-mob) and the just punishment of the law, surely the second also calls for an immediate constraining intervention by a superior force? If Rene Girard is right in seeing deep compassion for the victim as the most distinguishing mark of Christian faith,[17] how is peace-building achieved and love shown by shunning the use of force to stop the abuse and suffering of the powerless and forlorn victim? How is justice furthered by refusing to capture and bring to trial those responsible for the horrendous crime of ethnic cleansing?

The peace church argument seems to be that, when it comes to using force to 'bring punishment on the wrongdoer' (Rom. 13:4), Christians should not be involved: 'Let the state do it, if it must: the state as Rome or Nebuchadnezzar (Jer. 25:9, 27:6), and hence as a servant of God.'[18] However, in a participatory democracy, Christians, along with other faith people and secular believers, *are* the state. They cannot opt out of responsibility for controlling the human inclination towards anarchy, and yet, at the same time, benefit from the rule of law. Would that not be sheer hypocrisy? Of course, the motives and means have to be carefully scrutinised at all times. That, too, is a responsibility of citizenship.

Conclusion

So, I continue to reflect on the two major issues, which perhaps more than any others highlight the dispute between peace-church people and those who find they cannot follow them all the way. In the first place, abstention from the use of force to solve conflict is undoubtedly part of the witness to the Gospel. In particular, it is a powerful way of exposing the dynamic tendency of coercive power to find devious and deceitful ways of justifying itself. The tendency of power to corrupt is taken very seriously indeed. At the same time, through this way of witness-

---

[17] *I See Satan Fall*, chapter 14.
[18] Alan Kreider in a personal note to the author.

ing, the state is also taken seriously precisely by constantly calling its belligerent actions into question. It should by now be a
matter of agreement among all Christians that the church's mission to bring the Gospel of Jesus Christ to all people cannot be
executed in any way by the use of coercion. The furtherance of
Christian faith by the compulsive agency of the state is a contradiction. The most the Christian community can hope for from the
state is that it maintains a legal system of religious non-discrimination that allows the Gospel to be proclaimed without ideological pressure or political interference.

Secondly, however, there are real-life situations (we have tried
to depict some of them), where the choice between using violence of some kind and not using it is unreal. As members of a
human community that still lies 'fast bound in Adam's night',
and not withstanding our fervent prayer to be used as reconcil-
ers, we cannot escape from being sullied by the corporate sin of
the human race. So, however much one may advocate, and seek
to put into practice alternative strategies of non-violent action,
there remain situations where not to choose physical force actually contributes directly to surplus violence. We are tainted by
living in a fallen world, even before we sin ourselves. We too live
under judgement, at the same time that we live by grace and forgiveness. To withdraw into isolated communities is not an
option for Christians, for it would imply a denial of our humanity by denying the humanity of those from whom we have separated ourselves. It would also make impossible the mission
mandate to make disciples of all peoples and to serve them in
their need.

So, if (rightly) disciples of Jesus have no option but to be
involved faithfully in the world as salt and light,[19] it cannot be
possible to shun all recourse to violence for oneself, whilst allowing others (presumably non-Christians) to use violence to hinder
the spread of evil. Surely this would amount to an inconsistency
bordering on hypocrisy, unless one was willing not to intervene
physically when one's daughter was threatened with rape or her

---

[19] Alan Kreider, 'The challenge to faithful involvement' in *Handling Problems of
Peace and War*, pp. 74–75.

grandmother with brutal assault. I do not think that a contextual interpretation of Jesus' saying, 'do not resist an evildoer' (Matt. 5:39), can be pressed to mean 'never defend those entrusted to your care from the action and consequences of gratuitous aggression'.

The final verdict has to be, in my opinion, that the peace-church tradition, in so far as it counsels complete abstention from any use of force, is so nearly right, but not quite. It seeks too neatly to resolve the tension between human solidarity in unrighteousness and the kingdom of perfect righteousness by pretending that, here and now, one can live exclusively in the latter. Having said that, let those who disagree be mightily careful not to be corrupted by a pragmatic, so-called realist approach to social ethics, which so easily is manipulated by those whose self-interest is to maintain themselves in power.

CHAPTER 8

Mission as Prophecy: A Voice from Latin America[1]

Introduction

Gradually Christians in the West are becoming aware of a remarkable new event in the history of the Church. It has been called the coming of the 'Third Church'.[2] The first church was the Christian community during the first three centuries after Christ, existing as a minority religious group. The second church was the institution that became established in the heartlands of Europe after the conversion of Constantine. The third church is the Christian community that has come into being beyond the West. It is now the majority church, representing a post-European Christianity.[3]

These three manifestations of the Christian faith correspond to three phases of Christian missionary outreach. Each expresses a different relationship between the Gospel and political power. During the period of the early Church prior to Constantine, the Christian

---

[1] I would like to recognise that the distinctly prophetic nature of mission was brought home to me afresh recently by a student of the Protestant Institute for Mission Studies in Budapest, Hungary, Monika Csiszer. I would like to thank her for her insights.

[2] The description comes from the title of the book written by W. Buhlmann, *The Third Church* (Maryknoll: Orbis Books, 1977).

[3] For example, Lamin Sanneh, *Whose Religion is Christianity? The Gospel beyond the West* (Grand Rapids. Eerdmans, 2003).

message was spread from the periphery of the Roman empire to its very heart. The Acts of the Apostles was written by Luke, one of Paul's travelling companions, partly to tell the story. It begins in Jerusalem, a small town in a troublesome province on the eastern edge of the empire, and ends in the capital city. Christians were also spreading the message of Jesus Christ, East into Asia and South into Africa. There is a strong tradition that the Apostle Thomas reached as far as India, perhaps even before Paul reached Rome.[4]

During the second period, when the Christian faith became consolidated throughout Europe, the movement could be said to have run from the centre to the periphery. It went from those places secured under the authority of the empire to the outlying districts, still inhabited by the 'barbarians', those not yet brought into the sphere of 'civilisation'.[5] This direction became even more obvious during the spread of Christianity beyond Europe from the sixteenth century onwards. As the imperial, colonial enterprise demonstrated, the European nations possessed superior force and were able to impose their governance and religion on other peoples, whose own empires were in decline. From a European perspective, the Gospel was flowing from the centre of the world to those on the edge. The latter were often not able to resist the pressures to be converted.[6] The story of the modern mission movement (late eighteenth century to mid-twentieth century) highlights this trend even more emphatically. As in the case of mission after Constantine, during this period the assumed civilising power of Christian faith motivated thousands

[4] See, for example, Michael Nazir Ali, *From Everywhere to Everywhere: A World View of Christian Mission* (London: Collins, 1991), chapter 2.

[5] The Celtic missions were, perhaps, an exception to this general progression, in that they were initiated on the periphery and went to the periphery, see George G. Hunter, *The Celtic Way of Evangelism* (Nashville: Abingdon Press, 2000).

[6] As is often the case, there were notable exceptions. The most obvious, perhaps, was that of Japan at the end of the 16th century. Having initially responded favourably to the Christian message, the rulers acted with ferocity to stamp out the emerging Christian community. By the middle of the 17th century, it had all but disappeared. The story is captured powerfully in the novel of Shusaku Endo, *Silence* (London: Peter Owen, 2003). One may contrast this experience to that of nearby Philippines, where the Catholic Church became a powerful force alongside the Spanish civil government.

of missionary volunteers to cross the European frontier to reach the remotest parts of the globe.[7]

The third phase of mission engagement has begun to happen within the last fifty years. As the younger churches of the global South have taken full charge of their own lives, they have become ever more conscious of their mission responsibilities. Today, thousands of people are involved in mission beyond the borders of their own nations. Many of them are evangelising and planting churches in the nations of the West. In so far as they often come from impoverished countries, it is possible to speak once again of this 'reverse' mission moving from the periphery to the centre. In truth, it is also happening from the periphery to the periphery.[8]

Until the last two decades of the twentieth century, Western Christianity has been dominant. Mission has been seen largely as emanating from the West and having as its object the rest of the world. However, in a short space of time, the situation has changed dramatically.[9] The 'Third Church' is now making its presence felt, not least in the number of missionaries going to the original sending nations. The changes can also be traced historically by looking at the way in which the agendas of international bodies like the World Council of Churches, the Anglican Communion and other world confessional bodies have evolved to reflect the concerns of the younger churches.

---

[7] Again, it is necessary to point out that were exceptions, most notably that of Korea. Korea was never a colony of any Western nation. It would be a travesty of mission history to pretend that all Christian evangelism was encouraged and supported by the colonial powers. For example, there were significant occasions in the history of the British rule in India, when the colonial administration opposed Christian outreach, see Jeffrey Cox, *Imperial Fault Lines: Christianity and Colonial Power in India, 1818–1940* (Palo Alto: Stanford University Press, 2002).

[8] The transference of passion and energy for mission from the West to the rest is recounted in a number of books, for example, Philip Jenkins, *The Next Christendom: The Coming of Global Christianity* (New York: OUP, 2002), Grace Davie, *Europe: the Exceptional Case.*

[9] I am not competent to comment on the situation of the RC Church in this context. From outside, one receives the impression, which may be superficial, that the long hegemony of the European interpretation of Christianity remains dominant. This could change, one supposes, were a non-European Pope to be elected.

Lamin Sanneh emphasises two special characteristics of this new emerging situation that place the future of world Christianity in new circumstances. The Church of the South is *post-Constantinian*. In the main, it has rarely enjoyed a special relationship with the organs of state. It is true that in some parts of the world, due to the particular history of colonial conquest, the Church still exerts a considerable influence on the moral, social and cultural life of various nations. This is most evident in Latin America. However, it rarely has any formal constitutional link to the state. In political terms, it holds no institutional sway over governments. By and large, it is the church of the poor, those who are economically and politically insignificant.

The church of the South is also *post-Enlightenment*. The Christian faith has developed outside Europe (including North America and Australasia) on the margins of the fierce struggle between secular forces and Christian believing that has taken place in those societies. In the West, it might be said that the Church has undergone a process of refining, so that its power and authority have been stripped away and its system of belief subjected to immense critical scrutiny. This process, as recounted in the first four chapters of this book, has gone so far that Christians outside Europe wonder whether the very heart of the Gospel has not been abandoned and the Christian community altogether lost its nerve.

On the other side, some Western Christians and most of those imbued with secular habits of mind find it almost impossible to understand the beliefs and mentality of the younger churches. In spite of evidence to the contrary, the notion that the West occupies the vanguard of intellectual and cultural progress remains so strong that the beliefs of so-called developing[10] peoples are

---

[10] The very term, *developing*, implies a goal which other communities ought to aspire to. It also indicates that they have a lot of ground to catch up. The definition of *developed* is given by the nations of the West, in terms of economic growth, technological achievement and democratic governance. According to the criteria used by Western agencies and institutions, non-Western nations are, by definition, behind and, therefore, inevitably sub-standard, mediocre and incompetent. One cannot imagine a better example of how language is exploited to maintain the present power-relations between the 'advanced' and 'backward' nations.

considered to belong to a more primitive stage of human social evolution. Likewise, the Christianity of the churches of the South is patronisingly judged to be crude, unsophisticated and credulous. Significantly divergent histories often lead to mutual incomprehension.

Now, the future of Christianity in the West may well depend on how the Western churches relate to this new phenomenon. It is certainly likely that the so-called 'opinion formers' in the West will increasingly misunderstand and misrepresent the Christianity of the Third Church (as indeed they do of orthodox, mainstream Christianity still being practised in Europe). David Smith sums up the challenge in the following words:

> The task of the churches in the North in this situation is clear: faithfulness to Christ would demand that they become increasingly counter-cultural while offering a consistent, unflinching challenge to the stereotyping and misrepresentation of Southern Christianity, whether this comes from government briefings or media images. In addition, a missionary church would bear costly witness to the fact that the deep spritual sickness afflicting the rich North might actually be healed when the voices from the other world are heard and understood.[11]

The reason for the challenge is that the West continues to interpret the whole of life through the categories of the Enlightenment and modernity. There is a consensus that the typical European liberal society, built on secular educational principles, humanist moral values and technological sophistication, is the forerunner of societies everywhere. They are, in other words, everyone else's future. The only worthwhile goal, apparently, is a Western-style democracy, a consumer-society and a privatised faith with ultra liberal dimensions.

There is no question but that the spectacular growth of the church in Africa, parts of South and East Asia and Latin America, to be followed quite possibly in Central Asia, is a new reality

---

[11] *Mission after Christendom* (London: Darton, Longman & Todd, 2003), p. 131.

within the history of the Christian faith. Something quite novel is happening that profoundly affects the second Church. Where will this version of Christianity situate itself? Will Christians belonging to the European tradition of Christianity decide to listen to their brothers and sisters from the South, or choose to ignore them? Will they continue to drift towards a faith thoroughly revised under the impact of modernity and post-modernity, one which appears to be increasingly indistinct from the finest of humanist aspirations, or will they learn something fresh from the uninhibited, joyous and dedicated practices of the churches that once they brought to birth? How heavily does Constantinianism and the secular aspects of the Enlightenment weigh on the future of the Western church?

I believe that a new awareness of the Third Church is an opportunity for the Second Church to reevaluate its own position in relation to the history of the last three centuries and, in particular, to the rapid and widespread cultural drift of the last fifty years. If it does not do so, there is a strong possibility that it could cease to exist altogether. There are, however, encouraging signs that groups of Christians in the West are seriously looking at alternatives to the conventional Christian institutions and ways of operating that have long predominated in their context. One might cite as examples the new ways of being church that are emerging under titles such as, 'missional church' or 'base ecclesial community'.[12]

In this chapter, I want to explore the impact, both actual and potential, of one strand of Christian faith strongly represented in the Third Church, particularly in Latin America. It embodies a crucial, yet still not central, dimension of mission: the prophetic voice. As the notion has been variously interpreted, I begin with an outline of how the task of the prophet is portrayed in the Bible. This will provide the background and setting for a discussion of this particular contribution to mission made by the Latin American church.

[12] See Darrell L. Guder, *The Continuing Conversion of the Church* (Grand Rapids: Eerdmans, 2000); Margaret Hebblethwaite, *Base Communities: An Introduction* (London: Geoffrey Chapman, 1994); Milfred Minatrea, *Shaped by God's Heart: The Passion and Practices of Missional Churches* (San Francisco: John Wiley, 2004).

The prophetic message

Some people claim that the imagery surrounding prophetic mission is overused and even abused. There is certainly a danger of mere rhetoric, particularly when the (prophetic) message appears to contain almost nothing but denunciation and condemnation. The prophet runs the risk of self-righteousness as he or she turns the warning of judgement on others, by definition the unrighteous.

Nevertheless, the Christian faith is prophetic through and through.[13] Paul speaks of the church being built upon the foundation of the apostles and prophets (Eph. 2:20). There is much material in the New Testament on the prophetic calling, not least in the Book of Revelation. There is also considerable warning about the menace of false prophets. However, it is natural to think first of the phenomenon of prophetic witness in the history of Israel from the eighth century BC onwards.

The nations of Israel and Judah found themselves, at that time, in an ambiguous historical context. On the one hand, due to the long period of political stability they were exceedingly prosperous. Jeroboam had reigned, uninterrupted, for 41 years and Uzziah for 52. Resources had been spent on capital projects and the manufacture of 'consumer-goods' not wasted in unprofitable wars. On the other hand, Assyria, the 'superpower' of the moment, was waiting in the wings for an opportune time to extend its power and control.

The content of the message

What the prophets had to say to the leaders of the nations touched on all aspects of life. They declared what God thought about the people's religious life, economic practices, moral con-

---

[13] In the New Testament the word 'prophet' occurs 144 times and 'prophecy' 19 times. It is used of the Old Testament prophets, John the Baptist, Jesus Christ, Zacharias, Simeon and Anna (in Lk. 1–2) and Christian prophets in the early church, see C. H. Peisker and Colin Brown, 'Prophet' in Colin Brown (ed.), *Dictionary of New Testament Theology*, Vol. 3 (Carlisle: Paternoster Press, 1986); Anthony C. Thiselton, *The First Epistle to the Corinthians* (NIGTC) (Grand Rapids: Eerdmans, 2000), pp. 956–965, 1128–1168.

victions and foreign policies. The message can be usefully sum-
marised around three recurrent themes.

THE CONDEMNATION OF IDOLATRY

The first and most fundamental concern was that God's people
were abandoning their respect for the one, true, liberating God.
They had become deeply involved in a variety of idolatrous
practices. We may identify two principal kinds. Some dutifully
observed all the rites prescribed by the law, but also used ritual
in an attempt to manipulate God for their own personal ends.
They banked on the fateful hypothesis that outward obedience
would bring automatic blessing. However, they ignored the deep
moral implications of God's revealed will. They allowed religious adherence to become divorced from the obligations of care
and justice for the whole community. Due to their faithful com-
pliance with the law's requirements, we might call them the
'respectable' idolaters.

Then, there were those who changed the religious rites to
invoke the name of pagan deities. As they wished to keep their
options open, they included Yahweh in the pantheon of the gods
meriting homage. We might call these the 'radical', or heterodox,
idolaters. Either way, they had effectively lost touch with the life
and demands of the true God.

The effect of their spiritual 'adultery' (becoming joined to
other gods or ideologies) (Hos. 2.1–13) was, firstly, *immorality*.
Other religions, based on fertility cults, positively approved of
the exploitation of women, girls and boys in religious prostitu-
tion. The practice was carried over into Israel and Judah.
Secondly, idolatry issued in many kinds of *unjust* action. The
weak were exploited through the system of bonded-labour,
through which their future income was mortgaged against the
debt they had already accumulated. The property of the vulnerable was expropriated. Violence was meted out to any who resis-
ted. The leaders of the people had massively forsaken the sacred
trust God had given them of protecting the defenceless members
of the community.

It is important to bear in mind that idolatry is the first and most basic of all sins (compare Rom. 1.18).[14] Once the people lost respect for God, they cast aside his ways and invented their own brands of belief:

> For fools speak folly, and their minds plot iniquity: to practise ungodliness, to utter error concerning the Lord' (Isa. 32:6).

The consequence was to brush aside the moral demands of God and find a religion more to their taste, one which would justify their abuse of power.

THE WARNING OF THE CONSEQUENCES OF IDOLATRY

The prophets cautioned the people, laying out in detail what would happen if they did not change the situation and put into practice the action God required of them. There would be, for example, economic disaster. Not for the last time in history, when all seemed well in the nation's financial performance, an economic crash of epic proportions was on its way (Isa. 32:12–13). As a result, a life-style of self-gratification, focused on pleasure-seeking for its own sake, would come to an end. The pursuit of a hedonistic way of life would be seen as the great illusion that it inevitably is (Isa. 32:13). The people would also find that there was no security, either in their own military strength or in armed alliances with other nations, against external hostile intentions.

The people were implored to repent of their idolatry, their exploitation of the weak and their selfish, self-absorbed way of life, and return to the God of the covenant. He had promised blessing to those who chose to honour him beyond the wildest dreams of those who sought their pleasure wholly within the material world. The prophetic message was tinged with great sorrow and compassion (Isa. 1:18, Mic. 6:3), yet it was quite uncompromising. It urged, cajoled, reasoned and warned the

---

[14] It is not, as Milbank claims, being deprived of life as a gift, which leads to violence (see *Being Reconciled*, pp. 26ff.). Both loss of an original delight in God and a corrupted and thwarted will are serious aspects of sin. However, they are effect rather than cause. Paul interprets idolatry as *exchange*, the decision to change the reality of the created universe for one's own imagined creation. This is not so much loss of the gift of life, as God intends it to be, as its deliberate refusal.

people. Every choice the people made was infused with a sense of destiny: either for life, or for death. There was no way they could escape into a religiously or morally neutral zone of their own making.

THE PROMISE OF NEW BEGINNINGS

This is an aspect of the prophetic message, which is simetimes overlooked. God will send a true liberator, who will deliver the people from their foolish ways and restore to them genuine wisdom. Then, they will listen again to God's authentic word, clearing their minds of false religious junk. God will pour out his Spirit, who will transform the natural order, bring justice to the community and end fear by bringing a real security to all:

> See . . . princes will rule with justice . . . The minds of the rash will have good judgement . . . A spirit from on high is poured out on us, and the wilderness becomes a fruitful field . . . Then justice will dwell in the wilderness and righteousness abide in the fruitful field. The effect of righteousness will be peace . . . My people will abide in a peaceful habitation, in secure dwellings and in quite resting-places' (Isa. 32:1, 4, 15–18).

So, Isaiah and the other prophets spoke unequivocally on subjects like military alliances, consumerism, the corruption of legal processes, economic injustices, the religious justification of oppression and the manipulation of God for personal gain. In delivering their message, they were not calculating or prudent; they were not cautious, discreet or guarded in what they said. They did not try to balance the interests of the different social classes.

Now, the prophets' calling was not to take upon themselves the task of changing the political and economic situation. Rather, it was to tell those, given responsibilities to exercise on behalf of the people, what God requires (Mic. 6:8), whether they would hear or whether they would close their ears (Ezek. 3:27).

A voice from Latin America

The purpose of this section is not to pretend that the Christian community in that part of the world is necessarily more virtuous than the Church in the West. It lives, of course, under the same word of judgement and grace. Any indication of a superior right-eousness has no place among God's people, however clear they may be about the call to proclaim God's just demands. The issue concerning prophecy is about one part of the world church read-ing 'the signs of the times', and then sharing its understanding of the Gospel and its mission vision with other parts. Three main areas stand out, where the Latin American church can appropri-ately challenge the church elsewhere to assume its prophetic mission.

A fresh reading of Scripture

One of the most characteristic emphases of the Latin American church has been its rediscovery of the Bible as a book of prophecy in the sense we have been describing. We may note three crucial points that are often made.

THE POOR ARE THE MOST AUTHENTIC INTERPRETERS OF THE TEXT
In many ways, the poor[15] have a more profound understanding of the text than many people who have dedicated their lives to its study. This is not true in the sense of a formal *mastery* of schol-arly competencies, such as expertise in the biblical languages, acquaintance with the historical context, knowledge of extra-bib-lical sources or theories to do with its compilation. Rather, they have often shown a greater *receptivity* to its message. The poor are more familiar with the world of the Bible in that it seems to have been written so often from their point of view. They find it easier to accept that the message really is good news. Its word of

---

[15] The meaning of the poor in Latin American theological reflection has been dealt with in hundreds of books and articles. It may be summed up simply and cogently by a Peruvian woman, living in a shanty town, who expressed the feel-ings of her community in the words, 'we are a people hungry for bread and hungry for God.'

liberation speaks directly to their circumstances. They are the ones who are addressed.

The hermeneutical imperative for a context, in which a critical intellect dominates, appears to be that of distinguishing different layers of tradition, with a view to setting out the most authentic beliefs of the original communities within their most likely historical context. The essence of the matter for the poor, however, is to read the text as a call to transformative action. For some, then, viewing the Scripture as a library of ancient texts, with a certain historical and cultural interest, takes centre stage. For others, encountering the Scripture as an uncompromising, contemporary call to repentance, hope and change predominates. The perspective (or pre-understanding) from which the reading takes place shapes the interests in what is heard and how it is interpreted and applied.

THE SCRIPTURE CONTAINS A MESSAGE OF CONTINUING REVOLUTION. The Latin American reading, I would suggest, is more radical than the self-styled radical theologies manufactured in the West. The latter often manifest a capitulation to the latest social or political trend. They may be characterised by their polemic against 'established' or 'conservative' theologies (liberation theology sometimes being included), because according to their interpretation the latter belong to another age and discredited thought processes. However, when they in turn become the latest approved and prevailing radicalism, they are often not noticeably self-critical. Owing to a general assumption that the word of Scripture is relative to its context, they lack those powers of discernment given by a text received as God's transcendent word. The inclination to pick and choose which word they wish to hear from the text blunts its prophetic capacity to deliver people from substituting their own desires and ideas for God's purposes.

At least in intention, the Latin American church has rediscovered the practical potential of the biblical, prophetic message to challenge all forms of idolatry, be these fundamentalist, liberal or radical. Experience seems to show that those who handle the Scriptures with respect and expectation, including the willingness to be challenged by the hard sayings, are more likely to discover its practical, liberating power than those whose hermeneutic obliges them to stand in judgement on the text.

THE CONTEMPORARY MEANING OF THE TEXT IS MORE IMPORTANT THAN THE ORIGINAL

This statement sounds provocative. One has to be careful not to be misunderstood. There is *no* contemporary word without the Word of the Bible. However, it is possible to dissect the Hebrew and Greek texts with great erudition and yet remain unchanged. The Boff brothers set out the issue with clarity:

> Liberative hermeneutics reads the Bible as a book of life, not as a book of strange stories. The textual meaning is indeed sought, but only as a function of the practical meaning. The important thing is not so much interpreting the text of the Scriptures as interpreting life 'according to the Scriptures'. Liberative hermeneutics seeks to discover and activate the transforming energy of biblical texts. In the end this is a question of finding an interpretation that will lead to individual change (conversion) and change in history (revolution). This is not a reading from ideological preconceptions: biblical religion is open and dynamic thanks to its messianic and eschatological character.[16]

Naturally, prophetic mission is not taking the text and making it agree with whatever suits the latest political opinion. That is, indeed, an ideological reading. Such a strategy is unnecessary, for the message, as authentically heard from the text, can be trusted to set out the truest account of liberation that will ever be forthcoming.

A fresh interpretation of history

Latin American Christians attempt to understand Europe's territorial expansion and the Church's missionary venture from the

---

[16] *Introducing Liberation Theology* (Tunbridge Wells: Burns & Oates, 1987), p. 34.

'underside of history'.[17] In other words, they have been interpreting the significant historical events of the last half millennium from a non-European perspective. As they would say, it is
the victims of European aggression who undertake this interpretation. They are the ones who, in terms of the politics of power
and influence, still remain on the 'edge of humanity'. Quite simply, the vast masses of the Southern continents are insignificant.
They are not relevant, but their continued existence in abject
poverty remains a permanent embarrassment. They are the
objects of the West's occasional charity and perennial injustices.

They see the world divided into a centre and a periphery. The
centre has been occupied by the continent of Europe, which has
been in the ascendancy since the late fifteenth century. As
Enrique Dussel has perceptively put it, the premise of Western
civilisation has been the aphorism, *vinco ergo sum* (I conquer,
therefore I am). Through superior military strength and more
advanced scientific and technological knowledge, Europeans
have consecutively conquered territories, nature, raw materials,
markets, political life, technological innovation and space. Only
by understanding the historical development of Europe and by
extension the USA and, in particular, the inner dynamic of the
capitalist system of economic life, can one appreciate the causes
of the increasing poverty and misery that afflicts the majority of
humankind.

The Latin American church challenges Christians in the West
to decide where they situate themselves with regard to the
motives, goals and effects of the globalisation processes. How do
they understand mission in this global context? Could it be that
they have so compromised their stance concerning the idolatry
of materialism and the injustices of economic exploitation that
they cannot hear the Gospel as 'good news to the poor'? What
might the prophetic message of repentance and conversion mean
in this context? What might the consequences be? It is a curious
fact that in some Western nations the church is strongest in the
most affluent areas, whereas in the global South the church is

---

[17] The Spanish phrase is *el reves de la historia*. Literally this means the backside or
other side of history. Figuratively, it means reverse, as in failure, misfortune or
adversity.

growing fastest among the poorest of the poor. How does one make sense of this puzzling phenomenon in terms of the unity of all Christians in Jesus Christ?

Since the collapse of communist regimes in Europe in 1989, Marxism might now seem a curiosity of recent history. As a way of organising society politically and economically it has failed in practice. Nevertheless, given the power of its analysis of human alienation and economic exploitation within the capitalist system, Christians might still wish to ask whether its evaluation of social relations in terms of the fetishism of commodities[18] still speaks prophetically to an economic order driven by the consumption of goods.

A fresh engagement with culture
One of the most sensitive and complex issues facing the church's mission thinking and practice is 'enculturation', i.e. finding ways of expressing the Gospel that is simultaneously appropriate to particular cultures and faithful to the apostolic message of Jesus Christ. The original introduction of Christianity into Latin America was largely a disaster. Tragically, the Spanish and Portuguese *conquistadores* used religion as a weapon to control the subjugated peoples. They succeeded in destroying to a great extent the cultures of the original inhabitants.[19] For nearly 500 years the indigenous peoples were not allowed to bring any of their traditions into relation with the Gospel. The result was a transplanted European church and widespread syncretism, in which Catholic piety, focused on Mary and the saints, was mixed

---

[18] Marx argued that in a capitalist economy material objects are invested with a certain value and power, which exist independently of human beings. Interpersonal relations are shaped by the production processes which create material goods. Within a market economy, human relations are mediated by inanimate objects. The value of the worker is the value of his or her product. We treat each other principally as buyers and sellers of commodities and services rather than as fellow human beings. The whole operation alienates people from their true humanity.

[19] See Enrique Dussel, *Historia de la Iglesia en America Latina: Coloniaje y Liberacion, 1492–1972* (Barcelona: Nova Terra, 1972), p. 51.

with indigenous beliefs and practices, centred on the rhythms of nature.

Protestant mission, which began with Bible distribution early in the nineteenth century, was fiercely anti-Catholic. Religiously, the evangelical pioneers believed that the task of evangelism was to rescue the people from the darkness of their superstition. Culturally and politically, the challenge was to educate the people in the Anglo-American traditions of freedom, democracy, work as a vocation and sound economic practices.[20] In the second series of objectives, they were aided and abetted by the more liberal elements of the local oligarchies.

The first wave of Pentecostalism, beginning in the early years of the twentieth century, was the most indigenous expression of the Gospel. Of all non-Catholic churches the original Pentecostal churches have been least influenced by imported models of Church life and structures. In their communities they have seemed to be able to meet the needs of some of the poorest groups in society, in particular those of economic migrants moving from the countryside to the mega-cities, perhaps the most dislocated members of humanity. So successful has been their mission in this respect that one commentator wittily summed up the situation by saying that the Catholic church has taken a preferential option for the poor, but the poor have opted for the Pentecostal churches.[21] However, having spoken about their ability to relate the Gospel successfully to a specific context and a special need, with regard to styles of leadership, they have probably been too indigenous.

---

[20] See Jean-Pierre Bastian, 'Protestantism in Latin America' in Enrique Dussel (ed.), *The Church in Latin America: 1492–1992* (Tunbridge Wells: Burns & Oates, 1992), pp. 313ff. Unlike the US administration's foreign policy of encouraging, if necessary by the sanction of force, feudal, authoritarian states to adopt Western liberal democracy, the missionaries in Latin America believed that democracy was only achievable through the internalisation of Christian values.

[21] See Philip Berryman, *Religion in the Megacity: Portraits from Two Latin American Cities* (Maryknoll: Orbis, 1996); Jose Miguez Bonino, *Faces of Latin American Protestantism* (Grand Rapids: Erdmans, 1995), chapter 3; Edward L. Cleary, 'Latin American Pentecostalism' in Murray Dempster, Byron Klaus, Douglas Petersen (eds.), *The Globalization of Pentecostalism: A Religion made to Travel* (Oxford: Regnum Books, 1999).

There are no easy answers to the questions that arise when the Gospel is transplanted from one soil to another. However, the Latin American church, having suffered from the implicit arrogance of a missionary movement that believes that its version of Christian faith marks the universal standard, is more aware of the ways in which the Gospel can be easily confused with transitory cultural customs and values. Throughout the Latin American church, Christians debate the question of how the Gospel relates to Amerindian religious life. On the one hand, the prophetic nature of the Gospel message cannot be compromised. On the other hand, those elements of the indigenous religion, which, because of their human quality, express truth about God and the universe, should be recognised. It may be that Christians in Europe, reflecting on the reality and nature of implicit religion in its many guises, can learn something about contextual mission from the experience of the Latin American church.

The call to prophetic mission

Listening to the church in Latin America as it strives to understand and live by the authentic Gospel is not a matter of accumulating information about remote and exotic happenings. Christians there may have experience and wisdom to share that will help the church elsewhere be more faithful and effective in mission. I conclude, therefore, by outlining four issues that may provoke thought and action in other parts of the world.

God's salvation deals with contemporary manifestations of sin

Mission and evangelism to be effective depend on the ability of Christians to identify forces that underlie current manifestations of conflict, violence, fear and despair among different sectors of society. If, as I have attempted to demonstrate, idolatry and injustice are the most basic sins, how do they show themselves in human communities?

Perhaps one of the most important elements in a contextually relevant theological programme would be to acquire the skills needed to read the signs of the times. As well as listening to social and cultural disciplines, as they analyse current human problems, Christians training for leadership in the churches will need to develop a persuasive theological evaluation of the predicaments of contemporary society.

Ultimately, however accurate secular interpretations of reality may be, without touching upon the deep spiritual malaise that afflicts a world that finds a personal God of justice and compassion deeply threatening, they will not be able to move beyond a certain level of explanation. From the perspective of the reality of God's salvation in the world, they will appear superficial, able to deal mainly with the symptoms of the diseases, not the underlying causes. Therefore, theological education should focus on a programme of applied faith, which combines in a creative and flexible way ordinary human experience, social science disciplines and mature Christian reflection on the contemporary significance of the apostolic message of Christ.[22]

The goal of evangelism is to liberate people from the idols of our time
The Gospel is good news about the best possible way of being human! If the analysis of society provided by the critique of idolatry is true, the Gospel will always offer a relevant alternative to many of the dominant values of a society that has distorted God's good order and created its own disorder. For example, the 'good life' promoted by a consumer culture is a terrible parody of the 'fullness of life'. It is a case of seeking the wrong treasure in the wrong place.

The Gospel story affirms that one finds real satisfaction in life by losing it for the sake of Jesus and the reign of God. In one sense, conversion to the values of the kingdom is painful, for it does require death to the natural inclinations of the selfish self. On the other hand, it is also the gateway to discovering the true purpose of life, which is to take the gentle yoke of Christ and learn the meaning of freedom by following him (Matt. 11:29–30; John. 8:31–32).

Freedom is paradoxical. Common-sense suggests that free-

---

[22] See Peter Penner (ed.), *Theological Education as Mission* (Schwarzenfeld: Neufeld, 2005).

dom is dependent on acquiring skills, possessions, a good rep-
utation, financial security and a tolerant environment.
However, such a view, dominant in many cultures, confuses
freedom with independence. To be truly free one needs to lose
one's reliance upon such matters. These are dependent on circumstances, often beyond our control. Therefore, our hold on
them is always precarious. Freedom is possible, ultimately,
only by exchanging an uncertain security in transitory goods
and fickle human beings for the true and living God. Freedom
is always beyond the grasp of those who wish to make sure of
it for themselves.

The church is the community of liberated people
One way of thinking of the church, in the light of the prophetic
message about idolatry, justice and a future hope, is as a people
collectively aware of and resistant to the destructive forces of our
times. These include the kind of economic and social fatalisms
that give the impression that only one kind of economic system
and one kind of society is feasible in the twenty first century. This
kind of church seeks to overcome everything that militates
against the gift of life and well-being, such as child-labour, boy
soldiers, debt insolvency, absence of clean water, preventable
diseases, domestic violence, trafficking of prostitutes, alcohol
and drug dependency, abortion and euthanasia.

The church, however, has to be conscious of the tensions
within its own communities and the ways in which it may be
substituting cultural captivities for the authentic message of
Christ. To what extent do its institutions, programmes and pronouncements (whether we call them prophetic, or not) promote
or hinder belief that liberation in Christ is possible? We live in a
world inclined to be suspicious of grandiose claims, used to
engaging in searching social and cultural analysis and prone to
be critical of institutions that give the impression of being self-
serving. It may not be the end of history; it is assuredly the end
of the age of innocence!

The way the church behaves, how it organises its life, how it
conducts its worship and makes decisions indicates, in every

case, what it believes. Those things it fails to do give evidence of
its priorities. Never before, perhaps, does the watching world
expect such high standards of consistency among Christians than
at the present time. Too often the modern generation experiences
betrayal, a sense of having one's trust abused, of not knowing
whether there is anything or anyone on whom one may rely. Can
the church offer a community that is utterly trustworthy? This
means a rigorous honesty that does not buy favour by issuing
false assurances or making exaggerated claims. Its promises must
be equal to its ability to keep them. Let it be said of Christians,
'they never let us down'.

Jesus Christ is the only true liberator

Through experience, Latin Americans, in different contexts and
for diverse reasons, are acutely aware of the ease with which
human beings distort the image of God and manipulate religion
for their own benefit. There seems to be an innate human tendency to turn religion into another 'commodity' that can be used
to satisfy felt needs, justify beliefs already held or compensate
for weakness and powerlessness. There have been, and are, too
many 'attractive' faces of Jesus Christ: the benign Christ of the
social elites or the miraculous Christ of the peddlers of prosperity, the wise Christ of the religious mystics or the indulgent
Christ of the libertarians. But, there are too few 'disfigured' faces
of Christ: 'so marred was his appearance, beyond human sem-
blance' (Isa. 52:14). This face is produced by the agony, despair
and torment of human suffering. It is sculpted on an instrument
of torture by the sheer brutality and corruption of human evil,
borne in his own person.

However, as the prophetic theology of Latin America has
constantly reiterated, the Christ of the canonical Gospels, of
concrete history, of the biblical texts is not open to manipulation. Above all, however laudable the contextual motives, he
cannot be turned into an innocuous Christ: one that fits too
comfortably into a particular pattern of culture. This is God's
only Son, the visible image of the invisible Father and Creator
of all. Any other image that diminishes this one is false to real-

ity. He, alone, witnesses to the truth, speaks the truth, is the truth. There is nothing spurious, untrustworthy or deceitful in him. So, Christ's disciples have to be constantly on their guard against fabricating counterfeit christs,[23] of whatever hue or shade.

The call to prophetic mission is not an invitation to an easy life. The Latin American church has rediscovered, what the early church knew all too well, that the truth of the Gospel may be profoundly unpopular and mightily resented. What is good news to the genuinely poor, 'those who are contrite and humble in spirit' (Isa. 57:15) is bad news for those who hide the poverty of their (affluent) lives by creating their own religion. Down the years, prophets have not exactly been welcomed with open arms!

---

[23] There is plenty of evidence that the early church had to be constantly vigilant against distortions of the authentic image of Christ (for example, Matt. 24:24; Col. 1:15–20, 2:8–9; 2 Thess. 2:9–12; 1 Jon. 2:18, 4:3).

CHAPTER 9

The Gospel in Context:
the Case of Same Gender Relations

A controversy within the Christian Church worldwide is intensify-ing. It concerns the willingness of some Christian communi-ties to recognise an equal status for same-gender unions as that currently afforded to heterosexual couples. Given the profound significance of sexuality in human relations and the current obsession of Western culture with all matters sexual, the debate is engendering strong passions. The threat of severe divisions in the Church is real, since there are widely different assumptions about how Christians know what practices are permitted or encouraged on the basis of their faith.

Some suggest that the matter is not terribly important. The Church, they say, tends to become over-excited about sexual issues. In reality, there are much more important matters to attend to, such as the critical mission challenges that are explored elsewhere in this book. However, I will argue that the question of homo-sexual[1] relations is, as a matter of fact, a classic case of the tension which exists for the Christian faith between the Gospel and culture. As such, it is not peripheral to the peren-nial missionary obligation under which the Church lives and moves and has its being. Indeed, it is an excellent example of an

---

[1] The use of the word in hyphenated form is intended to indicate a same-gender relationship of which sexual activity is a part. This is to distinguish the term from a relationship of exclusive male (or female) companionship, but which is devoid of sexual acts. The purpose is descriptive, not evaluative.

issue – the Gospel in context – which penetrates to the heart of missiological reflection.

I will address the debate primarily from within the parameters of Christian thought and action. Thus, I will assume that people on both sides of the dispute accept that there is a recognisable Christian framework of belief that is binding upon conscience and practice, even though its content may be disputed.[2]

The Problem

It might appear strange that Christians could disagree so profoundly about what is good and right belief and practice regarding same-gender sexual relations. After all, dissension is only of recent occurrence. In the Church's long history, there has been an uninterrupted consensus regarding this matter: physical intercourse between human beings is intended only for a man and a woman within marriage as a lifelong commitment. Any sexual engagement outside of this context is regarded as contrary to God's intention for his special creation. The ground for the Church having taken this stance is that, prima facie, the New Testament testimony to Jesus Christ, by which the Church lives, seems to be transparently clear on this matter.

For this reason, many Christians in the younger churches find the permissive stance of some Christians in the West to be incomprehensible. To advocate the blessing of same-gender relationships in certain circumstances seems to them to be an evident betrayal of God's revealed will and an abject capitulation to the thinking of secular society. In other words, for them, the matter represents a clear conflict between what the Gospel demands and what the culture permits or promotes, which has to be resolved in favour of a faithful, and if necessary costly, witness to the Gospel. The issue is as unambiguous as the Church's duty to

[2] There is another discussion with people who live by secular assumptions. Initial points of contact and agreement will be harder to come by. As there are few commonly held views, the process of discussion is likely to be more diffuse and protracted. Nevertheless, at another time and in another context, such a dialogue is important, even urgent, and by no means an exercise doomed to failure. However, it is not the focus of this present presentation.

campaign, for example, against all forms of racism and child exploitation.[3]

However, what may seem strange is now a reality. A number of Christians believe intensely that the debate has shifted, so that old certainties have to be re-examined in the light of new circumstances. There are a number of lines of argument. First, the traditional, uniform interpretation of the key biblical passages has to be re-evaluated. In the light of greater knowledge of the social and cultural background to the New Testament, and with more sophisticated linguistic and hermeneutical tools available, one may discover a more nuanced understanding of the kind of practices condemned by Paul.

Secondly, it is an historical fact that ethical standards evolve over a period of time for any but the most static societies. In Western culture, changes can often be traced to the influence of the Christian faith, as Christians are constrained by their faith and by circumstances to rethink the traditional stances. The abolition of feudalism and slavery are classic examples of a deep shift of perspective brought about by a more informed understanding of the implications of Christian belief. Radical changes have also taken place in considering the nature and purpose of punishment. A warm and generous recognition of the equality of ministry between men and women is now taken for granted by many Christians in all churches. By analogy, it is argued, acceptance of homo-sexual relationships will happen inevitably, when the Church eventually becomes convinced of the theological and cultural reasons for removing unwarranted discrimination against them.

Thirdly, this development in ethical awareness reflects society's accumulated experience of the depth of human commitment possible between people of the same gender. It appears to be a fact of nature that same gender attraction, to the exclusion of heterosexual relationships, is just as real for a minority of people as the latter is for the majority. Hence, if they are excluded from forming these bonds, and expressing them phys-

---

[3] For many Christians living in Africa the biblical witness is much more uncompromising in this instance than in the case of polygamy. Some Western Christians seem to see the clarity of the issues the other way round.

ically in a manner similar to that of heterosexual couples, their very nature (as created by God) is denied and God's handiwork despised.

Fourthly, as a consequence of the progress in understanding, the kind of missionary and pastoral challenges faced by the Church today is quite different from that pertaining in apostolic times. The Church has no alternative but to reflect deeply on the contextual relevance of its message and practices. It cannot simply repeat verbatim texts written in vastly different contexts.

Finally, and to complete the hermeneutical circle, our attitude cannot be the same as that of Paul. In today's society, the Gospel demands a different outlook and strategy. Mission in the way of Jesus Christ requires, in the changed circumstances of the twenty-first century, a compassion for the religiously excluded similar to that he exercised in the first century. To be faithful to Jesus Christ in our generation requires the exposure of religious intolerance and bigotry just as it did in his day.

So, whether one believes that acceptance of homo-sexual relations represents a refusal of the cost of discipleship or whether one is convinced that, on the contrary, it means a faithful witness to the love of Christ in a new situation, the dispute is about the Gospel and context. In fact, it is an exemplary instance of the issues involved in seeking to resolve the tension between the two. As such, it is profoundly germane to the Church's mission at the frontiers of contemporary society.

The Main Issues

Christians opposed to the legitimacy of any kind of homo-sexual practice argue that there is only one plausible way of interpreting those passages in the New Testament which most explicitly touch the subject (namely, Rom. 1:26–27, 28, 32; 1 Cor. 6:9–11, 18–20; Eph. 4:19; 1 Tim. 1:9–11). They interpret these texts to state that any sexual practice, taking place outside marriage, falls under God's judgement, for it reflects the choice of a way of life (life-style) that belongs to the realm of death (Rom. 6:13–14, 19–22; Col. 1:13), doomed to perish. Such practices belong to the

'old age' (1 Cor. 2:6–8) from which Christ, by his death and resurrection, has set us free. They may be expected of those whose
moral compass is not pointing in the direction God has set for
abundant human life and who have not experienced new life in
Christ.

Homo-sexual practices are part of an 'ungodly' life, in the
sense of being cast adrift from a consciousness of the moral standards God requires.[4] They reflect a way of thinking which
upholds a personalised ethic: any action whose consequences do
not harm other sovereign individuals is morally permitted. Thus,
from the perspective of the Christian faith, homo-sexual practice
is evidence of an unregenerate nature. It follows from the kind of
thinking that is conformed to the patterns of this world (age), a
thinking which has not yet been transformed by the new life
available in Christ (Rom. 12:2). It springs from ignorance (Eph.
4:18) about the true life offered by grace to all who believe and
act on the Gospel (Rom. 8:5–14).

From this understanding of the New Testament teaching it follows that the Christian message in respect of currently sanctioned sexual behaviour is counter-cultural. Whether the culture
is first century Greco-Roman or twenty-first century European,
the Gospel is opposed to it on this matter. One of the prime missionary tasks of the Church is to discern what in contemporary
culture is to be affirmed and supported and what has to be resis-
ted (1 Thess. 5:21–22). Such a task requires a clear understanding
of the content and implications of the Gospel, for its author is
both the Creator and Judge of all human aspirations.

On the other side of the dispute are those who believe that
homo-sexual practice, in some circumstances, is compatible
with, or even expressive of the Gospel. For them the application
of Scripture to contemporary realities is not nearly so unproblematic. Given the missionary imperative of including those sexually attracted to their own gender in the offer of the Gospel and

---

[4] Anthony Thiselton summarises the attitude as a manifestation of 'post-modern'
assumptions: 'Once humans have reconstructed God in accordance with its religious and power preferences, as Feuerbach and Nietzsche knew full well, they
are free to reconstruct ethics and conduct in accordance with their moral and
social preferences,' *The First Epistle to the Corinthians*, p. 446.

the pastoral imperative of caring for them in the fellowship of the church, a way has to be found of negotiating the texts that does not damage either the authority of the Gospel or personal experience of a given nature.

To further this end, two different approaches to the texts have been adopted. In the first one, it is suggested that proper exegesis will show that the traditional interpretation is not valid. The condemnation of homo-sexual practices in the teaching of the early Church cannot refer to the kind of relationships envisaged today, for they were not practised in the society of that time.[5] Precisely because all ancient cultures were prejudiced against acknowledging that same-gender unions, when lifelong commitments, were as valid as heterosexual ones, such relationships could not happen. Therefore, the practices to which Paul refers can only be those which actually took place, namely casual liaisons.[6]

Most serious advocates of homo-sexual practices today also reject irregular, superficial and fleeting alliances. Therefore, when they read the key texts, they do not necessarily have any misgivings about accepting the injunctions, for they have resolved any possible conflict by paying attention to a perfectly legitimate contextual interpretation. Contemporary culture helps us to understand the text better by suggesting relevant questions that will be missed by those who too hastily assume a uniform interpretation.

In the second approach, a different method is adopted. Even admitting that the texts may cover all homo-sexual relationships *per se*, both those practised at the time and those that have evolved in different cultural circumstances, does not mean that the teaching is morally binding today. It is a fact that the way the Church has understood and applied the Scriptures has, in many instances, changed over time. Previously, interpretations have

---

[5] This line of argument is advanced by, among others, R. Scroggs, *The NT and Homosexuality* (Philadelphia: Fortress Press, 1983), J.B. Nelson, 'Sources for Body Theology' in Jeffrey S. Siker (ed.), *Homosexuality in the Church: Both Sides of the Debate* (Louisville: Westminster-Knox, 1994).

[6] Either with young adolescents or adult male prostitutes.

been vigorously defended and implemented that today no Christian would want to accept.[7]

As already mentioned, certain attitudes to women is perhaps the most prominent example. From the perspective of a more morally enlightened society ways of understanding certain texts have changed. The important lesson to be learned from the history of interpretation is that individual texts must not be isolated from the key elements of God's saving actions through Jesus Christ. Scripture cannot be read as if every text carried equal weight. Each has to be related to the greater whole. In other words, interpretations have to be justified on the basis of the hermeneutical keys chosen. In the case of women, the key is the equality of men and women, created in the image of God. Certain passages (as the creation narratives of Genesis 1 and 2) have been re-evaluated in the light of the assumption that equality means not only equivalence of dignity and worth (the biblical view) but also of opportunity and practice (the contextual addition).[8]

A similar strategy should be adopted in the case of homo-sexuality. Experience shows that two people of the same gender are able to exhibit the same kind of caring, unselfish, reciprocal, gratuitous love that is the mark of the very best heterosexual marriages, which in turn reflect the creative and redeeming love of God. It seems, therefore, blasphemous to deny the evidence of a love so profound that one can only conclude that its origin and inspiration is divine.

So, by way of summary, what is at stake between the two parties in the dispute is the actual meaning and application of texts within the grand narrative of the Gospel of God's saving acts in Jesus Christ. These texts have to be measured in part by the

[7] 'As with the equality of women, as with the emancipation of slaves, the thing which at first was supposed to be 'incompatible with scripture' finally turns out to be demanded by the heart of the Christian Gospel itself. That is how it so often is. But how bizarre that so few see it in advance.' Jeffrey John, *The Church and Homosexuality: Post-Lambeth Reflections*, p. 13.

[8] In the history of interpretation this is sometimes called the *sensus plenior* – the fuller meaning, already contained implicitly in the text but at a later stage made explicit by the Spirit to the church.

author's original intention. However, their meaning is also determined by their relationship to key hermeneutical principles that become evident as interpreters of Scripture listen also to what the Spirit is saying to the Church through elements of contemporary culture. In other words, the dispute is about how one handles the text in context.[9] The sections that follow are attempts to clarify further the different elements of the discussion. As will be noted, it is not possible to remain neutral with regard to the conflicting opinions expressed. I hold a position which I believe is right. All that can be demanded is fairness and charity in describing views, with which one disagrees, and an openness to one's own views being challenged.

The Gospel and Context – an epistemological question

This chapter is arguing that the issue of same-gender sexual relations is, for Christians, essentially a matter of how one correlates the Gospel and a particular culture. Part of the discussion depends on how one answers the following question: is it possible to arrive at a clear view of the Gospel without immersion in

---

[9] There is another approach, which having conceded that the traditional interpretation of the texts cannot be gainsaid, nevertheless concludes that the Church today is not bound by what amounts to the particular, religious (Jewish legalistic) and cultural captivity of Paul. This is a variation of the second option, but is more cavalier towards and dismissive of the integrity of the texts. Unlike the second approach, it adopts an *extrinsic* hermeneutical key, namely the alleged witness of the Spirit in the development of moral values through history, by which the validity of the witness of the Spirit through Scripture is judged. Thus, Eugene Rogers confesses that 'the argument I offer is . . . an attempt to *retell and renarrate bits of the Christian story* so as to reveal the coherence of Christian thought with a practice of marriage broad enough to include gay and lesbian couples . . .' and 'we must mine Scripture and tradition under the Spirit, who will *rule new rules for us*', Eugene F. Rogers (ed.), *Theology and Sexuality: Classic and Contemporary Readings* (Oxford: Blackwell, 2002), p. 219 and p. 238 (my emphases).

Owing to the acute epistemological difficulties of such a position, which will be touched on in the chapter, and the fact that it is not the argument used by the most careful advocates of the compatibility of the Gospel with homo-sexual practices, I intend to disregard it for the purposes of this discussion. It could be that further consideration of such a stance belongs naturally with an examination of secular approaches to the issues of same gender relations.

culture obscuring one's vision to such an extent that clarity is lost
and confidence in a true understanding is undermined? Does
context always, inevitably, distort the way we state the Gospel?
An affirmative answer to these questions is the prevailing view
of many in the Church. The answer is itself a reflection of culture.
For a series of historical reasons 'perspectivism' appears to be the
most dominant account of how one should evaluate claims to
know the truth.

Perspectivism is a theory in epistemology. It argues that
claims to knowledge basically reflect a particular situation in the
world. No method of understanding the features of our experience – no form of rational or empirical procedure – can be said
to enjoy a privileged epistemic status. Historically speaking
most, if not all, so-called facts have proved to be interpretations
of experience from someone's point of view. Hence, beliefs once
held to be unequivocally valid have been shown to be mere
perspectives on life that, in the course of time, have had to be
either seriously revised or abandoned altogether. The claim to
be able to possess unambiguous and decisive knowledge is an
illusion of 'Enlightenment' philosophy and dogmatic theology.
Perspectivism is a deeply suspicious reaction to the claim that
we can have access to self-evident, assured knowledge about a
reality, independent of our preferences and aspirations. It
ridicules the notion that we can have a view 'from nowhere' (or
everywhere).

As a consequence of this major shift in cultural consciousness,
we must admit that it is now necessary to recognise multiple
ways of seeing. Each one is perfectly valid in its own right and,
even if it is not our way of viewing reality, has to be respected
and, to a certain extent, conceded. In contemporary society it is
intolerable to tolerate only one way.[10]

---

[10] This way of thinking underlies the attempt by some Church leaders to diffuse
the controversy over homo-sexual relationships by calling for reconciliation
between opposed groups as a kind of 'peaceful co-existence' within the body of
Christ. However, it is a superficial move, as it seriously undervalues the meaning of reconciliation. In a way analogous to the assumptions behind the 'Truth
and Reconciliation Commissions' (South Africa, Chile), reconciliation is condi-
tional upon being able to ascertain the truth of the matter.

Perspectivism in one form or another has become a persuasive force in modern ethical discourse.[11] And yet, if applied directly to the questions of Gospel and culture, it becomes self-defeating and incoherent. Absorption in culture is self-evident. To be human is to be a cultural being. However, there is no logical extension of this fact to the acceptance of a radical relativism, by which all opinions are allowed a moral equivalence and all views of the Christian faith are given some credence. Such a line of argument would deny the possibility of recognising a distinction between Gospel and culture and, ultimately, of being able to make sense of the notion that we are immersed in culture! Naturally, although relativism remains immensely attractive to our generation, no one is a relativist in practice. Everyone defends some absolute, even if it is the absolute that all perspectives are relative to time and place.

In the circumstances of our discussion, those Christians who wish to defend the legitimacy of same-gender sexual relations do so, as a matter of fact, on the basis of a 'non-contextually' determined view of the Gospel. In debate with 'traditionalists' they undoubtedly appeal to what they consider a more comprehensive understanding of the Gospel: one which is not to be equated simply with social and psychological forces that coincidentally have shaped their thinking. Were this not so, their 'Christian' defence of homo-sexual practices would be incomprehensible. They acknowledge the fact that we are perfectly aware of our ability to stand apart from our situation to reflect upon it critically.[12]

Christians of all persuasions, therefore, believe that the Gospel is the major factor in this critical endeavour precisely because it affords a perspective, which is independent of our likes and dislikes and our putative power-struggles. In our arguments, both for and against homo-sexual relations, we appeal to the meaning

[11] It underlies, for example, principled defences of relativism, subjectivism and some forms of consequentialism in contemporary moral debate; see Peter Singer (ed.), *A Companion to Ethics* (Oxford: Blackwell, 1993), chapters 19, 38 and 39.

[12] Such a stance implies the defence of objective knowledge against those who advocate its inevitable, socially-conditioned bias; see Roger Trigg, *Rationality and Religion* (Oxford: Blackwell, 1998), pp. 29ff.

of the Gospel as an external truth which compels belief irrespective of our inclinations. The Gospel and our culture can be effectively separated. Arguments for homo-sexual practices stem
from the belief in an unconditional moral good. Perspectivism
may be culturally attractive. It is, however, an intellectual red-
herring. In practice, we are all fiduciary and moral absolutists.
The debate, therefore, is led into a complete dead end by those
who wish to suggest that stances are mainly formed by particular cultural influences.

The Gospel and Context – a hermeneutical question
Given the fact, then, that all Christians make unqualified claims
about the Gospel, and yet appear to be in deep conflict over particular interpretations, is it possible to discover a basic message
(a core) such that to deny it would imply a severe rupture with
the Christian faith and community? For all kinds of 'post-modern' reasons - the deconstruction of power and authoritarianism,
'languagegames', post-Kantian idealism, Hegelian historicism –
it is fashionable to answer no. The denial, however, is little more
than a theoretical ploy, as it cannot be defended in practice.

Discovering the meaning of the Church's mission always
involves a struggle for the true Gospel. If an appeal to a core
message is ruled out in principle there is no position left from
which to criticise present understandings and present alternatives. Critique always implies a better perspective, according to
some implied independent set of criteria. Without a reliable
statement of God's truth, the prophetic task of the Church would
not be possible. Thus, the Church would not only be unable to
debate meaningfully the issue of same-gender relations, it would
also be impotent to pronounce on issues of social justice or
engage in a serious dialogue with people of other faith traditions. This is the main reason why the debate about homo-
sexuality is of profound missiological concern: it illustrates
acutely and poignantly the tensions between the Gospel and
culture. So, then, the choice is not between a Gospel nucleus or
none at all. It is a matter, rather, of which explicit or implicit
nucleus we subscribe to.

Antiquated though the pursuit of the core truth of the Gospel may appear, it is unavoidable. The only satisfactory way of engaging in the task is by a diligent, self-critical reading of the biblical text, seeing that the Christian Church has never recognised a more favourable source of knowledge for gaining access to God's view of things. Of course, all readings have to be keenly aware of the different elements of the hermeneutical circle: the conceptual assumptions that all interpreters take to their study of the text, their daily praxis and the questions that all contexts pose to the Gospel. Nevertheless, it is necessary to insist that there are principles and criteria for understanding the original intention or natural meaning of the writings, which are not merely a matter of private opinion or arbitrary cultural preferences. In this way, Christians who disagree about the nature and implications of their faith can have an intelligent debate about a source of knowledge and understanding external to themselves. The alternative would be either an unprincipled struggle for power, with no agreed means of arbitration, or mindless moral indulgence.

The Gospel and Context – an exegetical question

In seeking to resolve disputes between Christians, such as the present one, there is no alternative to direct exegesis of the biblical text in searching for the implications of the Gospel. This will involve paying attention both to the relevant passages and to the wider context in which they are set. Not everyone may agree on the most important texts. Nevertheless, if one wishes to maintain intellectual integrity, at least those texts which specifically mention same-gender sexual relations have to be addressed. They are as follows:

> For this reason God gave them up to degrading passions.
> Their women exchanged natural intercourse for unnatural,
> and in the same way also the men, giving up natural
> intercourse with women, were consumed with passion for one
> another. Men committed shameless acts with men and
> received in their own persons the due penalty for their error.

And since they did not see fit to acknowledge God, God gave them up to a debased mind and to things which should not be done (Rom. 1:26–28).

Do you not know that wrongdoers will not inherit the kingdom of God? Do not be deceived! Fornicators, idolaters, adulterers, male prostitutes (malakoi), sodomites (arsenokoites) . . . – none of these will inherit the kingdom of God (1 Cor. 6:9).

The law is laid down not for the innocent but for the lawless and disobedient . . . for the murderers, fornicators, sodomites (arsenokoites), slave-traders, liars, perjurers and whatever is contrary to sound teaching that conforms to the glorious gospel of the blessed God, which he entrusted to me (1 Tim. 1:9–10).

At first sight, the direct textual references seem to be slender in the extreme. How is it possible to build a whole moral case on such a paucity of witness? In one sense, the references are fortuitous; they come as part of a particular argument, which presumably Paul did not have to repeat. However, the context of the discussion in which they are embedded is far from incidental. In the case of Romans, commentators agree that the passage begins with the phrase, 'For the wrath of God is revealed from heaven against all ungodliness and wickedness of those who by their wickedness suppress the truth (Rom. 1:18).' The rest of the chapter is an elaboration of the meaning of 'ungodliness' (asebeia) and 'wickedness' (adikia).

Asebeia is identified with idolatry, defined by the words, 'they exchanged the truth about God for a lie and worshipped and served the creature rather than the Creator' (Rom. 1:25). Adikia is identified with 'things that should not be done' (poiein ta me kathekonta) (Rom. 1:28). As frequently pointed out, asebeia and adikia are intimately related. People engage in the things that ought not to be done, because 'they (do) not see fit to acknowledge God' (Rom. 1:28). Paul's argument can hardly be disputed: immoral actions spring from a mentality that has distanced itself from knowledge of God and God's truth. Ethical action clearly depends on one's epistemic commitment. But knowledge of God and his ways are not confined to some esoteric world of privileged revelation. It is plain, visible, and knowable in the created world (Rom. 1:20) and (as Paul argues later) in conscience also (Rom. 2:15).

God's judgement falls upon all who perform acts that contravene God's creative intentions for his world. The judgement takes the form of confirming people in the consequences of their own choices. Three times Paul repeats the phrase, 'God gave them up . . . (Rom. 1:24, 26, 28)' Judgement, in a sense, is self-inflicted. It is the suffering that follows from a way of life chosen in defiance of the created order:

> Idolatry finally debases both the worshipper and the idol. God's judgement allows the irony of sin to play itself out. The creature's original impulse toward self-glorification ends in self-destruction. The refusal to acknowledge God as Creator ends in blind distortion of the creation.[13]

Prominent among the things that ought not to be done are the 'degrading of their bodies among themselves . . . degrading passions . . . unnatural intercourse . . . men committing shameless acts with men.' It would be anachronistic and sophistic to deny that Paul has in mind every kind of same-gender sexual practice. E. P. Saunders says:

> When we turn to Paul, we are not surprised that he condemns all homosexual activity, nor that he specifies both the active and passive partners . . . (In 1 Corinthians 6:9) Paul names both the effeminate partner, the malakos, 'soft' one, and the active one, the arsenokoites. Some scholars propose that the words are uncertain as to meaning and thus that perhaps Paul did not really condemn homosexuality. The words, however, are quite clear. 'Soft' was a common term for the passive

---

[13] Richard B. Hays, *The Moral Vision of the New Testament: A Contemporary Introduction to New Testament Ethics* (New York: HarperCollins, 1996), p. 385.

partner, and nothing could be more explicit than 'one who buggers males.'[14]

Saunders closes his discussion of Paul's attitude to homosexuality by stating that 'the two condemnations of homosexuality show that he applied to his Gentile converts the standards of Judaism. Naturally he found them wanting: 'such were some of you' (1 Cor. 6:11). On the basis of an observation like this, some argue that Paul was still applying norms belonging to the old covenant. He was simply repeating standard Jewish morality.[15] His injunctions here do not spring from the Gospel perspective of the new covenant. There might be some merit in such an argument were it not for the fact that the contexts explicitly relate to both the Gospel and the new covenant. In other words, they are not isolated and incidental statements. They are an intrinsic part of a comprehensive discussion.

Working backwards, Paul's argument starts with an observation about the corrupt nature of human society. He then states that evil deeds carry within them their own self-destruction, displaying a universal, God-ordained moral law of cause and effect – 'they know God's decree, that those who practise such things deserve to die' (Rom. 1:32). Seeing that human nature is irrevocably contaminated by sin,[16] every human being is destined for condemnation and punishment – normal consequences for breaking the law. Ordinarily speaking, then, there is no hope for human beings bent on pursuing their own desires. Like the prodigal son, each human being chooses his or her own path in life, leaving home and wandering impetuously into harmful activities.

However, the far country is not the end of the story. Although

---

[14] *Paul* (Oxford: OUP, 1991), pp. 112–113.

[15] For example, William Countryman, *Dirt, Greed and Sex: Sexual Ethics in the New Testament and Their Implications for Today* (Philadelphia: Fortress Press, 1988), argues that the condemnation of homo-sexuality in the New Testament reflects the Old Testament's ritual laws on purity and impurity and, therefore, must be irrelevant today.

[16] It seems likely that the passage is a (midrashic-syle) commentary on the fall of humankind, an analysis of the nature of the primal sin; see *The Meaning of Freedom*, pp. 202–205.

ignored, despised and reviled, God has taken upon himself the task of restoring beings to their full humanity, an act they cannot perform for themselves. Instead of the normal procedure of judgement, conviction and appropriate punishment, God has shown another kind of justice. By bearing himself the full consequences of human degeneracy, he opens up the way for human beings to be liberated from self-inflicted ruin. This is what Paul means by the euangelion (gospel): 'it is the power of God for salvation . . . in it the righteousness of God is revealed' (Rom. 1:16).

The context, therefore, in which Paul supposedly applies an old covenant morality, is actually a treatment of the full significance of the new covenant, whose consequence is a new, resurrected life in Jesus Christ. The subsequent argument of Romans, especially chapters 6—8, focuses on God's way of liberation from the sinful deeds of the flesh through crucifixion, burial and resurrection with Christ and the gift of the Holy Spirit. It is inconceivable, therefore, that, when Paul speaks of 'sinful flesh', 'sin in the flesh', 'to set the mind on the flesh is death', he is not referring directly to 'the degrading passions' listed in the earlier part of his discussion of the Gospel (Rom. 1:26–31).

Though employing a different argument in 1 Corinthians, the comprehensive background is God's new righteous rule through Jesus Christ. This is what Paul means when he uses the term the kingdom of God (basileia). It is the new sphere of reality that has come about through the work of atonement of the Son of God. How could Paul be more explicit than to link the kingdom to the new life, available to all through the cleansing, sanctifying and justifying action of God (1 Cor. 6:11). 'Wrongdoers will not inherit the kingdom' (1 Cor. 6:9), because they have not availed themselves fully of God's means of liberation.

Likewise, in 1 Timothy, the reference to the different examples of the godless (aseboi) is set in the context of sound teaching 'that conforms to the glorious Gospel (kata to euaggelion tes doxes) of the blessed God' (1 Tim. 1:11). The list of 'the godless' is quite extensive (1 Tim. 1:9–10). There is no conceivable reason why the arsenokoitai should be considered any differently from 'slave-traders, liars, perjurers'. According to this passage, homo-sexual

acts, along with murder, committing adultery and bearing false-
witness, are contrary (antikeitai) to the Gospel.

Without being able to develop here all the implications of this
discussion, sufficient textual evidence has been given to demonstrate that the issue of same-gender sexual relations, although
only a part of human sinfulness, is, in the eyes of Paul, inextricably linked to God's provision of salvation in Jesus Christ. It is
wrong, therefore, to pretend either that Paul does not intend to
condemn every kind of relation in which members of the same
sex perform sexual acts together or that such actions have nothing to do with the Gospel.[17] On the contrary, such activity
belongs to the old order of death. It is one part of human beings'
slavery to passions, from which the Gospel is a glorious release:

[17] 'Repeated again and again in recent debate is the claim that Paul condemns only
homosexual acts committed promiscuously by heterosexual persons, because
they *exchanged* natural intercourse for unnatural'. Paul's negative judgement, so
the argument goes, does *not* apply to persons who are 'naturally' of homosexual
orientation. This interpretation, however, is untenable. 'The "exchange" is not a
matter of individual life decisions; rather, it is Paul's characterization of the
fallen condition of the pagan world', Hays, op. cit. 388; 'All of this is simply to
say that the judgement of Romans 1 against homosexual practices should never
be read apart from the rest of the letter, with its message of grace and hope
through the cross of Christ,' Ibid. p. 393.

Jeffrey John is one who argues that Paul's discussion of homo-sexuality, in the
light of present knowledge, is based on false premises: 'Paul must believe that
homosexuals wilfully choose their unnatural perversion . . . Yet we know that
this fundamental assumption on Paul's part is false. His belief that homosexual
acts are committed by naturally heterosexual people is untrue . . . We may
well . . . conclude that this false assumption on his part undermines any blanket
condemnation of homosexual practice on the basis of Romans 1', 'Christian
Same-sex Partnerships' in Tim Bradshaw, *The Way Forward?* (London: Hodder,
1997), p. 50. However, this reasoning completely misses the point, for he incor-
porates into the passage in Romans an assumption, which Paul does not make.
Paul is not talking about naturally heterosexual or naturally homosexual people.
The use of such a description would be anachronistic in the case of a first century writer. Paul is talking about anyone who exchanges the God-given world
of creation (*kata physin*) for a substitute world (*para physin*). Same-gender sexual
acts, whether carried out by bisexuals or homo-sexuals, manifest a human-con-
ceived world, an alternative to that created by God.

you were taught to put away your former way of life, your old
self, corrupt and deluded by its lusts, and to be renewed in the
spirit of your minds, and to clothe yourselves with the new
self, created according to the likeness of God in true
righteousness and holiness (Eph. 4:22–24).

Of course, there are many other passions. Christians may not be
selective about which immoral practices are denounced. If sexual
sins are highlighted to the near exclusion of other weighty viola-
tions of God's love and justice, the Church may well be guilty of
inconsistency and hypocrisy. At the same time, to minimise the
importance of right sexual relationships on the grounds that
there are more substantial issues of injustice and abuse is to
make a false choice. The Gospel is directed towards all forms of
dissonance between God's world of righteousness and our
world of unrighteousness.

The Gospel and Context – a pastoral question

As there are always serious tensions between the demands of the
Gospel and the seduction of culture, handling the strain and fric-
tion between them in individual cases becomes a serious pastoral
problem. As a community called to compassion and care, the
Church can never simply announce God's truth as if it were a
mere theological theory. Abstract and impersonal condemnation
of wrong is cruel and ugly. It can also be amazingly self-
righteous. The pastoral challenge is to support people who wish
to learn what it means to live according to the way of Christ in
the midst of the omnipresent pressures of culture. In the words
of Stanley Hauerwas, how do Christians fulfil their calling to be
'resident aliens'?

The deepest questions about same-gender relations probably
have more to do with this pastoral support than with the philosophical and theological matters that underpin one's basic outlook; although the latter are also crucial. On the one hand there
are many people who are convinced that, whatever the origin,
by nature they can only find their deepest human fulfilment in
relationship to another human being of the same gender. Certain

cultures reinforce this belief, by assuming that this is quite normal and there is nothing to be ashamed of. People are free and right to express themselves within this kind of bonding. Repression of sexuality is emotionally damaging. Any form of exclusion on the basis of 'orientation' is inadmissible discrimination against intrinsic rights. On the other hand apostolic teaching in the New Testament tells them that sexual activity in a same-gender relationship is a perversion of their nature – a deviation from God's good creation. To complicate matters even more, a number of Church leaders now tell them that their experience is more decisive than the implications of the Gospel.

The consequence seems to be that homo-sexually inclined people are forced either to deny their nature or ignore aspects of the New Testament's teaching. The latter is difficult, because it implies an arbitrary selection of what is to be believed and what discounted. The former seems impossible, for it cuts against what appears to be an inherited reality.

How can anyone resolve such a dilemma? How can the circle be squared? It would be foolish to pretend that there are easy answers. Insensitive moralising, glib solutions or compromise cannot be the ways forward. For the sake of continuing discussion, I would suggest that two complementary paths should be explored. Firstly, at the heart of the Gospel is a costly act of liberation that frees human beings from all that hinders God's offer of a distinctly new life in Christ. Though the Gospel message is clear about what constitutes God's standard for personal human relations, the emphasis is not on censure, blame and guilt, but on freedom, forgiveness, reconciliation and healing. Secondly, for the sake of ultimate human flourishing, it is crucial to recognise that certain culturally-inspired claims being made for homo-sexual experience are wrong, unhelpful and ultimately unkind, or even cruel.

There may have to be an irresolvable parting of the ways. It is not possible to reconcile the belief that God blesses a faithful[18]

---

[18] A.K.M. Adam argues that constancy is an overriding consideration in judging the legitimacy of sexual relationships as it mirrors or reproduces the character of God: see 'Disciples Together, Constantly' in Choon-Leong Seow (ed.), *Homosexuality and Christian Community* ((Westminster: John Knox Press, 1996),

homo-sexual union to the same degree as a life-long, hetero-sexual marriage with the belief that the former is a tragic distortion of the latter. The reason for this is given in the stark choice that confronts humanity, as it is compelled to live within the constraints of the reality of God's creation. The point at issue is put sharply by Richard Hays:

> The complementarity of male and female is given a theological grounding in God's creative activity. By way of sharp contrast, in Romans 1 Paul portrays homosexual behaviour as a 'sacrament' (so to speak) of the antireligion of human beings who refuse to honor God as Creator. When human beings engage in homosexual activity, they enact an outward and visible sign of an inward and spiritual reality: the rejection of the Creator's design.[19]

> Paul singles out homosexual intercourse for special attention because he regards it as providing a particularly graphic image of the way in which human fallenness distorts God's created order. God the Creator made man and woman for each other, to cleave together, to be fruitful and multiply. When human beings 'exchange' these created roles for homosexual

---

pp. 121ff. In the words of David McCarthy, 'through his theological framework of constancy and covenant, same-sex unions are not merely justified but are considered an efficacious sign of God's covenant-making and gracious self-giving to the world', 'The Relationship of Bodies: A Nuptial Hermeneutics of Same-sex Unions' in *Theology and Sexuality*, p. 203. This argument, however, is flawed. It begins back to front by searching for a positive attribute of 'successful' homosexual unions – constancy. It then exalts this into a key virtue. Subsequently, the key virtue is transformed into an overriding ethical principle. It is further identified as a characteristic of God. Finally, it is made synonymous with God's most fundamental relationship with his creation – covenant faithfulness. This is a very confused justification of homo-sexual unions, since it entirely begs the proper question: does God's covenant faithfulness actually permit such unions? Constancy cannot make a relationship acceptable, if there is good reason to doubt the validity of the relationship in the first place. Constancy is required for a relationship to succeed. It cannot, however, be the ground of that relationship.
[19] *The Moral Vision*, p. 386.

intercourse, they embody the spiritual condition of those who
have 'exchanged the truth about God for a lie.'[20]

It may well be that the Church will have to divide, seeing that
those who are convinced that the Gospel is clear in its teaching
and must take precedence over culture cannot accommodate
those who believe the contrary. The split is about the most fundamental of all questions: the nature of reality. Which relationships correspond to God's ordering of life, and which violate it?

Listening carefully to the contrary views of fellow Christians
is incumbent on all who believe in Christ. Therefore, those who
currently accept that the Gospel is unequivocal about the issue
of homo-sexuality must be open to having their views changed
by a more convincing interpretation. Likewise, those who
defend same-gender unions must be open to other explanations
of experience. Let us start with this second aspect of the dispute.

In the recent history of Western societies, homo-sexuality has
been considered a psychosexual disorder. The principal founders
of modern psychotherapy, Freud, Jung and Adler considered
that homo-sexuality was a neurosis, the expression of an unconscious and unresolved conflict arising in childhood. However,
this view has been challenged in recent years. It is not now
acceptable in medical circles to consider same-gender sexual
attraction as a malady or condition that requires treatment. On
the contrary, it is now viewed as a normal part of the natural
order. Some human beings, albeit a minority, are able constitu-
tionally to find true satisfaction only in relationships with a
member of the same gender. This is simply the way they have
been born.[21] There is nothing more out of the ordinary about this
than being born black or with blue eyes or dark hair, with an
ability to be a chess grandmaster, play a musical instrument or
run a sub-four minute mile. Clearly, in this view, discrimination
on the basis of sexual 'orientation' would be grossly unjust, for it

---

[20] Ibid. p. 388.

[21] 'Homosexuality (is) a blameless natural condition', Andrew Sullivan, 'Alone
Again, Naturally: The Catholic Church and the Homosexual' in *Theology and
Sexuality*, p. 283.

would be penalising someone for a trait over which they have no control. In other words, homo-sexuality is part of the natural order.

The alternative view is that homo-sexual attraction is part of a natural order gone wrong. It represents a confused sexuality, the exchange of a normal relationship with one that simulates the real article with an artificial and contrived substitute. In other words, it is a disorder, a pathological state of affairs. If this diagnosis is correct, homo-sexually inclined men or women need healing, in order to find their true humanity and identity. To pretend that something unhealthy is sound is not an act of kindness, for it may cause, for the person affected, further trauma.

According to this understanding, a homo-sexual disposition indicates an early psychological malformation, whose effect is to arrest a proper process of growth into normal sexual differentiation. It has been suggested by authorities such as Anna Freud that homo-sexual desire is the result of a person seeking to repair an early fractured sexual identity. During childhood, the person concerned has not been able to achieve a proper identification with his or her own gender. It is a way of compensating for a relationship between father and son or mother and daughter that has gone astray. It is the symptom of a failure to come to terms with one's true humanity. It is, first and foremost, a tragedy – a state of affairs from which a person needs to be set free.

The most authentic and caring response to homo-sexuality is to acknowledge the real truth, for a proper diagnosis of reality is the beginning of genuine freedom. The most compassionate pastoral accompaniment, therefore, is to support a homo-sexual person in the agonizing process of re-encountering their true masculinity or femininity, i.e. their true nature as human beings. If it is true that their 'orientation' is dysfunctional, such a process must be able to bear fruit. In the celebrated words of Albert Einstein, 'God does not play dice.' As one might expect, this interpretation of same-gender sexual attraction is fiercely contested by the homo-sexual movement. Following certain postmodern trends, it is seen as a perversion of scientific investigation in the interests of maintaining a measure of control over a predetermined social order.[22] In other words, science is being used to regulate society in conformity with a particular social consensus. This is said to be typical of the mindset of modernity which is founded on a belief in a universal rationality, itself part of an unchanging natural order, most clearly expressed in the success of the scientific enterprise.

It is not fortuitous that the change of opinion about homo-sexuality coincided chronologically with the beginnings of the post-modern attack on the pretensions of post-Enlightenment rationality. It is a typical example of the vast cultural shift that has been taking place over the last 40 years. The first argument in favour of homo-sexual relations is negative: neither religious authority, nor a self-confirming rationality, nor science is able to demonstrate that this kind of relationship is contrary to nature. Indeed, the argument from an intrinsic natural order is itself suspect.[23] Post-modern thinking has released the human spirit from the notion of an essential reality, so that it might create its own. The choice, therefore, between homo-sexual and hetero-sexual relations is a matter of the right of the individual to construct his or her own world. Each world is as valid as the other. This is all that needs to be said, except that society through its laws should recognise the equivalent status of the choices made and therefore legislate for equal rights.

In the last half-century there has been a huge cultural shift away from the notion of a standard sexuality to the propriety of sexual choice (also covering bisexuality, trans-sexuality, transgender sexuality and inter-sexuality). Choice is warranted basically. It is justified on the basis of a self-evident experience. All arguments to the contrary are the product of a cultural prejudice, the epiphenomena of a particular historical trajectory, which is no longer believable. Evidence strongly suggests that the shift has not come about as the result of scientifically established research findings. Such findings, if they tell against the cultural

---

[22] The research of Michel Foucault into particular human institutions is paradigmatic of this point of view; see *Descartes to Derrida*, pp. 251–267.

[23] The Christian gay and lesbian movement tends to maintain a belief in a given, created order, partly in order to maintain that homo-sexual orientation is inborn.

consensus, are simply rejected as socially unacceptable, intentionally distorted to promote a particular social agenda.

If this analysis of the present situation is accurate, we can see that the issue of homo-sexuality is not only about the Gospel or culture in a narrow sense, but actually goes to the heart of how we reason about reality and how we form value systems. To accept the ontological equivalence between hetero-sexual marriage and homo-sexual unions is to endorse a comprehensive epistemological shift. The problem for Christian faith is that this same epistemological shift cannot be applied to the Christian Gospel without changing its nature and content absolutely. The question, therefore, to defenders of homo-sexual relations within the Church is what justifies them in their selective epistemological stance.

The Gospel and Context – a question of communication

It is an unfortunate aspect of the dispute that arguments are vitiated by a loose, and often polemical, use of language. We leave aside the ascription of 'gay' to inter-male sexual attraction, only noting in passing that a word of joy in the English language has been, in the opinion of many, inappropriately abducted. Likewise, the designation 'gay liberation' to refer to a movement which aims to secure rights for homo-sexuals poses questions about the true nature of liberation. More significant in the present climate of attrition is the use of the words 'homophobia', 'bigoted' and 'fundamentalist'[24] to refer to those who oppose homo-sexual behaviour.

Phobia has two senses: an irrational fear of or an abnormal aver-

---

[24] Other words in the glossary of aggressively misused terms in this context are 'inclusive', 'progressive', 'tolerant' and 'broad-minded'. Space does allow an adequate analysis of the way in which these terms are used in a purely declamatory sense. It should be obvious to a moment's thought, however, that they are being used tendentiously, for they simply beg the question: at what point will the most liberal person actually draw a line? Unfortunately, the most self-proclaimed liberal can be extremely intolerant and exclusive of views that contradict his or her own. It is time to recognise that the use of these words does not advance an argument, but only furthers abuse and defamation.

sion to something or someone. It is commonly used, for example, of foreigners – xenophobia , open spaces – agoraphobia, spiders – arachnophobia, or technology – technophobia. However, it may be appended to almost any object of which human beings have a groundless, senseless or confused dread or hostility.

As soon as the clear (dictionary) definition is spelt out, it becomes obvious that the blanket accusation of homophobia against all who believe that same-gender sexual practices are improper and undesirable contradicts reality. The non-acceptance of homo-sexual practices is not groundless, absurd or confused. (This chapter attempts to show why.) It cannot be said to spring necessarily from an irrational fear or abnormal aversion. In fact, the accusation of homophobia is itself muddled if applied as a generalisation to all who believe that homo-sexual relations are wrong. It would be as nonsensical as accusing those who believe adultery is wrong of 'adulterophobia'. Unfortunately, the word 'homophobia' has become a blunt weapon in an acrimonious and painful campaign to overturn the unanimous conviction of the Christian faith over two thousand years that homo-sexual practices are contrary to God's revealed will for the flourishing of his people. Its use should be repudiated as an untrue description and, therefore, as a misleading and abusive tactic.[25]

Likewise, bigoted is used improperly. It refers to someone who is prejudiced against or intolerant of another's opinion, without any just cause. It may be applied to someone who is plainly ignorant of or deliberately misrepresents the opinion of another, or who refuses to acknowledge overwhelming arguments in favour of a belief. It cannot be applied to someone who simply disagrees, on good rational grounds, with the opinion of another. In the case of the debate about homo-sexuality, to call others bigoted is simply to vilify them. Again, as it is strictly untrue, it muddies the waters of the debate. Its use is wholly unworthy of a serious discussion on a vital and sensitive issue.

---

[25] Michael Levin believes that an antipathy to homosexuality is not a matter of hate or a desire to harm, but a desire to avoid, which may itself have a biological basis, see 'Homosexuality, Abnormality, and Civil Rights' in *Public Affairs Quarterly* 10 (1996), pp. 31–48.

Finally, the term fundamentalist is used to describe those who adhere to a particular interpretation of the relevant biblical texts.[26] Its use in this context, however, is quite inaccurate. Fundamentalism may be appropriately used of any interpretation that treats all texts as having equal worth or which does not acknowledge the significance of different literary genre for understanding meaning or which ignores the historical, social and cultural background to the text or, finally, which tends always to a literalist construal of language. It is wholly out of place as a description of the careful, linguistic, grammatical, intra-canonical and historically-sensitive exegesis of renowned biblical scholars. Their work is not to be judged on the basis of any preconceived view of what texts can or cannot mean. It can only be assessed on the basis of proper exegetical principles which are open to confirmation or refutation within their own terms, not within the confines of an extrinsically predetermined belief-system.

The use of this and similar language does not advance any argument at all. Indeed, it acts as a substitute for proper reasoned discourse. Those who resort to name-calling invite the suspicion that their stock of good reasoning is low. In a debate of high calibre, noone should have to defend themselves against false accusations. *Ad hominem* arguments shift the focus of a discussion away from proper evidence and logically consistent thoughtprocesses. The use of rhetorical language is counter-productive in that it gives the impression of hiding weak or vacuous arguments. The cause of careful deliberation will be immeasurably furthered by all sides in the dispute pledging abstinence from the use of loose epithets.

The Gospel and Context – a missiological question

Finally, we return to the claim made at the beginning that this issue of homo-sexual relations illustrates a profound missiologi-

---

[26] 'In a notorious pronouncement, the Lambeth Conference of 1998 embraced exactly this kind of selective fundamentalism, by declaring that all homosexual acts are incompatible with Scripture,' Jeffrey John, *Permanent, Faithful, Stable: Christian Same-sex Partnerships* (London: Darton, Longman & Todd, 2000), p. 7.

cal dilemma and cannot, for that reason, be sidelined as of secondary importance to the mission of the Christian community. Our thesis is based on the supposition that the proper stance of the Church towards practising homo-sexual couples is determined by a proper assessment of the relationship between the (unchanging nature of the) Gospel and changing cultural values. Mission always takes place on the frontier between the two. It is a task that has to be reviewed and renewed in every generation, for the philosophical and moral views of particular cultures change over time.

It is a matter of intense debate how far Western cultures are in the process of being transformed by a paradigmatic shift from a 'modern' to a 'post-modern' consensus. There can be little doubt, however, that the last 40 years has witnessed a profound modification of views, above all in the area of sexual morality.[27] The Christian Church, if its mission is to be effective, needs to be well-informed about the causes, nature and effects of these changes. Then, again, the Church has a responsibility to assess continually its understanding of the Gospel message it has been commissioned to announce to all peoples. To claim that the message is unchanging is not the same as claiming that any one particular interpretation is indisputable. There is a proper 'struggle for the true Gospel' in all areas of the Church's witness. This may involve sharp disagreements and painful estrangements, as has been seen in cases like the ordination of women, the legitimacy of war, marriage and divorce, social justice and the poor. Sometimes, the main issue between Christians is how to understand the implications of the Gospel when (a) there are significant shifts in what a particular culture tolerates and (b) issues arise where there is no clear, direct response from either the biblical text or the witness of the Church's tradition.

For the sake of consistency, the approach to biblical interpretation must be uniform across all the disputed areas of the Church's mission. It is inconsistent, for example, to quote verbatim texts like Isaiah 58 as a foundation for Christian attitudes to

---

[27] This is the central thesis in Callum Brown's analysis of the incredibly swift loss of influence among the younger generation of the Church's teaching about ethical propriety, see *The Death of Christian Britain* (London: Routledge, 2001).

the poor and excluded and to refuse the Pauline texts as a foundation for Christian attitudes to homo-sexuality. This, surely, would be a supreme example of 'selective fundamentalism' i.e. a quotation of Scripture or a dismissal of Scripture to fit one's preconceived view of what is right in culture.

If this argument about the Church's mission is sound, then the present debate about homo-sexual practice has a direct relevance to the Church's calling to announce the good news of Jesus Christ. It is regrettable, and inimical to a proper examination of what faithfulness to the Gospel of Jesus Christ requires in present circumstances, that some leaders in the Church should seek to pre-empt a proper 'disputation' by proposing to ordain or consecrate homo-sexuals and bless, or even perform a service of 'marriage' for, same-sex couples. It betrays a failure to listen properly to alternative views. The failure to wait until a significant section of the Church has come to a common mind on this issue does invite the accusation of 'heresy' in its linguistic sense of a sectarian opinion out of communion with the Church's common teaching.

In the Western world, the Church is under enormous cultural pressure to redefine its teaching on sexuality; some would argue, in order to make its message more relevant to the growing social consensus of the peoples whom it is trying to reach with the Gospel. It would be wise, however, to reflect long and hard on the right way to respond to this particular dispute between the Gospel and culture. Otherwise, the Church may not only fragment once again, but also look extremely foolish.

If the witness of history has any bearing on this matter, it shows that when the Church yields to the constraints of society, more often than not the Gospel is compromised. Is this not a fundamental lesson to be learnt from the European churches' syncretistic compromise with political power? There is little evidence to suggest that adaptation to the moral consensus of a society has done anything to halt the Church's steady decline. The Polish philosopher Leszek Kolakowski summarises admirably the dilemma of contextualisation in any given 'world'. The implications for mission reflection and practice are immense:

> That there are few (Christians), however, is not a symptom of
> any 'crisis' of Christianity, but confirmation of something it
> says about itself: that it is difficult to measure up to its
> demands. If there is a crisis, it is a permanent one; it is an
> indispensable way of being for Christianity, or perhaps an
> expression of the more general and universal 'crisis' in which
> we all find ourselves, having been driven out of paradise.[28]

An entirely different voice, from a wholly unexpected source,
makes a similar point. The author of the following statement is
self-confessedly both gay and an atheist!

> Knowingly to approve of gay bishops robs Christianity of
> meaning. It is time that convinced Christians stopped trying to
> reconcile their spiritual beliefs with the modern age and
> understood that if one thing comes through every account we
> have of Jesus' teaching, it is that his followers are not urged to
> accommodate themselves to their age, but to the mind of
> God . . . Jesus was never reluctant to challenge received
> wisdoms that he wanted to change. He gives no impression
> that he came into the world to revolutionise sexual mores.[29]

According to the early creeds, the Church is 'one, holy, catholic
and apostolic'. This is both a statement of reality in the purposes
of God, but also a constant missionary calling in every generation to live out this reality. There are excellent reasons – some of
which have been explored here – to suggest that formal acceptance by the Church of homo-sexual relationships will severely
jeopardise this missionary vision and vocation.

---

[28] 'On the So-Called Crises of Christianity' in *Modernity on Endless Trial* (Chicago:
The University of Chicago Press, 1990), p. 94.
[29] Matthew Parris, 'No, God would not have approved of gay bishops,' *The Times*
(London), 9 August 2003.

CHAPTER 10

———

Mission Post-everything? A Postscript

The title of this final chapter is chosen somewhat with tongue in cheek. However, there is a serious intent in discussing the content to which it refers. Both academics and ordinary mortals apparently love to refer to the present time by a liberal use of the prefix, 'post'. It did not take long to reach 10 common descriptions of this age.[1] In the area of culture, we have the most overworked epithet of all, 'post-modern'. To this may be added, with a tiny stretch of imagination, 'post-post-modern' to describe an emerging social 'paradigm'.[2] In the social and political arenas, we find 'post-ideological', marking the end of the communist regimes in Europe, and 'post-colonial', which heralds resistance by former colonised peoples to Western-centred constructions of the human world.

Philosophy adds the tag 'post-foundational' to convey a shift in theories of knowledge from the model of a building secured on immovable foundations to that of a web. We should not think of knowledge any longer in vertical terms, as if we were build-

---

[1] For the record, and somewhat playfully, we might add 'post-Fordism', 'post-structuralism', 'post-Marxism', 'post-Freudianism' and almost anything else that describes the aftermath of a social or intellectual tendency, current, fashion, style or mode!

[2] Paradigm is a word highly valued in the pantheon of descriptive designations in historical and cultural analysis. It is the rough equivalent of model, but sounds much more splendid.

ing an edifice from the base upwards. The horizontal spread of an inter-related network of beliefs is a more appropriate image. Francis Fukuyama has famously termed the triumph of a liberal capitalist world-order 'post-history'. His intention is to convey the impression that all social forces and trends have converged into a final synthesis, thus making history, as a record of the clash of opposing ideals, redundant.

Finally, in the area of studies about which this book has been written (missiology) a number of labels are being used to describe a significant change in the present fortunes of the Christian faith. 'Post-Enlightenment' refers to Christian communities that are working out the meaning of their faith in contexts largely unaffected by the rancorous dispute between faith and reason that has its origins in the eighteenth-century reappraisal of the role of religion in public life.[3] 'Post-Christendom' describes the reality of the Church outside Europe, wherever it has been free from alignment with political power. Likewise 'post-Western' is an explanation of the geographical (and cultural) location of the majority of the Christian population worldwide. More narrowly, 'post-Christian' is an interpretation of the religious situation in Europe now that the majority of its inhabitants no longer follow the beliefs and practices of the Christian faith.

In so far as these epithets are meaningful descriptions of solid events in the real world, it may be helpful, and even important, to engage with the actual realms of life they profess to define. In considering the future of the Christian faith, understanding the various contexts in which it is being professed is a high priority. If Christian communities are to represent truly the governing principles of Jesus Christ in daily living, they have to discover the reality of the situation in which they are embedded.

'Post' as a prefix attached to a number of descriptive words reveals a typical attitude to life. It suggests a way of trying to cope conceptually with a world of rapid change, flux and uncertainty. It is an attempt to get a handle on a series of processes, developments and discoveries that pass swiftly before our eyes before fading into the past. We constantly live *after* whatever

[3] See *Whose Religion is Christianity?*, pp. 22, 26, 62.

course of events was predominant yesterday. Life is experienced as a kaleidoscope of events, activities and ideas which are here today and gone tomorrow. Describing our present moment as 'post' is one way of trying to make sense of the fleeting nature of current affairs. It seeks to find some pattern in complex, evolving conditions of life. It also sustains the impression that human life has a destiny, that it is proceeding in a meaningful direction.

Post-modern or post-critical?

How may Christians respond to this 'cult' of the 'post'? To what extent is this kind of designation helpful? Are Christians, perhaps, in a better position to read the signs of the times in a way that does justice to what is unfolding on our planet? In one crucial sense I believe that they are, if one accepts that the most significant feature of our world is that it is 'post-critical'.

Immanuel Kant once said 'our age is, in especial degree, the age of criticism and to criticism everything must submit'. He was speaking about the age of Enlightenment. More fittingly it could have been called the age of Doubt. Its philosophical mentor was Descartes, who sought to establish an utterly secure method of escaping from all uncertainty regarding the ability to know something truly. His attempt has generally been considered a failure. Today most people would argue that by starting from their own observations, experience and reasoning, human beings cannot expect to reach an absolute certainty about any subject. The most they can hope for is a balance of probability. Peter Sedgwick, alluding to the thought of the philosopher David Hume, comments that 'reason becomes at best a means whereby we can limit the possibility of our beliefs straying too far from the bounds of good sense.'[4] In other words, we must be careful not to claim too much validity for either our thinking processes or the conclusions to which our thought brings us. Every statement that purports to be fact is disputable and endlessly revisable.

Given the intense recent criticism of the project of modernity,

[4] *Descartes to Derrida*, p. 25.

not least by Christians of quite different theological persuasions,[5] for attempting to gain an irrefutable understanding of the whole of reality through reason alone, it is important to bear in mind the intensely critical strand that informs the whole enterprise. Underneath a superficial confidence in the methods of science to deliver certain knowledge, there lies a continuous sceptical tradition, which automatically challenges all claims to truth and submits them to a rigorous disputation. Post-modernity is but the latest in a long line of intellectual movements, whose chief characteristic has been the modification or deconstruction of conviction, assurance, beliefs and truth-claims. Among others, we may count romanticism, anarchism, existentialism, phenomenology and nihilism.[6]

Thus, the critique of modernity that accuses it of the overweening desire to discover finally and unequivocally the meaning of everything by rational reflection on experience may be misplaced. Even though the scientific enterprise of the last four centuries may have put us firmly in touch with a real world, modern thought has been plagued by a nagging doubt that quite frequently erupts into despair or cynicism. The spirit of criticism constantly eats away at confidence.

However, if (as Kant maintained) everything must be subject to critique (including, incidentally, reason itself[7]), there must be a valid source from which any critical assessment can claim to be warranted. The important question is not: can any particular claim stand up to criticism? Rather, it is: is the criticism justified?

---

[5] See, for example, Lesslie Newbigin, *The Gospel in a Pluralist Society* (London: SPCK, 1989); Thomas F. Foust, 'Lesslie Newbigin's Epistemology: A Dual Discourse? in Thomas F. Foust (et al., eds.), *A Scandalous Prophet: The Way of Mission after Newbigin* (Grand Rapids: Eerdmans, 2002), pp. 153–162; Nam-Soon Kang, *'Terrorism of Truth?* The Challenge of Postmodernism and its Implication for Religion in the New Millenium' and Bert Hoedmaker, ' Religion beyond Modernity: A Missiological Perspective' in Philip Wickeri (et al, eds.), *Plurality, Power and Mission: Intertextual Theological Explorations on the Role of Religion in the New Millenium* (London: The Council for World Mission, 2000), pp. 135–154, 155–180.

[6] See *'Terrorism of Truth?'*, p. 137.

[7] See *On Kant*, pp. 54–55.

Here, we come back to the hypothesis that we are now living in a post-critical world.

The contemporary belief that the search for a self-evident and self-sufficient foundation for knowledge of the world has proved futile now leads to a sense of instability, flux and the loss of bearings. The metaphor that has been used is that of a raft 'that floats free of any anchor or tie'.[8] Human understanding is adrift on the open sea with only a limited set of charts to aid navigation. Moreover, repairs to the craft have to be made at sea, using whatever materials happen to be at hand. There is no possibility of returning to the security of the dry dock, where a thorough investigation of faults and damage may be undertaken, and the best materials, tools and expertise are available.

The present cultural mood in those societies that have deeply experienced the modern project is now one of extreme uncertainty concerning the possibility of knowing the truth. It is often pointed out that all our beliefs are relative to time and place. There is literally 'nowhere' that transcends specific, contingent circumstances. Clearly, transient human beings cannot view things from God's vantage-point. Therefore, all beliefs are endlessly revisable, according to the shifting 'somewhere' from which we perceive life. But, here is the rub! Unless there is some guarantee that critical judgements are not quite arbitrary, how is criticism possible at all? Criticism implies that there are viewpoints more justified than the ones being contested. If we are all equally 'at sea', steering our own raft without a compass that assures us of the right direction, how do we know that other rafts have chosen a wrong course?

The logic of a society which is hypercritical of all claims to understand the true nature of reality is that it becomes post-critical. Such a tendency undermines the grounds for being able to distinguish between truth and error. One strand of post-modernity accepts this logic and seeks to readjust its conception of life accordingly. This element is consistently sceptical about claims made by individuals or communities to have a *better* under-

---

[8] See Ernest Sosa, 'The Raft and the Pyramid' in Ernest Sosa and Jaegwon Lim (eds.), *Epistemology: An Anthology* (Oxford: Blackwell, 2000), p. 136.

standing of life than other people do. Such claims, it is said, cannot be distinguished from the most blatant forms of propaganda, for they are no more than instruments in the continual struggle of some humans to dominate others. If 'postmodernists question the value of truth because they consider it impossible to evaluate the adequacy of knowledge claims with any certitude', and if postmodernists reject all criteria for distinguishing between truth and falsehood, because they imply a hierarchy of values that designate some as good and others as bad,[9] critical thinking is unattainable.

The situation is not made any better by the apparently modest proposal that 'specific local, personal, and community forms of truth' may be possible.[10] In fact, what is in mind is not truth but the consensus belief of a community at a specific place and time. This may well be a piece of fiction, as in the case of the Aryan heresy of a superior race perpetrated by the leaders of the Third Reich. If, 'as substitutes for truth, affirmative postmodernists emphasize . . . small narratives, community-based narratives, rather than grand narratives',[11] what stops these from being narrow, chauvinistic, patriarchal, ethnocentric and eventually leading to genocide?[12]

Christians and Truth – in practice

A number of contemporary Christians hold that post-modernity represents the greatest challenge to Christian faith of our times: 'since every religion implies truth, the rejection of truth itself shakes the very ground of religion'.[13] I think this is a superficial judgement. Post-modernity is a much greater challenge to its own stated sentiments. To use a graphic metaphor, it eats its own tail. Post-modern convictions are shot through with unconditional affirmations that sound remarkably like truth-claims. If,

[9] *'Terrorism of Truth?'*, p. 145.
[10] Ibid. p. 146.
[11] Ibid. p. 147.
[12] Chapter 6 of this book gives all too many examples of these destructive kinds of 'narrative'.
[13] Ibid. p. 143.

however, they are no more than a collection of self-generating linguistic signs and symbols without any correspondence to a real world beyond some collective inventive imagination, the statements made have no meaning. As, presumably, they cannot refer to any objective state of affairs, they are, according to subjective taste, equally valid and invalid. Thus, post-modern allegations about the modern project are, according to its own assumptions, strictly speaking empty.

Of course, Christians have to take seriously the kind of cultural mood that the idea of the post-modern conjures up: relativist, pluralist, indulgent and permissive. They will have to think again long and hard about suitable means of communicating the Gospel, appropriate styles of leadership, acceptable structures and the shape of communities relevant to a fragmented society. However, they do not have to compromise for a moment on the question of truth. This is so for at least three reasons. Firstly, truth simply exists. Some things are real, whilst others are figments of the imagination. If this were not the case, we would be unable to distinguish between psychological normality and abnormality. Moreover, it would be impossible to convict anyone of wrongdoing, since such a category simply indicates a particular and arbitrary moral and legal code that happens to be operated by the social and political elite of the moment. In any case, evidence of guilt would be inadmissible, as witnesses, presumably, would be unable to distinguish between a real, external world and their own internal world. Not even the most ardent post-modernist would want to live in such a world. When our life is being judged by others, we readily appeal to accuracy, objective valuation and justice. We would be the first to denounce as unacceptable the action of being turned down for a job on the grounds that there is no way of determining the facts set out in our curriculum vitae.

Secondly, to dismiss truth as a meaningless concept or as an instrument of power is to play an intellectual game. In everyday life, it is impossible to function without constantly appealing to its existence. It is not helpful either to distinguish between acting on the basis of truth and living *as if* truth existed. The second option has already conceded the point. If human life has to be conducted on the basis that there is truth, and yet truth, as a universally valid fact of life, does not exist, we human beings are in disarray. It means that to bring some sense of order and meaning to our existence we have to invent arbitrary beliefs and values. Such a state of affairs, not the appeal to objective and absolute truth, would lend itself to a constant struggle for power. Postmodernity encourages the very situation it wishes to denounce!

Thirdly, truth and human liberation and flourishing are inextricably linked. There is no alternative to the saying of Jesus that 'the truth will make you free' (John 8:32). This statement cannot be reversed to read, 'everything that frees is true', for it begs the question about the meaning of freedom (as we saw in chapter 1). It cannot be substituted either for some other slogan such as *arbeit mach frei* (work makes one free), famously inscribed over the entrance to Auschwitz. Liberation from all that destroys or demeans human life can only happen through acknowledging and submitting to the truth about the universe. If such is not available, neither is human liberation.

Christian mission in a post-critical environment

Our discussion thus far implies that the future of Christian faith depends, in part, on Christians maintaining an analytical, critical and constructive presence in every situation. From their own criteria, firmly rooted in God's revelation, they are called to a constantly critical engagement with the perceived wisdom, cultural customs and values of all societies. In a post-critical world, they may find themselves as the only reliable voice of conscience left. However, such a mission, to be wholly authentic, must include the willingness to assess and amend their own traditions and practices.

In this context, the Christian church worldwide is confronted by the missiological imperative of thinking through the implications of being a global community that in the Western world is post-Christian and in the rest of the world is post- (or non-) Enlightenment, Western and Christendom. This means, at the least, acknowledging that the forms of Christianity that have prevailed in Europe do not necessarily constitute either an ideal or a norm. It is true that they have been dominant and assertive. However, obedience to the truth that liberates demands that Christians evaluate together, vigorously and honestly, their own traditions.

So, one of the most pressing mission challenges facing a post-everything world is to discern what is true (i.e. genuine and faithful) Christian belief and practice and what is inauthentic and defective. The criterion is not basically relevance, suitability or fashion. Every Christian 'life-form' has to be judged by the stringent principles of the truth as it is in Jesus Christ (Eph. 4:20–21). The process of discernment can only be authentically universal as each part of the church accords to every other a comparable standing and an equally esteemed and influential voice. The objective of such a critical debate about what is the true path for mission is not necessarily to reach consensus, although the *sensus fidei* is an ideal to be aimed at (as we saw in chapter 9). Even widespread agreement is not the same as truth. The goal is always to follow in the way of Jesus Christ with the greatest integrity possible, whatever the circumstances. Determining what this means, as in the case of the use of violence (chapter 7), may lead to vigorous disputes between Christians before any resolution is possible. To contend for the truth in Christ is a healthy process as long as it is done with the maximum respect for the personhood of those with whom we may disagree.

To conclude, I would like to sketch, from my limited and flawed perspective, a brief agenda for mission post-everything. My perceptions are obviously open to dispute and correction. That is part of the debate. I offer them, on the basis of what has been written in this book, as a further stimulus, in the context of our post-world, to a continuing 'catholic' conversation. Sometimes they may be controversial. However, being provocative can be a productive way of ensuring a proper debate.

Evangelism

Bringing the good news of God's free gift of salvation in Jesus Christ to all people is now the touchstone of mission. No longer is it necessary to defend the assumption that mission is more than evangelism. It is also clear in most Christian circles that other aspects of mission (such as peace-building, compassionate service among the most vulnerable and advocacy on behalf of persecuted minorities) have evangelistic dimensions, in that they point to the transforming effects of God's unmerited love. However, the call to primary evangelism, understood as explaining the meaning of Jesus Christ for individual lives, seems to be in dispute in some Christian communities.

It is true, of course, that there are few Christians who would repudiate evangelism altogether. Seeing that the notion is linked linguistically and formally to the *evangel*, the good news of God's action to free humanity from the guilt and power of sin, it would be hard to discard evangelism without severely mutilating the whole Christian faith. Nevertheless, for a variety of reasons (some of which we explored in chapter 5) many churches do not pay much more than lip service to the imperative to make the Gospel known to all.

The basic problem is that Christians, particularly in the post-Christian West, have over-reacted to their own past misdeeds and to the naïve triumphalism of some sectors of the Church.[14] In place of evangelism dialogue is substituted. This is understood as a process of mutual learning and witnessing leading to common action. Unfortunately, although it has its own integrity, this is much less than the evangelism practiced by the early church, and in subsequent periods of missionary outreach. If, as I have argued elsewhere,[15] lack of boldness in evangelism is due mainly to a number of different fears, the cause may be the failure of the Church to proclaim the Gospel effectively to itself. The 'perfect love (that) casts out fear' (1 John 4:18) is manifest entirely and efficaciously in God sending 'his Son to be the atoning sacrifice for our sins' (1 John 4:10) and 'not for ours only but also for the sins of the whole world' (1 John 2:2). One can only conclude that

---

[14] Lynne Price, for example, seems to agree with the Jewish writer Marc Ellis that violence may be endemic to the Christian faith: 'Churches and Postmodernity: Opportunity for an Attitude Shift' in *A Scandalous Prophet*, p. 113. I hope that I have said enough in chapters 6 and 7 to dispel this misconception.

[15] 'Mission in the West: On the Calling of the Church in a Postmodern Age' in ibid. p. 126.

a Church that has basically substituted dialogue and the witness of deeds, indispensable though each is, for evangelism does not appreciate the depths of the meaning of God's love. The church does not have a choice to withhold the report of God's way of salvation, for it does not own it; the Gospel belongs to the world. Every person has a right to hear. 'Woe betide me if I do not proclaim the Gospel' (1 Cor. 10:16).

The failures of the past should not paralyse the Church's witness in the present. With regard to Christianity's abject defects, especially in the case of sanctioning force to compel belief or defend a social system, Miroslav Volf has argued powerfully that what is needed is more, not less, faithful commitment:

> The more the Christian faith matters to its adherents as faith and the more they practice it as an ongoing tradition with strong ties to its origins and with clear cognitive and moral content, the better off we will be. 'Thin' but zealous practice of the Christian faith is likely to foster violence; 'thick' and committed practice will help generate and sustain a culture of peace.[16]

Thus, when Lynne Price uses the term 'faithful uncertainty' to describe an appropriate Christian attitude to mission, I fear she is precisely falling into the trap of adopting a 'thin' version of the Gospel.[17] This is manifest paradoxically in her apparent uncertainty about the enduring truth of salvation in Christ alone and her certainty about the imminent work of the Spirit in all people (of good will?).

Given the Church's many errors and shortcomings, a chastened evangelism is appropriate. Chastened means being unassuming and sensitive, willing to listen, considerate, courteous and gracious. This is a long way, however, from rejecting or neglecting evangelism. The proper attitude is not uncertainty. It is after all the Spirit who convicts people of the truth of Jesus (John 15:26,

---

[16] 'Christianity and Violence' in *Reflections* (Yale Divinity School, Winter 2004), pp. 16–22.

[17] Naturally, in her case, this comment does not imply that she would advocate a culturally-manipulated form of the faith.

16:13–15). Evangelism post-everything requires the Spirit-inspired
ability to steer a path between arrogance and self-reliance on the
one side and indecision and ambivalence on the other.

Community

It has become almost commonplace in some missiological thinking to decry or marginalise the Church as peripheral to God's
mission in the world. In part this has an historical cause and, in
part, it is due to a profound shift of theological perspective. So
terrified are some Christians of the residual temptation to return
to some form of Christendom ideal that concern for the institutional body is almost abandoned. This is evident, for example, in
certain reactions to Lesslie Newbigin's statement that the Gospel
is *public* truth. Some interpret this to mean that the Church can
claim the right and duty to impose its views on public policy, or
that the Church is seeking once again to recover a certain status
and authority within the life of the state. There is some
justification for this fear. Some Churches which have been established by law as the national Church, even in a highly secularised environment find it hard to exist as a body which
professes a minority creed. It is painful to admit that the kind of
influence they once had has disappeared for ever and they now
live as aliens in a strange land.

Even more telling is the apparent discrepancy between the
claims made for the power of the gospel to transform situations
decisively and the reality on the ground. Michael Taylor, in his
reflection on the collection of essays looking at mission after
Newbigin, makes this point energetically:

> I would have welcomed a greater degree of astonishment that,
> if the gospel is as strong as a prophet like Newbigin suggests,
> after two thousand years of missionary endeavour, after
> Christendom, the Enlightenment, and modernity, it still leaves
> a divided, violent, and ambiguous world at much the same
> moral and spiritual level as it was.[18]

---

[18] 'Afterword' in *A Scandalous Prophet*, p. 242.

Even allowing for the fact that we cannot know what the world would have been like had the light of the Gospel never penetrated at all the world's inclination to prefer darkness, I think astonishment is an apt description of how Christians should feel in the light of the amazing message of hope, which they have been entrusted to share with all humanity.

Theological interests also play their part in minimising the place of the Church in God's purposes for the world. It has become commonplace to reject a sharp division between the Christian community as God's people and the human community, on the grounds that it represents an unacceptable dualism. When Christians make too sharp a separation between sacred and profane history they tend to self-righteousness and withdrawal from society. They see themselves as a special people, anxious to avoid contamination by worldly pursuits. The boundary between those inside and outside is made crystal clear. Criteria for membership of the redeemed community are strict. Humanity outside the elect people is bound in sin and without hope.

In place of such a scheme of salvation, more liberally inclined Christians propose a much more inclusive community. The edges between believers and non-believers are blurred. Faith becomes a matter of degree: its intensity stretches along a line from incipient to weak to moderate to strong to fervent. In line with the post-modern fondness for abrogating difference and opposites, this line of thinking feels comfortable with fuzzy lines and vague definitions. People are not put into categories but allowed to define their own faith-stance and determine whether they belong to the community of faith or not.

It is repeatedly said that the kingdom of God, not the church, is central to God's activity in the world. The kingdom is a wider reality. It includes all who serve God's purposes by compassionate action towards those who are suffering. They show by love in practice that they are already receiving the grace of Christ. Even though their faith may be fragile and their grasp of orthodox doctrine shaky, they will be accepted: 'come, you that are blessed by my Father, inherit the kingdom prepared for you' (Matt. 25:34).

There are good reasons for rethinking the position that the church has in God's ceaseless purposes for his creation. The major argument in favour of maintaining firm distinctions between the community that belongs to Christ and people out-side, who have not yet taken a decisive step of faith, concerns the nature of commitment. It is understandable that arguments for blurring the lines around the nature of belief should be advanced principally in the post-Christian West. It is one way of attempt-ing to staunch the severe haemorrhaging of participants in the rites and activities of the churches. People who do not attend, but still declare themselves to be Christians, somehow still belong.[19] Then again (as we discussed in chapter 3), long-lasting commit-ments are not features that one associates with a generally self-indulgent, post-generation-X populace. Whether one is in or out may be a matter of mood or even what other attractions are on offer.

In contrast to the permissive attitudes and life-styles of con-temporary Western cultures, the Gospel of Jesus Christ, along with its offer of the utterly free grace of forgiveness and salva-tion, makes considerable demands: 'no one who puts his hand to the plough and looks back is fit for the kingdom of God' (Luke 9:62). The demands of the kingdom of God cannot be met by individuals living in isolation. Every follower of Jesus needs both the encouragement and the discipline that is provided by the bond of a committed fellowship of fellow pilgrims. To set the kingdom of God and the Church apart has no basis in theory or practice.

The problems surrounding the history of the church are not intrinsic to its existence. They occur, whenever Christians fail to listen critically to the prophets reminding them of the demands of God's word. The church is God's people in transit. They are a body of travellers, for ever on the move. Whenever they settle into a comfortable routine or pattern, other considerations than the perpetual call of Jesus, 'come, follow me', take precedence.

---

[19] Grace Davie's famous conclusion that the population of post-Christian Europe still believes without belonging is turned on its head: the non-Church attending population now belongs, without believing!

The current notion of the 'emerging' church encapsulates the pattern of church life that is required by discipleship in the kingdom, constantly looking towards God's future. In every generation, the church is emerging afresh from the shape of the past to take on new forms appropriate to God's present missionary intention. There is a sense in which the church as the community of the kingdom, which stretches out into God's continuous future, already lives post-everything. This theological reality has to determine its structures and vision at every moment and in every circumstance.

Religion and conflict

The beliefs of Muslims are daily discussed by the media. The general attitude is ambivalent. The debate goes on at two levels. There is the theoretical question of whether the primary texts of Islam promote peaceful or forceful means to advance the cause of faith. There is the more practical question of how secular, pluralist, multi-cultural societies should handle a religion with an uncompromising message. The other side of this issue is the question of how Muslims should behave, when living as a minority community in a society where the majority are conditioned to be wary of religion in general.

Pragmatically a secular culture needs to tame and control religions, which are implacable in their proclamation of the rightness of their teaching. They are perceived to be dangerous, because they have not bought into the tacit consensus that a variety of beliefs, moral values and lifestyles makes for a healthy social order. The situation becomes more threatening when a religion refuses to conform to the post-Enlightenment common consent that faith is a matter of private conviction and has no place in forming public opinion, shaping moral attitudes or seeking to change the law. Simon Jenkins, writing in *The Times*, prior to the British general election of 2005, is typical of this approach:

> Arguments over abortion, stem-cell research and faith schools
> are shot through with normative values. Without them politics

would be a crude battle of interests. But it is a strength of British democracy that such debates are rooted in *a rationalist consensus*.[20]

The underlying assumption of this way of stating a prevalent view is that society needs to be delivered from the irrational dogmas of all religions and learn to live exclusively by the precept of secular rationalism. However, this widely canvassed view cannot meet the predicament of a pluralist society, where some communities fail to play by the rules of agnostic toleration. It is itself hopelessly inconsistent with its own inner conviction, in that it simply substitutes one faith for another (as we saw in chapter 2). Instead of banishing faith from the public arena, it succeeds in creating a new, nationally established creed.

Islam, then, presents a crisis for Western civilisation. The latter, having successfully brought (white) Christianity to heel, is now confronted with a faith that refuses to accept the secular consensus.[21] Just when Western societies have come to believe that they have moved into a post-Christian era, the Muslim community is determined to show that it is not yet a post-religious age.

The debate about a clash of civilisations, roused by Samuel Huntington's provocative book,[22] will continue. Vinoth Ramachandra sets out well-marshalled arguments to counter Huntington's theses about Islam.[23] However, the examples he gives concerning Islam's human rights record and perceptions of the West tend to negate his points. Moreover, he was writing prior to the destruction of the World Trade Centre, the Bali bombings, the slaughter of commuters in Madrid and London, the reaction of militants to the US-led invasion of Iraq and the arrival of President Bush at the White House with his rhetoric about democracy in the Middle East. Huntington's hypotheses

---

[20] *The Times*, March 23, 2005 (my emphasis).

[21] In different ways, this is also true of a number of churches growing among the immigrant populations of the large cities of Europe.

[22] *The Clash of Civilizations and the Remaking of World Order* (New York: Simon & Schuster, 1996).

[23] 'Islam and New Religious Wars?' in *Faiths in Conflict? Christian Integrity in a Multicultural World* (Leicester: IVP, 1999).

may be too sweeping and indiscriminate. However, there is enough smoke in the present controversy surrounding the so-called 'war on terrorism' to suggest that the fires of resentment, misunderstanding, racism, religious and cultural prejudice are more than flickering.

Some writers think that all religions have a propensity towards supporting violence. According to a recently espoused view,[24] the more religious believers seek to live by the letter of their foundational texts the more violent they are likely to be towards one another. Moderation in religion is futile, because it is ineffective in dealing with literal interpretations of the various scriptures and because it promotes tolerance for every kind of religious belief in the name of freedom and human rights. Liberal faith is, according to this perspective, an even more pernicious enemy of society, because the latter can only survive terror by ridding itself of religion altogether. Sam Harris and many others like him wish to live in a post-faith world. This perspective sounds suspiciously like a clash of civilizations; albeit one that crosses geographical and cultural frontiers.

How, then, is Christian mission to be pursued among people who believe passionately that the problem of religion and conflict is not in the interpretation of what a particular faith permits but in the very notion of belief in another reality beyond the universe? What do we say in a world, increasingly scared by the threat of indiscriminate violence, which believes that a post-terrorist world is only possible post-religion?

The Christian community has to resist being backed into a corner by those who offer false alternatives. The choice does not have to be between an extreme, sectarian interpretation of faith that despises every aspect of contemporary, permissive societies, a liberal emasculation of orthodox belief and a radical secular faith that scoffs at the existence of a reality beyond the material. It is not necessary to opt for either a refusal to engage with current irreligious cultures or to submit to their basic assumptions. The modern apologists for a religiously free human existence, or

---

[24] Sam Harris, *The End of Faith: Religion, Terror and the Future of Reason* (New York: W.W.Norton, 2004).

for 'thin' religion, are badly mistaken, at least as far as the Christian faith is concerned. As has been demonstrated with brutal clarity in the twentieth century, less religion does not equate with a greater regard for human persons. Were not the Gulag Archipelago and Auschwitz built upon the certainty that God was a human-created myth?

Selective quotation from the Bible in an attempt to show that Christianity is of necessity vicious and destructive is intellectually inadmissible. To use the Book of Revelation, for example, to demonstrate Christians' lust for the destruction of their enemies is to miss its point. The point is that justice is unreal, unless it is confirmed by judgement. However, the justice and judgement belong to God. Christians are never called to execute unbelievers for their unbelief. Not to distinguish between a suicide-bomber who believes that this form of death in the cause of 'righteousness' merits God's highest reward and the martyrdom of believers at the hands of others simply because they refuse to renounce the truth of God's salvation in Christ – 'the image of the beast could . . . cause those who would not worship the image of the beast to be killed' (Rev. 13:15) – shows much confusion. In the first case, evil people in the name of a twisted belief kill innocent passers-by in the act of killing themselves. In the second case, innocent people are killed solely on account of a true belief. Active slaughter cannot be equated with passive victimhood.

Radical discipleship – again?

In this world of gross inequalities, blatant injustices against powerless peoples, growing insecurities, inter-religious and interethnic conflicts, gratuitous offence against religious convictions, never-ending disruption of the world's eco-system, aggressive business practices and exploitation of the vulnerable poor, Christian mission has to focus, as never before, on Jesus' call to radical discipleship.

Discipleship means *following, witnessing* and *serving. Following* in the way of Christ, implies the desire to be like Christ in the world: consistently holy, compassionate, open, truthful, gentle, patient. It demands a practical spiritual life that counts on the Holy Spirit to transform and guide daily living. The constant desire of the disciple is to seek above all things the quality of life represented by the standards God sets in his domain (Matt. 6:33).

Being witnesses implies praying for and taking appropriate opportunities to present and argue for Jesus as God's only appointed means for breaking the hold that sin has on attitudes and behaviour and in bringing healing to broken and disordered lives. It signifies the formation of communities of disciples, which can act as a foretaste of the kind of society that will exist in the new heavens and new earth, which God has planned for those who love him.

Serving indicates a constant readiness to make oneself available for others in need. It will involve looking first to the interests of others rather than to one's own (Phil. 2:4). It may mean sacrificing quite legitimate pursuits (study, hobbies, domestic tasks, leisure activities), when the neighbour in need has no one else to turn to. It could entail being an advocate on behalf of disadvantaged, exploited, victimized or mistreated people.

Discipleship, inevitably, confronts every Christian with choices. In so far as we are able to order our own lives, we should regularly review our commitments to see how they shape up to God's high calling in Jesus Christ. In our use of money, time and gifts do we have a clear conscience that they are being used in the best possible way to serve others and glorify God? Nothing less than a clear conscience, when scrutinized by God's revealed will, is sufficient for a follower of Jesus.

I would suggest, therefore, that the threefold call to *follow, witness* and *serve* as the marks of faithful discipleship is the measure of mission in a post-everything world. This may not seem especially original or innovative. However, constantly changing circumstances supply plenty of novelty; whilst mission requires faithfulness to God's unvarying purposes for his creation.[25]

---

[25] There is an excellent summary of what integrity in mission should mean in 'The Editorial', *Mission Studies*, Vol. XIX, 2, 38, 202, pp. 7–8.

Bibliography

Hannah Arendt, *On Violence* (London: Penguin, 1970)

Isaiah Berlin, *Four Essays on Liberty* (Oxford: OUP, 1969)

Philip Berryman, *Religion in the Megacity: Portraits from two Latin American Cities* (Maryknoll: Orbis, 1996)

C. Boff and L. Boff, *Introducing Liberation Theology* (Tunbridge Wells: Burns & Oates, 1987)

David Bosch, *Transforming Mission: Paradigm Shifts in Theology of Mission* (Maryknoll: Orbis, 1991)

Tim Bradshaw, *The Way Forward?* (London: Hodder, 1997)

Callum Brown, *The Death of Christian Britain* (London: Routledge, 2001)

Colin Brown (ed.), *Dictionary of New Testament Theology* (Carlisle: Paternoster, 1986)

E. Bucar (ed.), *Does Human Rights Need God?* (Grand Rapids: Eerdmans, 2005)

Walter Buhlman, *The Third Church* (Maryknoll: Orbis, 1977)

Helder Camara, *The Spiral of Violence* (London: Sheed & Ward, 1971)

Albert Camus, *The Myth of Sisyphus* (Harmondsworth: Penguin , 1975)

Colin Chapman, *Whose Holy City?* (Oxford: Lion, 2004)

Paul Copan & Paul K. Moser (eds.), *The Rationality of Theism* (London and New York: Routledge, 2003)

William Countryman, *Dirt, Greed and Sex: Sexual Ethics in the New Testament and Their Implications for Today* (Philadelphia: Fortress , 1988)

Jeffrey Cox, *Imperial Fault Lines: Christianity and Colonial Power in India, 1818–1940* (Palo Alto: Stanford University Press, 2002)

Ralf Dahrendorf, *The New Liberty: Survival and Justice in a changing world* (London: Routledge & Kegan Paul, 1975)

Grace Davie, *Religion in Modern Europe: A Memory Mutates* (Oxford: OUP, 2000)

Grace Davie, *Europe the Exceptional Case: Parameters of Faith in the Modern World* (London: DLT, 2002)

Stephen T. Davis, *God, Reason and Theistic Proofs* (Edinburgh: Edinburgh University Press, 1997)

Murray Dempster, Byron Klaus, Douglas Petersen (eds), *The Globalization of Pentecostalism: A Religion made to Travel* (Oxford: Regnum, 1999)

John Drane, *Jesus and the Gods of the New Age: Communicating Christ in Today's Spiritual Supermarket* (Oxford: Lion, 2001)
   Do Christians Know How To Be Spiritual? The Rise of the New Spirituality and the Mission of the West (London: DLT, 2005)

Enrique Dussel, *Historia de la Iglesia en America Latina: Coloniaje y Liberacion* (Barcelona: Nova Terra, 1972)
   The Church in Latin America: 1492–1992 (Tunbridge Wells: Burns & Oates, 1992)

Jacques Ellul, *Violence: Reflections from a Christian Perspective* (London: SCM, 1970)

Shusaku Endo, *Silence* (London: Peter Owen, 2003)

Franz Fanon, *The Wretched of the Earth* (Harmondsworth: Penguin , 1970)

Duncan Forrester, *Apocalypse Now? Reflection on Faith in a Time of Terror* (Aldershot: Ashgate, 2005)

Thomas Foust (et al, eds), *A Scandalous Prophet: The Way of Mission after Newbigin* (Grand Rapids: Eerdmans, 2002)

Milton Friedman, *Capitalism and Freedom* (Chicago: University of Chicago Press, 1962)

Erich Fromm, *The Fear of Freedom* (London: Routledge & Kegan Paul, 1960)

Francis Fukuyama, *The End of History and the Last Man* (London: Hamish Hamilton, 1992)

Rene Girard, *I See Satan Fall Like Lightening* (Maryknoll: Orbis , 2001)

John Gray, *Liberalism* (Milton Keynes: Open University Press, 1986)

A. C. Grayling, *What is Good? The Search for the Best Way to Live* (London: Wiedenfeld & Nicolson, 2003)

Darrell L. Guder, *The Continuing Conversion of the Church* (Grand Rapids: Eerdmans, 2000)

Colin Gunton, *The One, the Three and the Many: God, Creation and the Culture of Modernity* (Cambridge: CUP, 1993)

S. Hall and B. Gieben, *Formations of Modernity* (Cambridge: Polity , 1992)

Sam Harris, *The End of Faith: Religion, Terror and the the Future of Reason* (New York: W.W. Norton, 2004)

Friedrich Hayek, *Law, Legislation and Liberty* (London: Routledge & Kegan Paul, 1979)

Richard B. Hays, *The Moral Vision of the New Testament: A Contemporary Introduction to New Testament Ethics* (New York: HarperCollins, 1996)

Margaret Hebblethwaite, *Base Communities: An Introduction* (London: Geoffrey Chapman, 1994)

Peter Hebblethwaite, *The Christian-Marxist Dialogue and Beyond* (London: DLT, 1977)

Martin Heidegger, *Being and Time* (Oxford: Blackwell, 1962)

Wolfgang Heinrich, *Building the Peace: Experiences of Collaborative Peace-building in Somalia 1993–1995* (Uppsala: Life and Peace Institute, 1997)

Andrew Heywood, *Political Ideologies: An Introduction* (Basingstoke: Macmillan, 1992)

George G. Hunter, *The Celtic Way of Evangelism* (Nashville: Abingdon Press, 2000)

Michael Hunter and David Wootton, *Atheism from the Reformation to the Enlightenment* (Oxford: Clarendon Press, 1992)

Samuel Huntington, *The Clash of Civilizations and the Remaking of World Order* (New York: Simon & Schuster, 1996)

Philip Jenkins, *The Next Christendom: The Coming of Global Christianity* (New York: OUP, 2002)

Jeffrey John, *Permanent, Faithful, Stable: Christian Same-sex Partnerships* (London: DLT, 2000)

Walter Kaufman (ed.), *Basic Writings of Nietzsche* (New York: The Modern Library, 1968)

J. Andrew Kirk, *Liberation Theology: An Evangelical View from the Third World* (London: Marshall, Morgan & Scott, 1979)

    Theology encounters Revolution (Leicester: IVP, 1980)

    God's Word for a Complex World: Discovering how the Bible speaks today (London: Marshall Pickering, 1987)

    Loosing the Chains: Religion as opium and liberation (London: Hodder & Stoughton, 1992)

    The Meaning of Freedom: A Study of Secular, Muslim and Christian Views (Carlisle: Paternoster Press, 1998)

    What is Mission? Theological Explorations (London: DLT, 1999)

    (Ed.), *Handling Problems of Peace and War: An Evangelical Debate* (Basingstoke: Marshall Pickering, 1988)

Leszek Kolakowski, *Modernity on Endless Trial* (Chicago: University of Chicago Press, 1990)

Alan Kreider, *The Change of Conversion and the Origin of Christendom* (Harrisburg: Trinity Press International, 1999)

    (Ed.), *The Origins of Christendom in the West* (London: T. & T. Clark, 2001)

Jamie L. Manson, *Reflections: Violence and Theology* (New Haven: Yale Divinity School, 2004)

David Martin, *On Secularization: Towards a Revised General Theory* (Aldershot: Ashgate, 2005)

Michael Martin, *Atheism, Morality and Meaning* (Amherst, NY: Prometheus, 2002)

David McLellan, *Ideology* (Milton Keynes: Open University Press, 1995)

David McLellan, *The Thought of Karl Marx* (Basingstoke: Macmillan, 1995)

Jose Miguez Bonino, *Doing Theology in a Revolutionary Situation* (Philadelphia: Fortress Press, 1975)

    Faces of Latin American Protestantism (Grand Rapids: Eerdmans, 1995)

John Milbank, *Theology and Social Theory: Beyond Secular Reason* (Oxford: Blackwell, 1990)

    Being Reconciled: Ontology and Pardon (London: Routledge, 2003)

David Miller (ed.), *The Blackwell Encyclopaedia of Political Thought* (Oxford: Blackwell, 1991)

Milfred Minatrea, *Shaped by God's Heart: The Passion and Practices of Missional Churches* (San Francisco: John Wiley, 2004)

Jurgen Moltmann, *Experiences in Theology: Ways and Forms of Christian Theology* (London: SCM, 2000)

Viggo Mortensen (ed.), *Theology and the Religions: A Dialogue* (Grand Rapids:

Eerdmans, 2003)

Richard Mouw, *The God who Commands* (Notre Dame: University of Notre Dame Press, 1990)

Seyyed Hossein Nasr, *Religion and the Order of Nature* (Oxford: OUP, 1996)

Michael Nazir Ali, *From Everywhere to Everywhere: A World View of Christian Mission* (London: Collins, 1991)
  Conviction and Conflict: Islam, Christianity and World Order (London: Continuum, 2006)

Lesslie Newbigin, *The Gospel in a Pluralist Society* (London: SPCK, 1989)
  Truth to Tell: the Gospel as Public Truth (Grand Rapids: Eerdmans, 1991)

Thania Paffenholz, *Community-based, bottom-up Peace-building* (Uppsala: Life and Peace Institute, 2003)

Christopher Partridge (ed.), *Dictionary of Contemporary Religion in the Western World* (Leicester: IVP, 2002)

Blaise Pascal, *Pensees* (Harmondsworth: Penguin, 1980)

David Peterson (ed.), *Witness to the World* (Carlisle: Paternoster Press, 1999)

Philip L. Quinn and Chareles Taliaferro, *A Companion to the Philosophy of Religion* (Oxford: Blackwell, 1999)

Vinoth Ramachandra, *Faiths in Conflict? Christian Integrity in a Multicultural World* (Leicester: IVP, 1999)

Nicholas Rescher, *Pascal's Wager* (Notre Dame: University of Notre Dame Press, 1985)

Eugene F. Rogers (ed.), *Theology and Sexuality: Classic and Contemporary Readings* (Oxford: Blackwell, 2002)

Alan Ryan (ed.), *The Idea of Freedom* (Oxford: OUP, 1979)

Willem Saayman and Klippies Kritzinger (eds.), *Mission in Bold Humility: David Bosch's Work Considered* (Maryknoll: Orbis, 1996)

Lamin Sanneh, *Whose Religion is Christianity? The Gospel beyond the West* (Grand Rapids: Eerdmans, 2003)

R. Scroggs, *The New Testament and Homosexuality* (Philadelphia: Fortress Press, 1983)

Peter Sedgwick, *Descartes to Derrida: An Introduction to European Philosophy* (Oxford: Blackwell, 2001)

Juan Luis Segundo, *Faith and Ideologies* (London: Sheed & Ward, 1984)

Choon-Leong Seow, *Homosexuality and Christian Community* (Westminster: John Knox Press, 1996)

Gerald Shenk, *God with Us? The Roles of Religion in the FormerYugoslavia* (Uppsala: Life and Peace Institute, 1993)

Jeffrey S. Siker, *Homosexuality in the Church: Both Sides of the Debate* (Louisville: Westminster- Knox, 1994)

Peter Singer (ed.), *A Companion to Ethics* (Oxford: Blackwell, 1993)

David Smith, *Mission after Christendom* (London: DLT, 2003)

Ernest Sosa and Jaegwon Lim (eds.), *Epistemology: An Anthology* (Oxford: Blackwell, 2000)

R.S. Sugirtharajah (ed.), *Voices from the Margins* (Maryknoll: Orbis , 1991)

Anthony C. Thiselton, *The First Epistle to the Corinthians* (Grand Rapids: Eerdmans, 2000)

Norman Thomas (ed.), *Classic Texts in Mission and World Christianity* (Maryknoll: Orbis, 1995)

Garrett Thomson, *On Kant* (London: Wadsworth, 2003)

Roger Trigg, *Reality at Risk: A Defence of Realism in Philosophy and the Sciences* (Hemel Hempstead: Harvester Wheatsheaf, 1989)

    Rationality and Religion (Oxford: Blackwell, 1998)

W. Warren Wagner, *The Secular Mind: Transformation of Faith in Modern Europe* (New York: Holmes & Meier, 1982)

Andrew Walls, *The Cross-Cultural Process in Christian History* (Edinburgh: T. & & T. Clark, 2002)

Amina Mohamoud Warsame, *Queens without Crowns: Somaliland women's changing roles and peace-building* (Uppsala: Life and Peace Institute, 2002)

David West, *An Introduction to Continental Philosophy* (Cambridge: Polity, 1996)

Philip Wickeri (et al, eds), *Plurality, Power and Mission: Intertextual Theological Explorations on the Role of Religion in the New Millenium* (London: The Council for World Mission, 2000)

David Wilkinson, *The Message of Creation* (Leicester: IVP, 2002)

Walter Wink, *Healing a Nation's Wounds: Reconciliation on the Road to Democracy* (Uppsala: Life and Peace Institute, 1996)

World Council of Churches, *Guidelines on Dialogue with People of Living Faiths and Ideologies* (Geneva: WCC Publications, 1979)

    The Nature and Purpose of the Church: A Stage on the Way to a Common Statement (Faith and Order Paper No. 181) (Geneva: WCC, 1998)

John Howard Yoder, *Nevertheless: The Varieties of Religious Pacifism* (Scottdale: Herald Press, 1971)

John Howard Yoder, *The Politics of Jesus* (Grand Rapids: Eerdmans, 1972)

    The Original revolution: Essays on Christian Pacifism (Scottdale: Herald Press, 1972)

    The Priestly Kingdom:Social Ethics as Gospel (Notre Dame: University of Notre Dame Press, 1984)

    What Would You Do? A Serious Answer to a Standard Question (Scottdale: Herald Press, 1992)

Index

rights, natural 4, 5, 41, 43, 135, 190,
194
Rousseau, Jean-Jacques 3

salvation 92, 95–96, 99ff., 107–109,
187, 190
Sanneh, Lamin 154
Saunders, E.P. 185, 186
scepticism 39, 81, 88
scientific enterprise, 3, 7, 70, 74
scientific method 72
secular, meaning of 2, 13, 26ff.,
37–39
secularisation x, 35ff.
secularism xiii, 1ff.
Sedgwick, Peter 203
sensus fidei 88, 209
Shakespeare, William 142
shalom, meaning of 125, 138
Smith, David 155
social contract 9
socialist tradition, the 4–6
spirituality 134
state, the 9–11, 84
surplus-value 18

Taylor, Michael 212
territory, significance of 60–61, 96,
117–119
terrorism 133

theism, xiii
theology, dialectical 17
natural 17–18
political 20
liberal 90, 162
Third Church, the 151, 153
tolerance 41, 71, 80, 127–128
translation 88
truth 12, 51, 58, 72–73, 74, 77, 88, 96,
98–99, 102, 206ff.

United Nations, the 117, 121, 141,
143
utilitarianism 54

violence 134ff.
Volf, Miroslav 211
von Hayek 10

war, holy 115–116, 122, 124
just 120–121, 126, 135, 138,
139–143
wealth, accumulation of 15
redistribution of 5–6
Western culture 11ff., 46, 69
World Council of Churches 30, 102,
153

Yoder, John Howard 134, 136, 137